Urban Economic Development

OTHER WORKS OF BENNETT HARRISON

*Education, Training, and the Urban
Ghetto, 1972*

*The Political Economy of Public Service
Employment, 1972 (co-editor)*

*The Economic Development of Harlem,
1970 (co-author)*

URBAN ECONOMIC DEVELOPMENT

Suburbanization, Minority Opportunity,
and the Condition of the Central City

Bennett Harrison

Department of Urban Studies and Planning
Massachusetts Institute of Technology

The Urban Institute • Washington, D.C.

LC 73-86699

ISBN 87766-098-0

UI 148-715-4

REFER TO URI 48000 WHEN ORDERING

List price: $10.00

The Urban Institute
2100 M Street, N.W.
Washington, D.C., 20037

ACKNOWLEDGMENTS

EARLY IN 1971, THE STAFF OF The Urban Institute's Metropolitan Labor Market Project, under the direction of Harvey A. Garn, recognized the need for a comprehensive survey of the still largely unpublished, and therefore inaccessible, literature on the decentralization of urban jobs, and the implications of this phenomenon for minority economic welfare.

In June of 1971, the author—who is currently Associate Professor of Economics and Urban Studies in the Department of Urban Studies and Planning at the Massachusetts Institute of Technology—was commissioned to conduct such a survey and pursue its major implications, following lengthy discussions with the project staff.

Suggestions on content, and constructive criticism of various drafts, were provided by Benjamin Cohen, Charlotte Fremon, Harvey A. Garn, Franklin James, Lawrence Sawers, Mahlon Strazheim, Raymond J. Struyk, Richard F. Wertheimer II, and Lorene Yap. Ernest Strauss and Jacqueline Swingle provided indispensable editorial and production assistance. None of these individuals is, of course, responsible for the views expressed here.

CONTENTS

TABLES

ix

FIGURES

ACRONYMS

ACIR, *Advisory Commission on Intergovernmental Relations*
CBD, *Central Business District*
CDA, *City Demonstration Agency*
CDC, *Community Development Corporation*
CED, *Committee for Economic Development*
EBCDC, *East Boston Community Development Corporation*
EDA, *Economic Development Administration*
EEOC, *Equal Employment Opportunity Commission*
GPO, *Government Printing Office*
HCC, *Harlem Commonwealth Council*
HUD, *(Department of) Housing and Urban Development*
MDA, *Metropolitan Development Agency*
MESBIC, *Minority Enterprise Small Business Investment Company*
NBER, *National Bureau of Economic Research*
NEPA, *National Environment Protection Agency*
OEO, *Office of Economic Opportunity*
OFC, *Opportunity Funding Corporation*
OMB, *Office of Management and Budget*
OMBE, *Office of Minority Business Enterprise*
SBA, *Small Business Administration*
SBIC, *Small Business Investment Company*
SEO, *Survey of Economic Opportunity*
SIP, *Special Impact Program*
SMSA, *Standard Metropolitan Statistical Area*

FOREWORD

From remote beginnings, which to the present urbanite would seem forlorn and futile, the city has been intimately tied to the human experience and has played a dominant role in the development of civilization. Yet, after all this time, what the city is, does, and means is only imperfectly understood, notwithstanding the formidable analytic tools which research now has at its command.

Part of the reason is that much of the information available about the city over time is not in an idiom suitable for technological analysis. Even in the short term, research is confounded by the infinitely various fragmentation of the city, by the intense complexity of its behavior patterns, and by the urgency of its highly apparent problems with housing, poverty, education, transportation, racial hostility, governance, pollution, and crime. With a combination of technical analysis where it is possible, and surmise where it is not, a "conventional wisdom" has sounded the "plight" of the central cities with overtones not far from funereal, and with prescriptions largely surgical.

It appears, however, that the central city may have been written off too quickly, based on too narrow a focus over too brief a time span and on too dated a view of the relationship between the economy of the city and the economies of the suburbs whose problems increasingly mirror those of the city. The notion that the suburbs are draining the city of jobs for those with low and medium skills is being seriously questioned by a number of recent studies. Proposals which seek to relieve ghetto poverty by dispersing the ghetto population into the suburbs consequently seem unduly optimistic; nor do they take into account the rising numbers of blacks who strongly prefer to preserve their own community identity and to solve their own problems in their own locales.

There are signs, too, that private interests increasingly support and share government's concern about the drab decline of the urban core and—as with Detroit's "Renaissance Center," notably—are willing to make large capital investments to redesign and rebuild downtown areas for greater convenience and more enjoyable working, shopping, recreation, and living. It is no longer a matter of mere renewal but of seeing the city and its people as a unit and of at least providing a focal point for the larger revitalization. It is a question of recognizing the depths of mutual interests in the vitality of the central city and of the urban area as a whole, of recognizing how the health of the city is related to long-term cyclical developments in the national economy, of continuously examining the evidence and bringing the definition of the city's problems closer to present realities, and of then gearing private and governmental effort to the best solutions that rationality can offer.

Toward these ends, the present study by Bennett Harrison makes a timely and pertinent contribution by presenting the published and unpublished literature in review, by setting the stage for a realistic redefinition of urban economic problems, by encouraging greater cogency in ensuing dialogs, and by presenting an able and persuasive argument that the economy of the central city, despite a fearful range of difficulties, is, even now, still viable.

William Gorham
President
The Urban Institute

PART I
SUBURBANIZATION: THE RECORD AND ITS INTERPRETATION

Chapter 1

INTRODUCTION

EVER SINCE THE LATE 1950s when Harvard launched its study of the New York metropolitan region,[1] interest in the spatial patterns of employment and population within metropolitan areas has been prominent in the literature of urban economics. Analysts have observed and measured a gradual dispersal of economic activity out of the urban core into the suburbs and, in some cases, into the gaps between urban areas.[2]

This decentralization is a direct result of the changes in core population and commercial density that accompany the economic development of cities.

Residential land-use competes with industrial, commercial, and other nonresidential land uses, and pushes commerce outward from the core by bidding up land rents. At the same time, population increases in suburban and nearby exurban areas attract market-oriented activities to locations at increasing distances from the core.[3]

---

1. The principal books emerging from this project were: Raymond Vernon, *Metropolis, 1985* (New York: Anchor Books, 1963); and Raymond Vernon and Edgar M. Hoover, *Anatomy of a Metropolis* (New York: Anchor Books, 1963).
2. Cf. John F. Kain, "The Distribution and Movement of Jobs and Industry," in *The Metropolitan Enigma*, ed. James Q. Wilson, (Cambridge: Harvard University Press, 1968).
3. Thomas Vietorisz and Bennett Harrison, *The Economic Development of Harlem* (New York: Praeger, 1970), p. 194. The location theory presented above, according to which industrial and residential location are jointly determined, is attributed to William Alonso, *Location and Land-Use* (Cambridge: Harvard University Press, 1964). In its greater generality, it seems preferable to John Kain's theory that residential location always adjusts to job location for those workers with the freedom to choose: "The locational decisions of most manufacturing firms are largely unaffected by the distribution of metropolitan population. Manufacturing determines the locational decisions of urban households, not vice versa" ("Distribution," p. 17). The difficulty of building models in which work sites and residences are simultaneously determined is perhaps best illustrated by the work of Irving R. Silver, one of Kain's colleagues, in "An Integrated Model of Residential and Work Place Mobility," *Northeast Regional Science Review*, vol. 1, 1971. Silver is trying to develop models in which the worker's choice of residence and choice of work site are made jointly. Success would yield labor supply curves for specific locations, which in turn would help determine the location decisions of employers.

These movements are facilitated and reinforced by technological changes such as the substitution of automotive for fixed-route transportation, by the introducing of mass production which makes heavy use of horizontal space, and by the use of queuing processes in handling materials. These changes have made suburban areas, with their presently lower land costs, competitive with central locations. At the same time, the high density development of the urban core places a further technological constraint on city investment possibilities.

The incredible durability of buildings and the difficulties of assembling land hinder employment expansion in central cities. The value in current use of a plot of land and the building upon it can fall considerably below the value of the land in best use without inducing conversion simply because of the expense of clearing the old structure. Land assembly presents difficulties in large part because inefficient, low use-value structures are normally not all lined up neatly in a row, but are interspersed with structures generating income adequate to justify their continued existence. Consequently, a new investment covering several tracts of land must be able to recover the costs of purchasing some profitable assets—and then destroying them—as well as the costs of purchasing and clearing obsolete structures. Furthermore, the assembling of several tracts of land must overcome attempts by owners of individual plots to capitalize on the necessity for including their own property in a larger development by setting a monopoly price. These assembly and clearing problems are likely to be more difficult, the older the central city.[4]

Perhaps the most interesting of the many institutional conditions acting to reinforce these processes is the high level of housing standards obtaining in most suburban areas and manifested in relatively stringent building codes. These standards make it virtually impossible for low-income migrants to the cities to afford suburban housing—even when land rents there are relatively lower than in the central city. The underrepresentation of such populations in the suburbs encourages the middle-class residents of the central city to suburbanize, or at least does not discourage them *from* suburbanizing.[5]

Thus, suburbanization is, in and of itself, neither unexpected nor does it necessarily reflect some socioeconomic pathology in the central city. Urban areas may simply be undergoing an evolutionary change of form. Yet many responsible academic economists—and a growing number of

---

4.   Roger Noll, "Metropolitan Employment and Population Distributions and the Conditions of the Urban Poor," in *Financing the Metropolis*, ed. John P. Crecine (Beverly Hills, Calif.: Sage Publications, 1970), p. 502. Raymond Vernon offers the most complete discussion of the underlying technological changes, in *The Changing Economic Function of the Central City* (New York: Committee for Economic Development, January 1959), Supplementary Paper No. 6, reprinted in *Urban Renewal: The Record and the Controversy*, ed. James Q. Wilson (Cambridge: Harvard University Press, 1966).
5.   Anthony Downs, "Housing the Urban Poor: The Economics of Various Strategies," *American Economic Review*, September 1969.

congressmen and editorial writers—clearly believe that suburbanization is one of the principal underlying causes of the "urban crisis." The deterioration of the central city tax base due to middle-class suburbanizing is described by Bradford and Kelejian in just such terms:

> The problems of U.S. cities—rising crime rates, demoralization of public school systems, increasing dirt and ugliness, etc.—are traced by many observers to the decline in the number of higher income residents. This "worsening" of the central city income distribution is attributed to the movement of wealthier families to the suburbs, a process which is, in turn, induced or hastened by deteriorating conditions in the central cities. If this description is true, it is not farfetched to say that *the* problem of U.S. cities is the self-feeding flight of the middle classes to the suburbs.[6]

When those whites who are able to support the city's tax base continue to move out, the parallel loss of jobs makes it more difficult for those left behind (principally the black and the poor) to find work.

> Low income white workers adapt their residential choices to their job locations and to available transit services. When their jobs are in suburban areas, an increasing trend, they invariably live in suburban areas. When Negro jobs are located in suburban areas, they must either be foregone [because of residential segregation] or they represent difficult, costly, and time-consuming trips from [the central ghetto out] to suburban workplaces.[7]

John Kain estimates that there were from 4 to 9 thousand jobs in suburban Detroit in 1952, and from 22 to 25 thousand jobs in suburban Chicago in 1956, which blacks were unable to accept because of suburban residential segregation.[8] Moreover, to the extent that those jobs which are suburbanizing most rapidly have the relatively lowest skill-requirements, the unskilled blacks who remain behind are at a disadvantage in competing with suburbanites even for the jobs which remain in the central city.[9]

This volume reexamines the evidence on the postwar suburbanization

6. David F. Bradford and Harry H. Kelejian, "An Econometric Model of the Flight to the Suburbs," *Journal of Political Economy*, May-June 1973.

7. John F. Kain, "The Big Cities' Big Problem," *Challenge*, September-October 1966, reprinted in Louis A. Ferman, et al., *Negroes and Jobs* (Ann Arbor: University of Michigan Press, 1968), p. 238.

8. John F. Kain, "Housing Segregation, Negro Employment, and Metropolitan Decentralization," *Quarterly Journal of Economics*, May 1968, p. 189. The critical assumption underlying these calculations is that if blacks had the same spatial distribution of residences as do whites, then black access to local jobs would be equal to that of an equivalent white sample. This is a questionable assumption: in a discriminating economy, the existence of large or even growing numbers of suburban jobs does not guarantee that nonwhites will be able to move into these jobs, even if they live nearby. We shall return to this later.

9. "Jobs traditionally held by Negroes appear to be suburbanizing at an equal, and very possibly at an above-average rate, while there is only token suburbanization of Negro households" (ibid., p. 191). At the same time, central city jobs are becoming increasingly skill-intensive. This is known as the "mismatch hypothesis."

of jobs and residences, with particular attention to the "mismatch hypothesis." Both phenomena are found to have been exaggerated and, to some extent, misunderstood. Urban activity is indeed decentralizing, but this is not in and of itself pathological. Moreover, both suburbanization and its consequences for minority poverty are subject to constructive policy intervention, if we so choose.

This view of suburbanization as a largely evolutionary and nonpathological phenomenon can be reconciled with the discussion of the relationship between suburbanization and the "urban crisis." Changes in urban form have created disequilibria in the urban system. These disequilibria call for resource reallocations which have been impeded by the spatial immobility of labor and capital. These immobilities are severe and difficult to overcome, at least in part because the changes in urban form have been accompanied by a proliferation of intrametropolitan governments. Each represents a jurisdiction with strong preferences about the kinds of people it wishes to accommodate. Even more seriously, each is individually incapable of managing (i.e., neutralizing or expropriating, as the case may be) "spillovers" from neighboring jurisdictions, such as environmental pollution or neighborhood blight. The traditional response of central cities to the loss of taxable revenues through decentralization was to annex the peripheral areas, but this is increasingly curtailed as those areas incorporate as independent political jurisdictions. Moreover, many of the institutional arrangements by which urban activity is organized (e.g., the intrajurisdictional administration of public services) may have been made obsolete by these disequilibria. Yet, even though the changes have become politically and economically apparent, public policy has not responded. That failure of policy constitutes the urban crisis.

To say that there has been a failure of policy is not to deny that many policy proposals exist. Two of the most important and widely publicized are the planned suburbanization of minorities and the suppression of plans to rebuild central city (especially ghetto) economies for fear of attracting low-income nonwhite interstate migrants whose relocation into the urban core would negate the benefits derived from the first policy. After the evidence on suburbanization has been presented, we shall therefore give some attention to these two proposals. The book will then turn to a technical, economic, and political analysis of the viability of the central city itself, focusing on proposals for reorganization and redevelopment, especially as they relate to minority economic opportunity. We will conclude with some suggestions for future research.

Chapter 2

THE SUBURBANIZATION OF EMPLOYMENT AND POPULATION

AN IMPORTANT DISTINCTION MUST BE MADE between two concepts which are often confused in the literature. The gradual dispersal of economic activity from the primary core of the city (as measured by the relative flattening over time of "density gradients," i.e., functions showing how the quantity of investment or employment per areal unit varies with distance from the core) shall be called "decentralization." But where this phenomenon crosses jurisdictional boundaries and has consequent implications for, say, fiscal policy, it will be described as "suburbanization." The former term, in other words, describes a technical-economic phenomenon whose existence is analytically independent of any particular political or institutional circumstances. The latter term, on the other hand, is literally defined only in some specific institutional context. This distinction serves to remind us that a complete analysis of the issues with which we are concerned will require attention to both analytical and institutional factors.

The Secular Trend

MANY RESEARCHERS GIVE THE IMPRESSION that the decentralization of urban jobs and residences is a comparatively recent phenomenon which is somehow closely related to the growing concentration of blacks in the central city. Mills (who, as we shall see, does not subscribe to this position) has summarized the conventional wisdom:

7

Much popular literature is written as though suburbanization were mainly a postwar phenomenon, induced by the peculiar circumstances of urban life in that period. For example, it is sometimes claimed that home mortgage insurance by the federal government has been mainly responsible for postwar suburbanization. Or, it is claimed, postwar suburbanization has resulted mainly from the attempt of whites to flee from the increasing numbers of Negroes in central cities. Finally, postwar suburbanization is sometimes attributed to the rapid growth of automobile ownership during that period.[1]

In fact, however, the process of suburbanization, (or "decentralization") has been underway since at least the beginning of the century. The figures in Table 1, taken from an Urban Institute study by Charlotte Fremon, indicate that the central cities' share of metropolitan manufacturing employment has been declining for at least this long.

Decentralization has been taking place for many years in population and in nonmanufacturing employment as well. Mills has estimated the intertemporal and intercity patterns of this long-run process through the use of urban density functions, defined as

$$D(u) = De^{-\gamma u}$$

where $D(u)$ is the population (or employment) density u miles from the

TABLE 1
CENTRAL CITY MANUFACTURING EMPLOYMENT AS A PERCENTAGE OF METROPOLITAN MANUFACTURING JOBS IN EIGHT SMSAs: 1900–1967
(1965 city boundaries)

Period	Percent Share	Changes
	%	%
1900–1918	88.6	—
1919–1938	77.3	−11.3
1939–1958	76.4	−0.9
1959–1966	66.7	−9.7
1967	60.8	−5.9

Source: Charlotte Fremon, *The Occupational Patterns in Urban Employment Change, 1965–67* (Washington, D.C.: The Urban Institute, January 1970, unpublished working paper), p. 11. This working version was later recast and in August 1970 was published, under the same title, as an Urban Institute Paper (URI No. 70000). To avoid confusion and to take advantage of some formulations which in the earlier version were more directly suitable to my present subject, my references are drawn exclusively from the January working paper.

1. Edwin S. Mills, "Urban Density Functions," *Urban Studies*, February 1970, p. 9.

TABLE 2
AVERAGE DENSITY GRADIENTS BY SECTOR
AND YEAR IN SIX SMSAs:
1910-63

	1910	1920	1929	1939	1948	1954	1958	1963
Population	.96	.94	.73[a]	.67[a]	.57	.46	.41	.36
Manufacturing	—	.95	.82	.77	.76	.67	.60	.48
Retail	—	—	1.02	.90	.76	.73	.58	.41
Services	—	—	—	1.12	.88	.81	.70	.55
Wholesale	—	—	1.43	1.24	1.01	.89	.77	.59

[a]Figures are for 1930 and 1940.
Source: Edwin S. Mills, "Urban Density Functions," Table 4.

urban center, D represents density *at* the center, e is the base of the system of natural logarithms, and γ stands for the rate at which density declines with distance from the center; this is the density gradient. The larger the estimate of γ, the more centralized is the spatial distribution.[2]

For the set of six metropolitan areas on which data from the early 1900's are available, Mills has estimated gradients for population and for four industry groups: manufacturing, retail, services, and wholesale. The results are given in Table 2.[3] It is clear that the six central cities have become less dense over time in terms of both population and employment. Has this decentralization process accelerated? It appears that

postwar density functions have flattened faster than prewar. However, a large part of the prewar evidence is from the decade of the 1930s, and it can hardly be doubted that the depression slowed up the rate of suburbanization. If one

2.   Since only two observations are available per area per period (i.e., central city and SMSA activity levels), it is possible to estimate but not to test the statistical significance of the two parameters D and γ (ibid., pp. 5–6). Basically, the parameters are specified as functions of the current area of an SMSA and its central city and the levels at various times of employment or population within the SMSA and its central city. Two nonlinear relationships are developed and solved simultaneously by an iterative procedure. Given the substantial amount of suburban annexation by central cities that has taken place in this century, specification of the *current* area (or, to be more precise, of parameters of that area, such as the radius of the central city) implies that Mills' estimates of *past* gradients are probably biased upward, thereby understating the degree of decentralization. If this logic is correct, then the trends estimated by Mills probably extend even further back in time than his actual base periods.
3.   In a presentation to the faculty of the Department of Economics at the University of Maryland in the spring of 1970, Mills reported population estimates for four metropolitan areas going back to 1880:

Year:	1880	1890	1900
Average Gradient:	1.28	1.10	1.03

considers population and compares the pre-1954 period with the 1954–1963 decade, or the 1910–1930 period with the 1948–1963 period, the rates of suburbanization are about the same. A fair conclusion from these data seems to be that most of the rapid suburbanization just after World War II was the result of the war and the preceding depression, rather than of basically new forces.[4]

The 18–20 year increments in Table 1 also indicate a diminishing pace of decentralization (if the Depression era is ignored). The sample areas have not, in other words, experienced notable postwar acceleration in a process that appears to have been operative for nearly a century.

Suburbanization from World War II to the Kennedy Era

DATA FOR THE PRE-WORLD WAR II period are extremely scarce. Economists seeking larger and presumably more representative samples have therefore concentrated their attention on the more recent past. Table 3 presents John F. Kain's (by now) well-known 1948–63 suburbanization series for population and four industry groups in forty large urban areas. We can obtain a better feel for the dimensions of this growth in the relative importance of the suburban economy from Table 4, which shows the 1948 base level and the average annual absolute changes over the three intervals tabulated by Kain. Certainly the most dramatic change has been in the central city's loss of manufacturing jobs. Over the nine-year period 1954–63, the forty central cities in the sample sustained a net manufacturing job loss of

TABLE 3
SUBURBAN SHARE OF SMSA EMPLOYMENT AND POPULATION FOR FORTY SMSAs: 1948–63
(1950 central city boundaries)

	1948	1954	1958	1963
Employment	%	%	%	%
Manufacturing	33.1	38.6	42.0	51.8
Wholesaling	8.2	14.5	20.7	28.6
Retailing	24.7	30.6	37.2	45.4
Services	15.2	21.6	26.1	31.3
Population	36.0	43.5	48.2	54.3

Source: John F. Kain, "Distribution and Movement," Table 10.

4. Mills, p. 12. Interestingly, his results (those reproduced here and much more detailed findings for the period 1949–63 on 18 cities) indicate a covergence over time in the degree of decentralization among sectors. In Table 2, in 1929 the largest entry is about double the smallest. By 1963, the largest is only 1.64 times the smallest. Moreover, while the manufacturing and population gradients were almost identical in 1920, the latter rose to between 1.33 and 1.46 times the former in the period after World War II. "This suggests, but does not prove, that the movement of people to the suburbs has attracted manufacturing employment rather than vice versa," as hypothesized by Kain (Mills, p. 12).

TABLE 4
LEVELS OF POPULATION AND EMPLOYMENT FOR 1948, WITH AVERAGE ANNUAL CHANGES 1948-63 IN FORTY SMSAs
(1950 central city boundaries)

	Central City				Suburban Ring			
	1948 level	1948-54 period	1954-58 period	1958-63 period	1948 level	1948-54 period	1954-58 period	1958-63 period
	-no.-	-no.-	-no.-	-no.-	-no.-	-no.-	-no.-	-no.-
Employment								
Manufacturing	118,652	218	-2,122	-3,462	58,805	2,396	1,262	4,180
Wholesaling	33,124	-85	55	-198	2,959	425	767	831
Retailing	61,048	-588	188	-985	19,992	896	2,263	1,931
Services	23,654	479	1,011	294	4,240	510	874	756
Population	899,625	464	25	-4,595	504,790	31,491	36,722	41,000

Source: Kain, "Distribution and Movement," Tables 3 and 5.

40 × [4 × 2,122) + (5 × 3,462)] = 1,031,920, while the forty suburban rings gained an almost identical number of such jobs. There is no doubting the severity of this transformation. The literature clearly shows that this decentralization of manufacturing has created much of the concern over the implications of suburbanization with respect to job-related income distribution.[5]

In a more recent study, Dorothy K. Newman has presented what she considers to be evidence of accelerating suburbanization. Over the period 1954–65, half of the new, private, nonresidential building in metropolitan areas (measured by percent of valuation of newly authorized permits) took place in the suburban rings of those SMSAs. For industrial buildings, the ratio was even greater—63 percent. Based upon this data (displayed in Table 5), Newman concludes:

These buildings represent a large capital investment, leading to substantial increases in suburban employment, especially in industry, retail and wholesale trade, and business, professional, and technical services. Many of the jobs created are within the capabilities of the people who need employment opportunities, but most of the new jobs are too distant and difficult to reach.[6]

Indeed, since construction costs (an element in permit value) tend to be higher inside cities than outside, "the higher ratio of outside to inside central city building . . . involves either more or larger building in the ring, and, consequently, even greater job opportunities than the permit value of new building construction itself would indicate."[7]

5. Kain adjusted his data for municipal annexations of peripheral "turf." It has been suggested that his treatment of annexation leads to exaggerated estimates of the degree of suburbanization. The issue is hardly academic; between the 1950 and 1960 Censuses, annexation accounted for about 83 percent of the growth in central city population in the United States (Benjamin I. Cohen and Roger G. Noll, "Employment Trends in Central Cities" [Pasadena, Calif.: California Institute of Technology, 1968], Social Science Discussion Paper No. 69–1, p. 4). Observing the extraordinary magnitude of this phenomenon, Kain decided (in conjunction with his collaborators on the RAND urban transportation study) to correct his metropolitan employment data for annexation: note that Tables 3 and 4 employ "1950 central city boundaries."

My own examination of the controversy suggests that the issue is moot, since estimates of intercity job decentralization appear to be insensitive to adjustments for annexation (for further discussion see the Appendix at the end of this chapter).

6. Dorothy K. Newman, "The Decentralization of Jobs," Monthly Labor Review, May 1967, p. 7.

7. Ibid. With respect to the jobs to be housed in these new suburban buildings, Newman's logic is unassailable if the labor/land ratio is not lower in the suburbs than in the central city. Data to measure such factor proportions are extremely difficult to generate; I would expect to find that—with land the scarcest of all central city resources—labor/land ratios would in fact be higher in the central city than in the suburbs.

One must also mention the jobs created by the construction of the buildings themselves. While the inadequacy and high cost of "reverse commuting" facilities unquestionably increase the relative inaccessibility of these suburban construction jobs to inner city residents, there is still another factor to contend with, one which is probably insensitive to location. I refer, of course, to racial discrimination in the construction trades.

TABLE 5

PERCENTAGE OF NEW, PRIVATE, NONRESIDENTIAL BUILDING OUTSIDE THE CENTRAL CITIES OF SMSAs: 1954-65

(1950 central city boundaries)

Areas	All Types	Business	Industrial	Stores	Office Buildings	Community	Educational	Hospital and Institutional	Amusement
						Type of Building			
All U.S. SMSAs	49%	46%	63%	53%	27%	45%	50%	36%	48%
Selected SMSAs:									
Atlanta	43	41	66	40	21	48	57	32	30
Boston	68	70	82	74	51	67	72	41	64
Chicago	63	61	73	67	39	66	69	58	75
Cleveland	58	59	60	73	37	44	61	33	57
Dayton[a]	62	66	56	78	53	49	28	56	99
Detroit	71	73	75	77	58	70	79	62	43
Indianapolis	44	50	61	52	21	40	46	10	52
Los Angeles	62	63	86	66	41	63	59	70	50
New Orleans[a]	42	49	58	66	10	37	35	44	41
New York	44	44	75	71	18	38	34	32	33
Philadelphia	67	69	76	72	51	68	72	43	72
St. Louis[a]	41	39	67	75	32	37	67	35	85
San Francisco	63	64	84	72	37	64	73	53	55
Washington, D.C.	64	62	84	89	47	64	57	61	94

[a] 1960–65.

Source: Dorothy K. Newman, "The Decentralization of Jobs," Tables 1 and 2. Excludes 1959. Based on a sample of over 3,000 permit-using places. The above table does not include all categories of new building.

Intracore and intrasuburban time series (or, for that matter, cross-section) data are virtually nonexistent. Kain has tapped what is perhaps the only source: a (then) ten-year time series on employment in Chicago industries, distributed by postal zip code zone.[8] He has partitioned the 55 postal zones of the central city into seven "rings" or areas, shown in Figure 1. Over the period 1958–63, Chicago lost a net 100,000 jobs. All of the inner areas of the city lost employment. Only areas "5 North" and "6 South"—the outermost regions of the central city—gained jobs during this period (the figures for each subarea are given in Table 11 below). Kain interprets this pattern as yet another indication of the trend toward suburbanization of industry.

The Mid-1960s: A Changing Pattern

UNTIL VERY RECENTLY, virtually all of the published empirical research on suburbanization—samples of which we have just examined—used 1963 as the terminal year of its statistical series. Policy discussions based upon these studies have, as a result, taken rapid suburbanization as a datum. Yet, during the post-1963 period (and particularly during the latter part of the decade), there was a significant change in the pattern. At the very least, the absolute declines in central city employment, including manufacturing, were reversed. In some metropolitan areas, the suburban share of SMSA jobs appears to have stabilized. In others, central cities have actually contributed more than half of new SMSA job growth, although the suburban share of SMSA employment continued to rise.[9] In testimony delivered to the House Ad Hoc Subcommittee on Urban Growth, Milwaukee's Deputy Commissioner of City Development recently quoted Chief Economist of the city of Boston, Alexander Ganz:

Since at least 1963, our large cities are no longer net losers of jobs. Even in the case of manufacturing, there has been a marked slow-down in the outflow of jobs. . . . Growth in business, personal and government service activities is more than offsetting the decline in manufacturing jobs. The present mix of industries in the large cities contains as large a share of rapidly growing activities as is the case in the suburban ring. Productivity in manufacturing in the large cities is

---

8. In fact, all states regularly collect such data from all employers covered by the Unemployment Insurance laws. These files are sampled by the Bureau of Labor Statistics for the construction of its *Employment and Earnings* series. Of all the participating states, to the author's knowledge, only Illinois publishes zip code summaries on a regular basis, and then only for the Chicago SMSA.

9. The latter result serves to remind us of a fact which is frequently underemphasized in discussion of the suburbanization of employment. Even by 1969, the great majority of SMSA jobs in the U.S. continued to be located within central cities. It is precisely because the average share of metropolitan jobs located in the central city is so large already, that even significant positive *incremental* growth in central city employment has not been sufficient to increase that share.

FIGURE 1

MAJOR SUBAREAS OF THE CITY OF CHICAGO

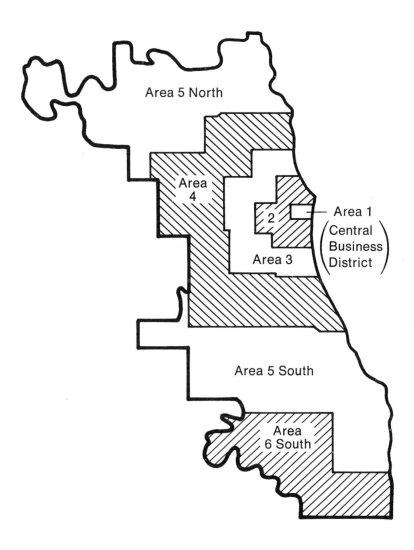

Source: John F. Kain, "Distribution and Movement," Figure 2.

rising as new equipment, new enterprises, and new processes displace obsolescent ones. Productivity growth in service activities in the large cities exceeds that in the suburban ring.[10]

Table 6 shows the changes in the suburban share of metropolitan employment in 10 SMSAs over the period 1959–67. Based upon unpublished Census data (which excluded government employment), the table indicates that, in five of the ten areas and three of the six industrial sectors in the sample, more than half of the net metropolitan job growth during the period

TABLE 6
EMPLOYMENT OUTSIDE THE CENTRAL CITY
IN TEN LARGE METROPOLITAN AREAS,
BY INDUSTRY: 1959 AND 1967
(1967 boundaries)

Area and Industry	Percent of SMSA Employment Outside Central City		Percent of SMSA Employment Growth Outside Central City 1959–1967
	1959	1967	
Atlanta	22	27	36
Baltimore	30	37	72
Boston	61	62	73
Houston	7	6	5
Kansas City	26	28	37
New Orleans	18	24	40
New York	15	19	49
Philadelphia	40	46	79
St. Louis	42	49	85
Washington, D.C.	39	49	70
Average	28	32	54
Manufacturing	37	41	79
Retail	32	41	78
Wholesale	16	22	68
Services	23	29	42
Finance, insurance, real estate	13	18	42
Others	27	28	31
Average	28	32	54

Source: U.S. Department of Labor, *1971 Manpower Report of the President* (Washington, D.C.: U.S. Government Printing Office, 1971), p. 90.

10. Alexander Ganz, "Our Large Cities: New Directions and New Approaches," reprinted by the Ad Hoc Subcommittee on Urban Growth, Committee on Banking and Currency, U.S. House of Representatives, *Hearings*, 91st Congress, 2nd Session, September 23, 1970, p. 122.

TABLE 7
AVERAGE ANNUAL RATES OF
EMPLOYMENT GROWTH IN THIRTY SMSAs,
BY INDUSTRY: 1958-63 AND 1963-67
(current boundaries)

Sector	Central City		Suburbs	
	1958-63	1963-67	1958-63	1963-67
Manufacturing	−1.3%	0.9%	6.0%	4.8%
Retail	1.0	0.6	7.7	4.6
Wholesale	−0.7	1.1	8.2	8.4
Services	2.6	2.4	7.9	5.9
Local government	1.6	3.1	—	—
Total	0.0	1.3	4.8	5.1

Source: Benjamin I. Cohen, "Trends in Negro Employment Within Large Metropolitan Areas," *Public Policy*, Winter 1972, Table 1.

took place inside the central city. The centralized orientation of public employment (see pp. 27–31 below) suggests that these results probably understate the performance of the central cities relative to their rings.

Benjamin Cohen, using the Censuses of Business, Manufacturing, and Governments, has updated his earlier collaborative effort with Noll. Table 7 shows the acceleration of central city job growth in 30 SMSAs over the period 1958–67, the first half of which was studied by Kain. For the group of 30 areas, the average annual rates of growth of central city manufacturing, retail trade, and services *rose* during the last half of the decade 1958–67; in the suburbs, however, the corresponding rates actually *fell*. For all industries, central city job growth—which had been completely stagnant during the earlier period—increased to an average annual rate of 1.3 percent. Cohen also examined each of the 30 SMSAs individually. For the four sectors which were studied so closely by Kain, Table 8 dramatically illustrates the reversal of trend. Whereas 15 of the 30 central cities had suffered an absolute decline during 1958–1963 in manufacturing, retail, wholesale, and service employment, only 5 central cities suffered such declines during 1963–67. Moreover, the turnabout was relatively more pronounced in manufacturing than in any other sector!

Charlotte Fremon has divided the period 1959–67 differently to eliminate the effects of the recession of 1963.[11] Her findings for 8 SMSAs for 1959–65 and 1965–67 are displayed in Table 9. While direct comparison

11. Charlotte Fremon, *Central City and Suburban Employment Growth, 1965–67* (Washington, D.C.: The Urban Institute, April 1970).

TABLE 8
NUMBER OF CENTRAL CITIES WITH
INCREASING AND DECLINING EMPLOYMENT,
BY INDUSTRY: 1958-63 AND 1963-67
(current boundaries)

	1958-63		1963-67	
	Decline	Increase	Decline	Increase
Manufacturing	19	11	9	21
Services	2	28	1	29
Wholesale	17	13	10	20
Retail	9	21	8	22
Total Employment	15	15	5	25

Source: Cohen, "Trends in Negro Employment," Table 1.

TABLE 9
AVERAGE ANNUAL PERCENTAGE CHANGE OF
CENTRAL CITY AND SUBURBAN EMPLOYMENT
IN EIGHT SMSAs
(current boundaries)

	Central Cities		Suburbs	
	1959-65	1965-67	1959-65	1965-67
	%	%	%	%
New York	1.1	2.0	4.8	4.5
Philadelphia	0.0	3.5	3.6	5.9
San Francisco	2.1	8.5	3.6	1.7
St. Louis	0.3	2.8	4.0	8.0
Washington, D.C.	2.8	3.4	7.5	8.7
Baltimore	0.2	3.8	5.2	12.8
Denver	2.1	4.6	7.5	10.8
New Orleans	2.4	3.7	7.1	7.1
Total, 8 Cities	1.1	3.0	4.7	6.0

Source: Charlotte Fremon, *Central City and Suburban Employment Growth, 1965-67*, Table 1.

TABLE 10
PERCENTAGE DISTRIBUTION OF JOBS BETWEEN CENTRAL CITIES AND SUBURBS IN THREE SMSAs: 1960 AND 1969
(current boundaries)

	Philadelphia		Washington		New York	
	1960[a]	1969[b]	1960[a]	1969[b]	1960[a]	1969[b]
Central City	56.5%	58.0%	63.1%	60.3%	81.5%	83.1%
Suburbs	43.5	42.0	36.9	39.7	18.5	16.9

[a] Based upon the 1960 Journey-to-Work Study from the 1960 Census; includes all industries and governments.
[b] Based upon unpublished data from the U.S. Equal Employment Opportunity Commission; covers all private firms with at least 100 employees.
Source: Kenneth Fox, unpublished Urban Institute draft, March 30, 1971.

between Fremon's results and those of Cohen (Table 7) is not possible,[12] there is some evidence that central city job growth *accelerated* during the period 1963–67.

Kain had observed that "the most rapid declines in central city employment are being experienced by the older, dense manufacturing centers of the North and East."[13] Kenneth Fox has found evidence that, even in these areas, employment decline turned into expansion during the mid-1960s. Fox's estimates for three older Northeastern areas—Philadelphia, Washington, and New York—are presented in Table 10. The data show that the central city's share of SMSA jobs actually *grew* in Philadelphia and New York. Fox's 1969 observations exclude government employment. For New York, Wilfred Lewis, Jr., has estimated a "suburban shift" of 17,875 government jobs between 1959 and 1965, relative to a *total* "suburban shift" of 136,947 jobs over the same period.[14] This government sector job loss was about 4 percent of the 1959 base period level (404,800 government jobs). The ratio of net manufacturing job loss attributable to suburbanization, compared to total manufacturing jobs in the base period, was also about 4 percent. Thus, for at least one "older, dense manufacturing center" over a recent six-year period, the relative severity of public sector employment suburbanization was no greater than that obtaining for manufacturing. Fox's conclusions for New York (and perhaps for Philadelphia) would

12. Fremon's data sources are County Business Patterns, The American Association of Railroads, and the U.S. Civil Service Commission. Moreover, she studies only 8 of the 30 cities analyzed by Cohen.
13. Kain, "Distribution and Movement," p. 17.
14. Lewis's "shift-share analysis" is discussed further on pp. 31 ff. below.

therefore probably not be vitiated by the inclusion of a public sector.[15]

Earlier, we mentioned Kain's study of employment change *within* the Chicago central city. I have been able to obtain more recent place-of-work data from the same source as that used in the Kain study. My results for 1963–68 are presented in Table 11, together with Kain's figures for the earlier period, 1958–63. A complete and thorough reversal of trend has taken place throughout the city of Chicago.[16] A net job loss of 20,000 in the earlier period turned into a net job gain of nearly 19,000 jobs in the next 5 years. *Every* geographic region of the central city (see Figure 1) experienced this reversal; in fact, only 4 of the city's 55 zip code areas suffered declines in employment. Even in the Central Business District the average annual rate of job growth switched from −1.0 percent to +1.7 percent. In the South Side ghetto, the respective rates of growth were −3.1 percent and +0.6 percent.

How might we explain what appears to be a cyclical pattern in the postwar process of suburbanization, centering on the year 1963? For one

---

15.   Fox himself is cautious about his interpretation of these findings: "At the very least, this result implies that in lieu of good data, our conventional wisdom is leading us dangerously astray." He also notes that the Equal Employment Opportunity Commission (EEOC) data's exclusion of small firms probably does not seriously distort the results "unless . . . there are many more jobs in establishments with less than one hundred employees in the suburbs than there are in the central cities. But even if *this* holds true, the finding that jobs in large establishments are becoming increasingly centralized in New York and Philadelphia runs against common beliefs" (Fox, unpublished draft, 1971). [Emphasis mine, B.H.] Location theory, of course, would lead us to predict that small plants would be relatively *more* centrally oriented than large plants, since their dependence on agglomeration economies (relative to internal economies of scale) is presumably greater.

16.   There were some modest changes in coverage between the two periods. The 1970 report from which my 1963–68 data were taken contains a complete time series from 1957, with the earlier data adjusted for such methodological variations. The differences between the original percentage changes reported by Kain for 1958–63 and percentages computed from the adjusted data seem inconsequential:

Region	Average annual pct. change, 1958–63 (Kain)	Average annual pct. change, 1958–63 (adjusted)
Cen. Bus. Dist.	−1.0	−1.0
2	−1.7	−1.6
3	−3.2	−3.0
4	−1.5	−1.7
5 North	4.9	4.8
5 South	−3.1	−3.2
6 South	1.1	1.0

(The figures here and in Table 11 are simple five-year averages, not compound rates of growth.)

TABLE 11
AVERAGE ANNUAL ABSOLUTE AND PERCENTAGE GROWTH IN EMPLOYMENT, BY SUBAREA: CHICAGO, 1958-68

Area	1958-63[a]		1963-68[b]	
	Number	Percent	Number	Percent
Central Business District[c]	−2,120	−1.0	3,458	1.7
2[d]	−5,065	−1.7	2,650	0.9
3[e]	−6,889	−3.2	161	0.1
4[f]	−4,903	−1.5	4,655	1.5
5 North[g]	4,538	4.9	5,510	4.2
5 South[h]	−3,922	−3.1	760	0.6
6 South[i]	304	1.1	1,282	4.0
Unclassified	−1,983	−2.4	89	0.2
Total	−20,040	−1.5	18,565	1.3

[a] Kain, "Distribution and Movement," p. 24.
[b] My calculations, from: State of Illinois, Department of Labor, Bureau of Employment Security, Chicago Area Labor Market Analysis Unit, *Employment Covered Under the Illinois Unemployment Compensation Act, 1957-1968* [The Postal Zone Study], Chicago, 1970.
[c] Includes zip codes 01–04 (all zips have the regional prefix 606).
[d] Includes zip codes 05–07, 10, 11.
[e] Includes zip codes 08, 12, 14, 16, 22.
[f] Includes zip codes 09, 13, 15, 18, 23, 24, 32, 39, 44, 47, 51, 53, 57.
[g] Includes zip codes 25, 26, 30, 31, 34, 35, 40, 41, 45, 46, 48, 56, 66.
[h] Includes zip codes 17, 19–21, 29, 36–38, 49, 52.
[i] Includes zip codes 27, 28, 33, 43, 55.

thing, it is not clear that the finding of uniformly rapid suburbanization in all urban areas during the earlier period 1948–63 is itself valid. An important variable not adequately handled by the earlier analysis is city size. Perhaps there are scale effects in the decentralization process itself. Kain, for example, did attempt to stratify his data to capture the effects of differences according to size classification, but he chose to do so along the dimension of SMSA population growth *rate*. This exercise generated results such as those shown in Table 12, and these led him to conclude that central cities located in those SMSAs with the fastest growing populations have been most successful in retaining their people and jobs. This is certainly true in absolute numbers, although not—as Table 12 indicates—for service employment. The scale effects are much more ambiguous, however, when *relative* central city-suburban growth is stratified according to the Kain scheme. Table 13 (which reports on only the most recent period) displays no clear scale effect. For manufacturing, the relationship between

TABLE 12

MEAN ABSOLUTE LOSSES OR GAINS IN EMPLOYMENT AND POPULATION FOR FORTY CENTRAL CITIES, BY OVERALL SMSA POPULATION GROWTH RATE: 1948–63

(1950 central city boundaries)

SMSA Growth Class	Manufac- turing	Retail	Wholesale	Services	Popula- tion
SMSAs with the fastest growing populations (n = 13)	−14,058	−2,562	3,794	9,331	111,000
SMSAs with medium population growth (n = 13)	−17,580	−9,043	−351	4,123	−60,000
SMSAs with the slowest growing populations (n = 14)	−66,705	−14,358	−6,493	11,458	−117,000

Source: Kain, "Distribution and Movement," Table 8.

[(average annual percentage suburban growth) − (average annual percentage central city growth)]

and SMSA size class (as measured by overall population growth over the period 1948–63) is U-shaped; for the other variables, it is hill-shaped. I am unable to find any reallocation of the "medium-growth" SMSAs which would leave us with two size classes displaying a uniform scale effect.

The usual problems with percentage growth rates—e.g., their sensitivity to the level of the base year population—are clearly present here. Cohen and Noll choose instead to specify size by the *level* of SMSA population

TABLE 13

DIFFERENCES BETWEEN AVERAGE ANNUAL PERCENTAGE EMPLOYMENT GROWTH IN THE RING AND IN THE CENTRAL CITY FOR FORTY SMSAs, BY OVERALL SMSA POPULATION GROWTH RATE: 1948–63

(1950 central city boundaries)

SMSA Growth Class	Manufac- turing	Retail	Wholesale	Services	Popula- tion
Highest growth rates	8.8	14.9	14.0	12.6	5.3
Medium growth rates	5.5	19.8	16.6	16.7	7.0
Lowest growth rates	6.0	11.7	15.2	8.4	5.7

Source: See Table 12.

in 1960, a theoretically preferable measure of scale. Thirteen of the SMSAs in their sample had populations of over 1.7 million at that time; the populations of the other 17 ranged from 0.8 to 1.7 million. "The aggregated data for all thirty metropolitan areas confirm the hypothesis of an absolute decline in central city employment[17] [but stratification] reveals that the hypothesis . . . is a valid generalization only for the very largest metropolitan areas."[18] Among the 17 "smaller" SMSAs, only 5 central cities experienced such a decline between 1958 and 1963, compared with 10 of the 13 central cities in the large SMSA group. Cohen and Noll hypothesize that their size variable is probably acting as a proxy for age and density. Older cities are likely to have relatively less productive infrastructure with which to support new industry, and relatively greater diseconomies of scale, manifested, for example, by congestion and pollution.[19]

Assuming the change in trend to be valid (if not fully general over all sizes of cities), it still remains to be explained. Several economists are currently attempting to relate urban growth to national, or aggregate, economic activity. There are cyclical effects in Kain's own data—although he apparently chose not to emphasize them in his forecasts or policy analyses.[20] The postwar suburban shares given in Table 3 are converted into differences and are so displayed in Table 14. These periodic rates of change in the suburbanization trends display a definite cyclical pattern, with a decline in the rates of employment and population decentralization

17. "Most large central cities are losing employment, both relatively and absolutely . . . ." John R. Meyer, John F. Kain, and Martin Wohl, *The Urban Transportation Problem* (Cambridge, Mass.: Harvard University Press, 1965), p. 54.
18. Cohen and Noll, p. 9.
19. David L. Birch has, with the aid of National Planning Association data files, tested this age hypothesis explicitly, developing in the process a theory of the "life cycle of the city." Younger cities have more room for expansion; "densities of [young] cities are roughly one-half the densities of the older cities." Having been built around road networks, younger, newer areas possess greater efficiency in the intracity distribution of resources and products, and are more attractive to auto and truck oriented people and firms seeking new locations. Birch stratifies a sample of 73 SMSAs into three categories: *old* (qualified as "metropolitan" before 1900), *middle-aged* (1900–1930), and *young* (after 1930): "The results strongly support the life-cycle notion . . . . The older the SMSA, the less rapidly it is growing in economic terms. Of particular interest is the absolute decline of retail trade and manufacturing in the older cities. In sharp contrast is the rapid growth of central city manufacturing in the younger cities regardless of size." (See David L. Birch, *The Economic Future of City and Suburb* [New York: Committee for Economic Development, 1970], CED Supplementary Paper No. 30, pp. 11–15.)
20. The possibility that his tabular results exaggerate the severity of suburbanization due to failure to control for differential effects of the business cycle on central city and suburban industry was indeed admitted by Kain (see "Distribution and Movement," pp. 17–18). However, I can find no further mention of the possibility or its implications in later sections of that paper or in any of his further work.

TABLE 14
PERCENTAGE INCREASE IN THE SUBURBAN
SHARE OF SMSA EMPLOYMENT AND POPULATION
FOR FORTY SMSAs: 1948-63
(1950 central city boundaries)

	1948-54	1954-58	1958-63
Employment			
Manufacturing	5.5%	3.4%	9.8%
Wholesaling	6.3	6.2	7.9
Retailing	5.9	6.6	8.2
Services	6.4	4.5	5.2
Population	7.5	4.7	6.1

Source: See Table 3.

during 1954-58 and a rise in the subsequent period. The period 1954-58 was preceded by one recession and terminated in another.

According to Cohen and Noll:

The relative performance of the large cities during the 1950's and early 1960's may have been more cyclical than secular. The decade following the Korean War was a period of relatively high unemployment, especially the period from 1950 to 1963 when the annual average national unemployment rate fluctuated between 6.8 percent and 5.5 percent. . . . . One would expect the performance of the central cities to have been relatively better in recent years, during which time the unemployment rate fell from 5.7 percent in 1963 to 3.8 percent during 1966-68.[21]

Cohen and Noll have suggested several plausible explanations of such hypothesized sensitivity of central job growth to the business cycle:

First, in periods of high excess capacity, firms tend to remove their least productive plants from production first. The rapid growth of employment in the suburbs prior to the high unemployment of the late 1950's suggests that the average age of capital in suburban locations was probably much lower than in central cities. . . . Consequently the suburbs could be expected to gain employment relative to the cities during a period of high unemployment.[22]

The second hypothesis concerns the relative weight employers give to the proximity of their labor force in deciding where to locate. Cohen and Noll

---

21. Cohen and Noll, pp. 19-20.
22. Ibid. Compare Kain's statement: "During slack periods, multi-plant firms generally reduce production most in their older and less efficient plants. It is likely that central cities contain a disproportionate amount of this older and less efficient capacity. Thus, cyclical effects might be especially pronounced in central cities" ("Distribution and Movement," p. 18).

believe that firms tend to locate near to the type of labor currently in short supply. In the recessions of the period under discussion, "unemployment rates did not rise nearly so much for professional and managerial personnel. The availability of employees in this category was therefore of relatively greater concern. One would therefore expect firms to be . . . more likely to locate in areas appealing to the middle income professionals living in suburbs."[23]

Some start has in fact been made in attempting to measure the linkages between urban and national economic growth. Based upon the results of a "shift-share analysis" of 15 cities for the period 1953–65 (the details of which will be examined later), Wilfred Lewis, Jr., concludes that national employment must grow at about 1.25 percent per year (which implies a rate of growth of real GNP of about 4 percent per year) in order to "keep the level of jobs in the 15 central cities studied here—and, by implication, large cities generally—roughly stable." National growth below the threshold will lead to net job losses in central cities.[24] For one metropolitan area (New York), for the period 1958–66, Thomas Vietorisz and I found that a 1 percent increase in the relative importance of the SMSA to the national economy (measured by the New York SMSA's share of national employment) was associated with a .28 percent increase in the central city's share of metropolitan employment.

We interpret these results to mean that the metropolitan area sectors which have most of their employment located in the central city are the same sectors for which the metropolis is most important nationally. The metropolis, in other words, derives its distinction vis-á-vis the nation from those of its sectors whose employment is most heavily concentrated inside the city, not in its suburbs.[25]

Others are presently attempting to construct metropolitan econometric models which can be linked with national models in order to simulate the processes by which national growth is transmitted to urban areas. In one such model, Norman Glickman has estimated employment functions for three sectors of the Philadelphia metropolitan economy for the period 1949–66: manufacturing, retail-wholesale-services, and "other."[26] Local manufacturing employment, for example, is specified as a linear function of local manufacturing production and a time trend. Output, in turn, is related to U.S. GNP. The fitted functions (with t-ratios in parentheses) are:

23. Cohen and Noll, p. 20.
24. Wilfred Lewis, Jr., "Urban Growth and Suburbanization of Employment: Some New Data" (Washington, D.C.: The Brookings Institution, 1969), unpublished manuscript, p. 20.
25. Thomas Vietorisz and Bennett Harrison, The Economic Development of Harlem (New York: Praeger, 1970), p. 196.
26. Norman J. Glickman, "An Econometric Forecasting Model for the Philadelphia Region," Journal of Regional Science, April 1971.

$$Q_{Phil}^{mfg} = -132.70 + 10.988 \text{ USGNP}; \ \bar{R}^2 = .984$$
$$(30.918)$$

$$E_{Phil}^{mfg} = 381.809 + .058 \ Q_{Phil}^{mfg} - 128.283 \ t; \ \bar{R}^2 = .645$$
$$(3.993) \qquad\qquad (4.788)$$

with Q, E, and t representing output (measured by value added), employment, and time, respectively. Substituting the first expression into the second and combining terms yields

$$E_{Phil}^{mfg} = 374.132 + 0.637 \text{ USGNP} - 128.183 \ t$$

Manufacturing employment in the Philadelphia SMSA is directly related to national output, with a diminishing time trend reflecting the decentralization phenomenon. GNP must (as Lewis found in his study of 15 urban areas) grow fast enough to offset the negative trend. Numerically, Lewis found that GNP must grow by at least 4 percent per year in order for SMSA employment to grow at all. Glickman's model for Philadelphia implies that real GNP had to grow by more than 5.5 percent in 1965–66 in order for manufacturing employment in the Philadelphia SMSA to grow at all.[27]

---

27. (1) $E = a + bG - cT$ with $G \equiv USGNP$

    (2) $G = \dfrac{1}{b} (E - a + ct)$

To find the rate of growth of USGNP at which local employment does not grow, totally differentiate (1) and set the result equal to zero:

    (3) $\Delta E = b\Delta G - c\Delta t = 0$

Thus, the required growth rate is

    (4) $\Delta G = \dfrac{c}{b} \Delta t$

In percentage terms, this is

    (5) $\dfrac{\Delta G}{G} = \dfrac{c/b}{\dfrac{1}{b}(E - a + ct)} \Delta t$

To compute annual required national growth rates, set $t = 1$. Therefore, the threshold rate of growth of GNP is inversely related to the current level of SMSA employment and to time. In other words, local growth (and, conversely, decay) will be inertial. Once local employment begins to fall, it will be progressively harder to reverse, in the sense that the required rate of national growth will get progressively larger.

    The example in the text is based upon the last year of Glickman's time series:

$$E_{Phil, \ 1965}^{mfg} = 550,000 \qquad\qquad t_{1965} = 17$$

$$\text{required \% } \Delta USGNP_{1965-66} = \dfrac{201.1}{\dfrac{1}{.637}(550 - 381 - 809 + [17 \times 128.183])} = 5.5$$

According to the model,

$$E_{1966} > E_{1965} \longleftrightarrow \text{\% } \Delta USGNP_{1965-66} > 5.5$$

In fact, $E_{Phil, \ 1966}^{mfg} = 575,000$ and $\% \ \Delta USGNP_{1965-66} = 6.5$

The Location of Public Sector Jobs

NEARLY ALL OF THE PRE- AND POST-1963 TABLES in this chapter have excluded government employment. Thus, policy discussions about sub-urbanization based upon the published literature must of necessity pertain exclusively to the private sector.[28] But what of the locational "propensities" of public employers?

The extraordinary growth of government jobs in American urban areas since World War II has only recently come to the attention of economists and policy makers.[29] Over the last decade, from two out of ten to over seven out of every ten new jobs in the nation's largest metropolitan areas were in federal, state, and local government (the average for 27 large SMSAs is 34 percent).[30] In fourteen SMSAs for which intrametropolitan public sector data are available, the proportion of such jobs which were located in the central city in 1966 was over two-thirds (see Table 15). In half of the SMSAs in the sample, central cities contained 70 percent or more of all SMSA public sector jobs. An older study of 1960 land-use maps in 39 metropolitan areas shows that, of eight major categories, "public administration" was by far the most centrally located, there being no significant *concentrations* of land allocated to public service use outside of the core areas of the SMSAs in the sample (see Figure 2).[31]

The implication of these cross-sectional data—that the central city orientation of public employment may at least partly offset the suburban-ization of private jobs—is further supported by appeal to the admittedly fragmentary time-series evidence. The latter, such as it is, has been assem-bled by Cohen and Noll and is presented in Table 16 below. Even in the central cities of the largest metropolitan areas (with their declining popu-lations), government employment has been growing over time. The only

---

28. In fact, the four sectors included in Kain's analysis constitute only about half of total urban employment, as he has acknowledged: "The Census data presented in . . . this paper may be providing a misleading picture of employment changes by focusing on those employ-ment categories that are decentralizing most rapidly" (Kain, "Distribution and Movement," p. 30). The excluded sectors—domestic service, the professions, public utilities, finance, construction, and government employment—*are* probably suburbanizing less rapidly than the four sectors analyzed by Kain. "Between 1958 and 1963," for example, "employment gains in construction, government and finance in New York City offset declines elsewhere, raising total employment within the city by over 50,000 jobs" (Roger Noll, "Metropolitan Employment and Population Distributions and the Conditions of the Urban Poor," in *Financing the Metropolis*, ed. John P. Crecine [Beverly Hills, Calif.: Sage Publications, 1970] p. 495).
29. Cf. Bennett Harrison, *Public Employment and Urban Poverty* (Washington, D.C.: The Urban Institute, June 1971), and references cited therein; and Harold L. Sheppard, Bennett Harrison, and William Spring, eds., *The Political Economy of Public Service Em-ployment* (Lexington, Mass.: Heath-Lexington Books, 1972).
30. Harrison, *Public Employment and Urban Poverty*, p. 2 and Table 1.
31. Louis K. Loewenstein, "The Location of Urban Land Uses," *Land Economics*, November 1963. Loewenstein also demonstrates the same result through an analysis of variance on the land use distributions.

TABLE 15
THE INTRAMETROPOLITAN LOCATION OF
PUBLIC SECTOR JOBS IN FOURTEEN SMSAs: 1966
(by place of work)

Metropolitan Area	Federal				State and Local				All Public Employment			
	Total	Central City	Ring	Central City as Percent of Total	Total	Central City	Ring	Central City as Percent of Total	Total	Central City	Ring	Central City as Percent of Total
Almeda-Oakland	84,548	74,062	10,486	87.6	139,205	82,763	56,442	59.5	223,753	156,825	66,928	70.1
Baltimore	17,436	12,587	4,849	72.2	74,276	44,024	30,252	59.3	91,712	56,611	35,101	61.7
Boston	46,257	29,797	16,480	64.4	109,063	38,800	70,263	35.6	155,320	68,597	86,723	44.4
Denver	22,440	16,254	6,186	72.4	55,477	25,097	30,380	45.2	77,917	41,351	36,566	53.1
Houston	14,914	14,472	442	97.0	71,647	61,969	9,078	87.2	85,961	76,441	9,520	88.9
Memphis	11,998	11,895	103	99.1	37,925	35,976	1,949	94.9	49,923	47,871	2,052	95.9
Montgomery	4,594	4,522	72	98.4	6,645	5,537	1,108	83.3	11,239	10,059	1,180	89.5
New Orleans	12,818	12,163	655	94.9	44,229	27,408	16,821	62.0	57,047	39,571	17,476	69.4
New York	122,585	104,449	18,136	85.2	539,668	383,730	155,938	71.1	662,253	488,179	174,074	73.7
Omaha	7,509	5,522	1,987	73.5	23,973	18,328	5,645	76.5	31,482	23,850	7,632	75.8
Philadelphia	79,917	63,144	16,773	79.0	166,121	81,107	85,014	48.8	246,038	144,251	101,787	58.6
Richmond	5,331	5,230	101	98.1	22,550	12,792	9,758	56.7	27,881	18,022	9,859	64.6
San Antonio	36,566	36,480	86	99.8	31,294	30,171	1,123	96.4	67,860	66,651	1,209	98.2
St. Louis	33,777	25,526	8,251	75.6	88,297	33,204	55,093	37.6	122,074	58,730	63,344	48.1
Totals									1,910,460	1,297,009	613,451	67.9

Sources: The Maryland Regional Forecasting Project, Professor Curtis Harris, Director; U.S., Bureau of the Census,*County and City Data Book*, 1967; U.S. Civil Service Commission Statistical Section, *Federal Civilian Employment in the United States, by Geographic Area*, May 1968. Reprinted from Bennett Harrison, *Public Employment and Urban Poverty*, Table 2.

FIGURE 2

INTRAURBAN LOCATIONAL PATTERNS
OF EIGHT MAJOR EMPLOYMENT
SECTORS IN 39 METROPOLITAN AREAS: 1960

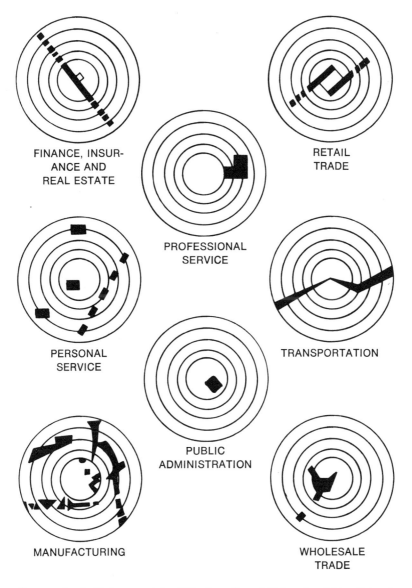

FINANCE, INSUR-
ANCE AND
REAL ESTATE

RETAIL
TRADE

PROFESSIONAL
SERVICE

PERSONAL
SERVICE

TRANSPORTATION

PUBLIC
ADMINISTRATION

MANUFACTURING

WHOLESALE
TRADE

Source: Louis K. Loewenstein, "The Location of Urban Land Uses," *Land Economics,* November 1963. Reprinted from Bennett Harrison, *Public Employment and Urban Poverty,* Figure 2.

TABLE 16
PUBLIC VERSUS PRIVATE SECTOR AVERAGE ANNUAL PERCENTAGE RATES OF EMPLOYMENT GROWTH FOR SELECTED PERIODS AND AREAS
(1963 central city boundaries)

	1958–63	1957/59–66	1957–62
Thirty SMSAs[a]			
Manufacturing			
Central Cities	−1.2%		
Suburbs	2.5		
Wholesaling			
Central Cities	−0.6		
Suburbs	2.7		
Retailing			
Central Cities	0.9		
Suburbs	7.8		
Services			
Central Cities	2.6		
Suburbs	7.6		
Seven SMSAs[b]			
Federal government			
Central Cities		1.8%	
Suburbs		2.4	
Eight SMSAs[c]			
Local government			
Central Cities			1.9%
Suburbs			6.9
Thirty SMSAs[c]			
Municipal governments in the 13 largest SMSAs			1.4
Municipal governments in the remaining 17 SMSAs			2.5

[a]Cohen and Noll, Table 3.   [b]Table 11.   [c]Table 7.
Source: Computed from figures in Cohen and Noll.

private sector central city growth rate in Table 16 which exceeds the three different government rates presented is services. In fact, the growth rate of the central city public sector has been so great that

the total gain in municipal employment between 1957 and 1962 in the thirty SMSAs taken together more than offsets the decline in the four private sectors discussed above between 1958 and 1963, changing the net decline of 33,000 new jobs to a net gain of 19,000. The further addition of Federal employment makes the gains even larger . . . .[32]

32.   Cohen and Noll, p. 12. Actually, as will be seen below in our study of Lewis's shift-share analysis, local government employment has also been "suburbanizing." But in this case (as Table 16 clearly indicates) the explanation lies in the truly extraordinary growth of suburban local government, not in central city force reductions.

In a study of fifteen urban areas over the period 1959–65, Wilfred Lewis, Jr., found that state and local government was among the fastest growing of all central city employment sectors, with federal government jobs in central cities growing somewhat more slowly.[33] In my own study of New York, between 1958 and 1967, local government accounted for the largest number of additional jobs in the city.[34]

Forecasting Future Rates of Suburbanization

WHAT OF THE FUTURE? WHAT SORT OF FORECAST does this empirical review permit? Many economists have interpreted the postwar historical record as indicative of *accelerating* suburbanization, and have predicted a continuation of this trend. Anthony Downs, for example, writes that

most new employment opportunities are being created in the suburban portions of our metropolitan areas, not anywhere near central city ghettos. Furthermore, this trend is likely to continue indefinitely into the future. . . . Nearly all *new* job opportunities will be located in suburbs . . . .[35]

while John Kain concludes that

the most central parts of metropolitan areas are losing employment to outlying areas and . . . this process is, if anything, accelerating. Slow growth and not infrequent decline of central city areas have accumulated to the point where absolute declines in central city employment are now commonplace.[36]

Thus, writes Kain, "my prognosis remains that of a continued decline in employment within the central cities of U.S. Metropolitan Areas."[37]

We have already learned in the first section of this chapter that suburbanization, whose origins we have traced back to at least 1900, appears *not* to have accelerated over the long term. We have also shown that the data generated by Kain to study shorter-term (postwar) suburbanization display definite cyclical behavior. Finally we have presented evidence for the post-1963 era which indicates at least a reduction in the rate of suburbanization.

Perhaps the most complete study of the acceleration question has been conducted by Wilfred Lewis, Jr. In a widely distributed (but as yet unpublished) paper, he has applied the technique of "shift-share" analysis to

33. Lewis, "Urban Growth."
34. Vietorisz and Harrison, *Economic Development of Harlem*, p. 204.
35. Anthony Downs, "Alternative Futures for the American Ghetto," *Daedalus*, Fall 1968, pp. 1335–36.
36. Kain, "Distribution and Movement," p. 27.
37. Ibid., pp. 36–37. Kain later qualified this prediction, saying that "because of the incompleteness of the data used . . . I would emphasize the speculative nature of these predictions and the need for more research."

the study of employment decentralization in urban areas.[38] The object of shift-share analysis is to break down regional economic growth into additive components reflecting the national, local, and industry-specific forces at work.

Lewis draws three principal conclusions from his analysis of the periods 1953–59 and 1959–65: (1) while the "suburban shift"—the amount by which a city's individual industries would have to grow in order to keep pace with the rates of growth of those industries in the SMSA as a whole—was significant for nearly every industry in all 15 cities, (2) national and regional growth were far more important than the suburban shift in explaining changes in central city employment,[39] and (3) "there is no evidence that the suburban shift is accelerating. The loss of jobs to the suburbs (after adjusting for other factors such as national and regional growth rates) was about the same in the more recent period as it had been earlier for the 12 cities for which data for both periods are available."[40] Table 17 displays Lewis's results for these 12 cities. Between the two six-year periods, the suburban shift factor increased significantly in Philadelphia, Newark, Portland, Paterson-Clifton-Passaic, and Minneapolis-St. Paul. It fell significantly in St. Louis, the District of Columbia, Denver, and New Orleans. There was virtually no change in New York, Baltimore and Atlanta. For all 12 cities, the suburban shift increased by only one-tenth of one percent between 1953–59 and 1959–65.[41]

The government, health, and education sectors were not included in the foregoing analysis because data for the earlier period were not available. How might their inclusion affect the results? For the later period, the

---

38. Lewis, "Urban Growth and Suburbanization of Employment." For a theoretical discussion of shift-share, see Harvey Perloff, et al., *Regions, Resources, and Economic Growth* (Baltimore: Johns Hopkins Press, 1960), pp. 70–74; and Edgar M. Hoover, *Introduction to Regional Economics* (New York: Alfred A. Knopf, 1971), pp. 292–95. For a description of a research design to study urban economic growth through a shift-share analysis, see Joel Bergsman, Peter Greenston, and Robert Healy, *Urban Economic Development and Growth Policy: An Agenda for Research* (Washington, D.C.: Urban Institute Working Paper, No. 200–5, February 1972).
39. "Of the various major factors, it is by all odds the national growth rate that explains most of the difference between higher and lower employment growth in a given central city at different times. . . . Comparing different cities at the same time, it is the regional growth factor—i.e., whether the city is located in a fast-growing or slow-growing [SMSA]—that primarily accounts for whether employment growth in a particular [central] city is high or low" (Lewis, p. 3).
40. Ibid., p. 16.
41. Robert Taggart, Executive Director of the National Manpower Policy Task Force and a research associate of George Washington University's Center for Manpower Policy Studies, is currently engaged in updating Lewis's shift-share results with more recent data on nine SMSAs for 1959–65 and 1965–68. Taggart reports that employment growth accelerated in six of the nine central cities (the three-year 1965–68 percentage growth rate exceeded the rate for the previous six years), and that Lewis's finding that national and regional growth dominate the suburban shift in explaining central city employment change is confirmed.

suburban shifts were as shown in Table 18. Although there was definite suburbanization within the previously excluded sectors (attributable almost entirely to the growth of local government in rapidly expanding suburban areas, an altogether predictable and nonpathological phenomenon), the job losses contributed by these sectors accounted for only a sixth of overall job losses associated with the suburban shift. The data are not yet available for determining whether suburbanization of these increasingly important urban service sectors is or is not accelerating.

In forecasting future suburbanization trends, it is important to distinguish between actual physical relocation of facilities on the one hand, and new suburban capital investment on the other. Given the very large fixed costs involved, firms are extremely reluctant to relocate plants, especially large ones.[42] When they do so, it implies very substantial interregional differences in operating costs and environmental conditions. An area whose plants are literally leaving is in very serious trouble indeed. Identifying the factors whose core-suburb differentials weigh most heavily in the relocation decision of firms can help governments direct public policy toward reducing the differentials, but this is likely to be an extremely difficult undertaking.

Locating *new* plant facilities in the suburbs is a totally different matter. The reason for it might be that the plants' principal markets are suburban, or it might simply be the "filling up" of the core (already discussed at length). Neither of these circumstances could be called pathological. To make central cities more attractive to at least some of these new facilities, public policy would have to focus primarily on the creation of new space and utilities. There is reason to believe that, given new developments in planning "three-dimensional space," central cities can provide these facilities.[43]

For at least one state (Michigan), it has been shown that net "shifts" in manufacturing location have consisted largely of expanding present facilities rather than of relocating.[44] Other area studies (for the San Francisco, New York, and Philadelphia labor markets) have found that "the numbers of businesses actually moving to the suburbs have been relatively small. The rapid growth of employment there is largely attributable to new business establishments or expansion of existing suburban plants."[45]

---

42. Cf. the statement of A. L. Bethel, Vice-President for Manufacturing, Westinghouse Corp., before the Ad Hoc Subcommittee on Urban Growth of the Committee on Banking and Currency, U.S. House of Representatives, *Hearings*, 91st Congress, 2nd Session, December 3, 1970, pp. 533–37.
43. See Chapter 7 for further discussion of this question.
44. Eva Mueller and James N. Morgan, "Location Decisions of Manufacturers," *American Economic Review, Papers and Proceedings*, May 1962.
45. U.S. Department of Labor, *1971 Manpower Report of the President*, p. 89 and the sources cited in footnote 6 on that page.

TABLE 17

RESULTS OF THE LEWIS SHIFT-SHARE ANALYSIS FOR TWELVE SMSAs: 1953–65

| | Civilian Non-Farm Employment in Central City[a] | | | | Composition of Change (Percent of Initial Employment) | | | | |
	1953	1959	1965	Change %	National Economic Growth	Industry Mix	Regional Shift	Suburban Shift	Total
	(thousands)								
New York:									
1953–59	2,949	2,779		− 5.8	− 0.2	5.1	− 6.6	− 4.0	− 5.8
1959–65		2,779	2,881	3.7	12.2	3.1	− 7.5	− 4.1	3.7
Philadelphia:									
1953–59	798	691		−13.4	− 0.2	1.1	− 5.8	− 8.5	−13.4
1959–65		691	667	− 4.1	12.2	0.6	− 7.0	− 9.8	− 4.1
St. Louis:									
1953–59	442	343		−22.4	− 0.2	1.6	−10.9	−12.8	−22.4
1959–65		343	334	− 2.6	12.2	− 0.3	5.7	− 8.8	2.6
Washington, D.C.:									
1953–59	221	225		1.6	− 0.2	6.9	13.9	−19.0	1.6
1959–65		225	254	12.8	12.2	3.7	13.6	−16.8	12.8
Baltimore:									
1953–59	363	326		−10.2	− 0.2	1.9	− 2.3	− 9.6	−10.2
1959–65		326	319	− 2.1	12.2	0.0	− 4.5	− 9.8	− 2.1

Newark:									
1953–59	343	307	320	−10.5	− 0.2	2.6	− 5.3	− 7.6	−10.5
1959–65		307		4.0	12.2	2.4	− 2.2	− 8.3	4.0
Atlanta:									
1953–59	208	226	280	8.5	− 0.2	3.2	12.5	− 7.0	8.5
1959–65		226		24.1	12.2	1.1	17.7	− 6.8	24.2
Denver:									
1953–59	160	165	180	3.1	− 0.2	4.1	13.1	−13.9	3.1
1959–65		165		9.2	12.2	1.0	3.2	− 7.1	9.2
New Orleans:									
1953–59	182	169	190	− 7.1	− 0.2	2.9	− 2.2	− 7.6	− 7.1
1959–65		169		12.3	12.2	1.2	2.9	− 4.1	12.3
Portland, Oregon									
1953–59	158	150	174	− 5.0	− 0.2	2.1	− 4.6	− 2.2	− 5.0
1959–65		150		15.7	12.2	0.0	10.8	− 7.4	15.7
Paterson-Clifton-Passaic:									
1953–59	111	102	103	− 8.0	− 0.2	− 4.4	9.7	−13.0	− 8.0
1959–65		102		1.4	12.2	− 0.5	8.9	−19.2	1.4
Minneapolis-St. Paul:									
1953–59	342	324	326	5.3	− 0.2	1.9	2.8	− 9.7	− 5.3
1959–65		324		0.8	12.2	0.8	0.7	−12.9	0.8
12-city total:									
1953–59	6,277	5,807	6,024	− 7.5	− 0.2	3.5	− 3.6	− 7.1	− 7.5
1959–65		5,807		3.7	12.2	2.0	3.3	− 7.2	3.7

[a] Non-farm employment, excluding government, education, and health services.

Source: Lewis, p. 12.

TABLE 18
SUBURBAN SHIFT IN
FIFTEEN SMSAs: 1959-65

Sector	Six-year job loss
All industries	−751,000
Manufacturing	−195,000
Retail trade	−174,000
Government	− 90,000
Education and health	− 36,000

Source: Lewis, p. 17.

Several recent doctoral dissertations, undertaken in connection with the modeling effort at the National Bureau of Economic Research (NBER), study the relocation of manufacturing plants within, into, and out of metropolitan areas, using Dun and Bradstreet data. Ray Struyk's study of the Boston area (defined as four central city and thirteen suburban analysis zones) confirms the hypothesis that "the patterns associated with new and relocating [plants] and their employees are clearly different."[46] Abstracting from these differences, and considering only the magnitudes of these relocations, we may distinguish four categories:

1. Of the 558 plants (employing 19,713 persons) located in the Boston region in 1965 which disappeared by 1968 (dying or emigrating), only 212 (with 7,404 employees) had been located within the Boston central city. This is 38.0 percent of the plants and 37.6 percent of the employees.

2. Of the 202 plants (6,199 workers) located in the central city in 1965 which relocated at some time over the next 3 years to another location within the region, only 62 (with 2,387 workers) moved to the suburbs; the rest moved to other sites within the city.

3. Over the same period, 18 plants (with 4,352 employees) moved into the city from the suburbs.

4. Finally, of the 440 plants (and 14,391 employees) which appeared in the region between 1965 and 1968 (newly born or inmigrating), 126 (with 5,897 workers) settled in the central city. This is only 28.3 percent

46. Raymond J. Struyk, "A Progress Report on a Study of Intrametropolitan Location of Industry," paper delivered to the Committee on Urban Economics, Resources for the Future, Cambridge, Massachusetts, September 1969, mimeographed. The results reported in this paper were at that time preliminary, "probably more important as indicators of the direction of further work in this area than as substantive results" (p. 23). Struyk—now associated with The Urban Institute—has recently co-authored a more complete study of industrial location in four cities (Raymond J. Struyk and Franklin James, *Intrametropolitan Industrial Location: The Pattern and Process of Change in Four Metro Areas* [New York: National Bureau of Economic Research, forthcoming]).

of the new plants, but fully 41.0 percent of the new jobs. Moreover, of the 17 analysis zones in the region, the two which accounted for more new plants and new jobs than any others were both central city zones.

In the larger study, involving Cleveland, Minneapolis-St. Paul, and Phoenix, as well as Boston, Struyk and James found additional evidence of the continued viability of the central city's manufacturing base and of the "naturalness" of decentralization.

While all four central cities sustained net absolute manufacturing job losses between 1965 and 1968, there were areas within each city whose relative shares of the SMSA's manufacturing jobs actually grew.

The single most important component of net employment change in the central city was the level of employment in establishments that were stationary throughout the period, not physical outmigration (evidence, perhaps, of the business cycle effect). Moreover, "natural increase" (births and deaths within the core and the ring) was "substantially more important" than actual migration in explaining the net decentralization of jobs. In particular, the suburbs exhibited far more jobs in "new" plants than did the central cities. On the other hand, "no evidence was uncovered that establishments located in core areas have a consistently higher propensity to die." Finally, "several industries consistently preferred centralized locations, and grew more rapidly at such locations than elsewhere."[47]

In a companion NBER monograph, which was also developed with the Dun and Bradstreet data—this time for New York City and for the period July 1967 to August 1969—Robert Leone arrived at a number of similar conclusions.[48] "What we have observed," he writes, "is clearly not universal decentralization." The core lost jobs in outmigrating plants which required more space to accommodate their one-story facilities, but it actually gained jobs in the home offices of many manufacturing companies.

Neither deaths nor mover origins were especially concentrated in the core. And "in virtually all industries, single-plant firms [which theory predicts would benefit most from agglomeration] had a strong and increasingly central orientation."

Finally, and most significantly, Leone found (as had Struyk) that in explaining the net decentralization of jobs, employment changes in stationary plants were more significant than employment changes associated with plant relocations.

47. Struyk and James, *Intrametropolitan Industrial Location*. The results reported here are still tentative.

48. Robert A. Leone, *Location of Manufacturing Activity in the New York Metropolitan Area* (New York: National Bureau of Economic Research, forthcoming). This, too, is still in preliminary, and therefore tentative, form.

These detailed studies of the supply of urban jobs reveal that net employment changes in the central city have five components: job gains through inmigrating plants, job losses through outmigrating plants, gains through new births, losses through deaths, and employment (capacity) changes in plants that do not move at all during the period of analysis. Perhaps the central finding of these NBER studies is that the growth and decline of stationary plants seems to dominate the process of employment change. This in turn reinforces the importance of further research into the hypothesis that national and regional business cycles affect core and suburban areas differently.

A recent study of the Philadelphia economy breaks down net employment changes in 1967 into those attributable to plant entries into and exits from the city, and plant relocations within the city.[49] During the year, 2,407 plants entered, while 1,931 exited. The net employment gain was 4,085 jobs (this varied from a loss of 1,061 jobs in the black North Philadelphia ghetto to a net gain of 1,141 jobs in the white working-class Frankford-Richmond section of the city). The modal entrant was in the wholesale and retail trade sector, as was the modal leaver. Of the incoming plants, 10.9 percent were in manufacturing, as were 10.7 percent of the plants leaving the city. In manufacturing, the plants which left tended to be somewhat larger than those which entered. Thus, although there was a net gain of 28 plants, the city's manufacturing sector suffered a net loss of 957 jobs. However:

> Although there was an overall decline in manufacturing employment, it is important to notice that many industries within this sector actually experienced net gains in the number of jobs. The gains were [greatest] in electrical machinery, food products, primary metals, and fabricated metals. In addition, ghetto and nonghetto areas appear to have benefited equally from these increases.[50]

A total of 2,076 plants with a paid work force of 72,698 persons relocated within the central city during 1967 (3,143 "mom and pop" stores with no paid employees also relocated at least once during the year). The high income white Northeast section lost 931 jobs this way, while, at the other extreme of the neighborhood distribution, South Philadelphia (predominantly black and Italian) gained 436 jobs through intracity plant relocations. The greatest amount of intracity relocation activity occurred in the service sector, followed by wholesale and retail trade. Manufacturing ranked far behind, with a relocation rate only a third as great as that of services.

The NBER and Philadelphia studies warn us that forecasts of employment

---

49. Kenneth McClellan and Paul Seidenstat, *New Businesses and Urban Employment Opportunities* (Lexington, Mass.: Heath-Lexington Books, 1972), chap. 3.
50. Ibid, p. 57.

decentralization should break down net changes into their component parts, in order to distinguish between nonpathological (*new* suburban) growth and actual suburbanization of jobs.

Finally, any forecast of future intrametropolitan industrial and commercial location should underscore the fact that the location of public employers is directly subject to government control, and that government employment is already the fastest growing sector of the urban economy. In the future, therefore, the availability of jobs in the central city need no longer be determined exclusively by "market forces," if indeed it ever was. The transformation of the urban economic base from goods production to service production does create certain short-term difficulties for a society reluctant to engage in large-scale income redistribution and transfer of tax revenues.[51] But in the long run, the tendency for the public sector to control (or at least influence) an increasing share of national product creates an instrument by which the central city job base can be maintained, assuming that to be a goal of social policy.[52]

APPENDIX: THE EFFECTS OF THE ADJUSTMENT OF TIME SERIES DATA ON ESTIMATES OF JOB DECENTRALIZATION

COHEN AND NOLL HAVE CRITICIZED KAIN'S adjustment procedure on both substantive and methodological grounds. Substantively, "the argument is often put forth [by Kain and others] that the flight of jobs to the suburbs has reduced the tax base of the central cities [which] leads either to higher tax rates or to a further exodus of jobs and people to the suburbs. For the purposes of examining this issue, employment data should not be corrected for annexation since the legal and political ability to annex significant new tax base is an important potential response to the challenge of diminishing tax resources."[53] Moreover, the use of constant city boundaries does not really help to maintain a sharp distinction between areas which are

---

51. Cf. William Baumol, "Macroeconomics of Unbalanced Growth: The Anatomy of Urban Crisis," *American Economic Review*, June 1967.
52. To the extent that the rapid growth of core public employment represents a form of political patronage or a kind of disguised welfare system—albeit one whose income payment (i.e., wages) is relatively high—there may be good reasons for discounting to some extent the instrumental value of public employment. Cf. Frances Fox Piven, "Cutting Up the City Pie," *The New Republic*, February 5, 1972.
53. Cohen and Noll, pp. 5–6.

more or less geographically accessible to residents of the core ghetto, a distinction which Kain clearly intended to make. "The cities with the most active [intercensal] annexation activity are precisely those that are most [spatially extensive] to begin with; relatively compact older industrial cities . . . have annexed no area at all."[54] Adjustments for annexation, in other words, do not make the employment data significantly more representative of a constant commuting range for ghetto residents; even under the 1950 boundary definitions, many central cities (e.g., Houston and Los Angeles) are already highly decentralized.

The methodological criticism first takes note of the role of Kain's hypothesis that "people follow jobs" (see above, page 3, footnote 3). Since the Census provides annexation information for population but not for employment, Kain chose to make the adjustment by assuming that jobs are annexed at the same rate at which population is annexed. By his theory of the relationship between household and industrial location, this assumption is clearly conservative, leading to an underestimate of the rate of job annexation. But "compelling evidence indicates that the bias operates very strongly in the other direction." Cohen and Noll estimate that, for the four industrial sectors studied by Kain, the ratio of employment to population in thirty SMSAs in 1960 was nearly 1.5 times larger in the central cities than in the suburbs.[55] Fremon discovered that this ratio actually rose between 1960 and 1967 in eight SMSAs she examined.[56] If annexed areas are more similar to suburbs than to the urban core in their land use and density characteristics, then actual job annexation will be relatively *lower* than population annexation. Thus, the Kain procedure actually *over*estimates the magnitude of job annexation. In other words, by using constant 1950 central city boundaries, Kain penalizes central city job growth after 1950.

Using Cohen and Noll's unadjusted data for 30 metropolitan areas, I have tabulated the suburbanization figures for the period 1958–63. The figures in parentheses in the following table are Kain's adjusted estimates (for forty SMSAs: 29 of the 30 used in the Cohen-Noll sample, plus Akron, Dayton, Fort Worth, Jersey City, Louisville, Memphis, Oklahoma City, Rochester, San Antonio, Seattle, and Tampa). Although the samples are not identical, the results are very close to being so; the differences could easily be due to sampling error. Thus Kain's procedure for eliminating annexation effects from the employment data does not appear to seriously overstate the rate of job suburbanization.

---

54.   Ibid., p. 6.
55.   Ibid., p. 5.
56.   Charlotte Fremon, *Occupational Patterns in Urban Employment Change, 1965–67*, p. 13.

SUBURBAN SHARE OF
SMSA EMPLOYMENT FOR
THIRTY SMSAs: 1958-63
(1963 central city boundaries)

	1958 %	1963 %
Manufacturing	40.8 (42.0)	45.4 (51.8)
Wholesaling	19.0 (20.7)	26.4 (28.6)
Retailing	36.3 (37.2)	44.2 (45.4)
Services	26.9 (26.1)	32.0 (31.3)

Source: Cohen and Noll, Table 3. Kain's adjusted figures (with 1950 central city boundaries), taken from Table 3 in the text, are shown in parentheses.

At the same time, this finding—while not formally inconsistent with Kain's theory of location (because the dynamic implications of that theory have been so casually specified)—lends little intuitive support to the proposition that "people follow jobs." Given the enormous extent of population annexation (83 percent between 1950 and 1960), extension of the central cities' boundaries to include these annexed people should—if Kain were correct—yield at least a close to proportional (or, indeed, extraproportional) increase in jobs, since it is the presence of the jobs in the annexed areas which allegedly attracted the people in the first place. For the Cohen and Noll estimates in the above table to be consistent with adjusted central city job increases of anything like 83 percent, suburban job growth during the five-year period would have to be in excess of 100 percent. This condition was, of course, not even approximated.

Chapter 3

THE SUPPLY AND DEMAND FOR CENTRAL CITY LABOR AND THE MISMATCH HYPOTHESIS

IN THE PREVIOUS CHAPTER, THE SPECIFIC PROBLEM of minority unemployment was never mentioned. Yet many seem to believe that the movement of jobs to the suburbs leads to increased minority unemployment in the core.[1] What assumptions underlie this belief? Are they valid? How *are* central city minority workers affected by the suburbanization of middle class whites and of industrial and commercial employers?

The Relative Availability of Central City Jobs

TWO PRINCIPAL ASSUMPTIONS SEEM TO BE AT WORK. The first concerns the supply of labor. By concerning themselves only with the demand for labor, and by inferring that suburbanization of this demand entails a reduction

---

1. Thus, for example: "most of the growth in new employment has been in the suburban ring and hence the low income groups [minorities] have had to resort to the local employment opportunities in the fairly stagnant industrial areas of the inner city" (David Harvey, "Social Processes, Spatial Form, and the Redistribution of Real Income in an Urban System," *Proceedings of the 22nd Symposium of the Colston Research Society* [London: Butterworth's Scientific Publications, 1970], p. 275). It is this belief more than any other which seems to undergird arguments for suburban open housing.

in central city employment, those who see suburbanization as the chief cause of continued ghetto poverty implicitly assume that the central city supply of labor is relatively fixed. This, however, seems not to be the case.

Wilfred Lewis, Jr. has created an index to measure the relationship between population and jobs within metropolitan areas:

$$\frac{\text{Jobs located in}}{\text{central city}} \div \frac{\text{Jobs located in}}{\text{the SMSA}}$$
$$\frac{\text{central city}}{\text{population}} \qquad \frac{\text{SMSA}}{\text{population}}$$

If the jobs-to-population ratio is the same in a central city as in its suburbs, Lewis's index will display a value of unity. Values greater than unity indicate that SMSA jobs are more highly concentrated in central cities than is SMSA population. Values of less than unity indicate the converse. Lewis's results for 1953 and 1965 are displayed in Table 19. In his own words:

It is clear that the central cities' loss of jobs appears distinctly less disastrous when compared to the population of potential job seekers than when looked at purely in terms of gross numbers. . . . The fact that the ratios are mostly greater than one—and substantially greater—shows that jobs, while they have been suburbanizing, are still substantially more highly concentrated in the central cities than is population, and this is true of almost all industries in almost all cities.[2]

Moreover, the fact that all but two of the industry groups in Table 19 show an increase in the Lewis index over the period 1953–65 indicates that "jobs in all cities and in almost all industries have been moving out more slowly than population, so that the number of jobs per inhabitant in the central city in 1965 equaled or exceeded the number there were in 1953."[3]

Charlotte Fremon has extended Lewis's analysis to 1967; her estimates of the jobs-to-population ratio in eight central cities are given in Table 20. Between 1960 and 1967, the ratio of central city jobs to central city residents increased from 45 percent to 50 percent. In none of the eight cities did the ratio decline. "Population, then, is still moving to the suburbs much faster than is employment."[4]

We have been using population as a proxy for labor force. Fremon has taken measurements of the actual central city labor force in five cities.

---

2. Wilfred Lewis, Jr., "Urban Growth and Suburbanization of Employment: Some New Data" (Washington, D.C.: The Brookings Institution, 1969), unpublished manuscript, pp. 24–26.
3. Ibid., p. 3. Lewis also observes that, "in light of what is so often said about the particular importance of suburbanization of blue-collar jobs, it is interesting to note that manufacturing . . . has also been moving to the suburbs more slowly than population" (ibid., p. 26).
4. Charlotte Fremon, *The Occupational Patterns in Urban Employment Change, 1965–1967* (Washington, D.C.: The Urban Institute, January 1970), p. 13.

TABLE 19
RATIO OF JOBS TO POPULATION IN
CENTRAL CITIES RELATIVE TO THEIR SMSAs,
BY INDUSTRY: 1953 AND 1965

Industry and SIC Code	1953		1965		
	Range	12-City Weighted	Range	12-City Weighted	15-City Weighted
Construction (15–17)	0.72–1.30	1.04	0.98–1.40	1.07	1.08
Manufacturing (19–39)	0.93–1.58	1.11	0.91–1.63	1.17	1.17
Food (20)	0.94–2.02	1.25	1.18–2.37	1.38	1.47
Textiles (22)	0.00–2.30	1.13	0.00–3.15	1.43	1.44
Apparel (23)	1.05–2.36	1.41	1.08–2.94	1.64	1.73
Lumber, furn. (24,25)	0.71–1.94	1.19	0.79–2.37	1.23	1.29
Printing (27)	1.11–2.00	1.39	1.14–2.58	1.53	1.62
Chemicals (28)	0.49–1.56	0.99	0.57–1.83	1.03	1.01
Machinery (35,36)	0.67–2.55	1.10	0.14–1.93	0.95	0.91
Transportation equipment (37)	0.08–1.50	0.40	0.17–1.59	0.52	0.60
Other	0.72–1.58	1.04	0.75–1.46	1.07	1.05
Transport & Utilities (40–49)[a]	1.13–1.67	1.31	1.25–2.26	1.48	1.51
Wholesale Trade (50)	1.14–2.01	1.42	1.06–2.27	1.47	1.51
Retail Trade (52–59)[a]	1.08–1.60	1.21	1.04–1.46	1.16	1.17
Finance, Insurance, Real Estate (60–67)	0.82–1.77	1.40	0.98–2.66	1.54	1.63
Personal and Business Services (70,72,73,75, 76,78,79,81,891,893)[a]	1.04–1.75	1.31	1.03–2.05	1.42	1.40
Total Above	1.09–1.54	1.21	1.06–1.70	1.28	1.30
Other Services (80,82,84, 86,89)[a]			0.27–2.10		1.30
Government (91–93)	not		0.96–2.21		1.19
Federal (91)	available		0.83–2.58		1.43
State (92)			0.00–3.68		0.86
Local (93)			0.80–2.15		1.11
Grand Total			1.06–1.77		1.28

[a]Details on the composition of each two-digit group are given in Lewis's paper.
Source: Lewis, p. 25.

Table 21 shows that the earlier results—more jobs than resident workers in central cities and an increase over time in this ratio, which implies a relatively greater centralization of SMSA jobs than of SMSA workers—are sustained when actual labor force is substituted for population. According to the figures given in Table 21, the central city economy apparently

TABLE 20
RATIO OF JOBS TO RESIDENTS IN
EIGHT CENTRAL CITIES: 1960-67

Cities	1960 Ratio[a]	1965 Ratio	1967 Ratio
New York	43.6	45.1	46.8
Philadelphia	42.3	41.7	44.9
San Francisco	51.8	61.0	72.5
St. Louis	54.7	59.1	65.5
Washington, D.C.	59.4	66.8	70.9
Baltimore	42.2	43.0	47.1
Denver	43.5	49.1	54.3
New Orleans	34.2	37.8	40.6
Total	44.8	47.0	50.0

[a] 1959 jobs, 1960 population.
Source: Fremon, *Occupational Patterns,* p. 15.

continues to generate more than enough jobs to accommodate the central city labor force (ignoring wages and skill requirements, for the moment). More recently, Thomas Welch has used 1960 and 1970 Census place-of-work data from twelve SMSAs to study changes in the central city/SMSA ratio of jobs to local labor force. For 1970, he found a substantial excess supply of inner city jobs in all twelve places (the relative central city excess supply was—as Kain would predict—somewhat greater for skilled than for nonskilled jobs). The analysis of 1960-1970 *changes* revealed *increases* over the decade in all the cities. This growth of the excess supply of central city jobs obtained for all occupations except sales workers, a predictable exception since retail sales is the industry which most closely follows

TABLE 21
RATIO OF JOBS TO LABOR FORCE IN
FIVE SMSAs: 1959 AND 1967

	1959	1967	
Area	(Central city)	(Central city)	(Ring)
New York	1.00	1.18	.70
Philadelphia	1.08	1.14	.68
St. Louis	1.35	1.52	.70
Washington, D.C.	1.34	1.70	.62
Baltimore	1.08	1.15	.81
Weighted Average	*1.05*	*1.18*	*.70*

Source: Fremon, *Central City and Suburban Employment Growth, 1965-67* (Washington, D.C.: The Urban Institute, 1970), pp. 6-7.

population movements. From these data, Welch concludes that labor force continues to suburbanize faster than jobs—even nonskilled jobs—thus reducing the potential competition for vacancies physically located within the urban core.[5]

However, although the supply of jobs physically located within central cities is growing, the employment of central city residents is actually falling! Figure 3 shows the average annual percentage rates of growth of central city jobs and employment of central city residents in Philadelphia, New York, St. Louis, the District of Columbia, and Baltimore. For the five cities, jobs grew over the period 1965–67 by an average annual rate of 1.5 percent, but employment of residents fell by a little over 0.4 percent! The results of a similar comparison undertaken by Wilfred Lewis for 14 cities over the longer period 1953–65 are displayed in Table 22. Negative entries in the last two columns of the table indicate that job growth exceeded the growth in the employment of residents.

These results all indicate that, instead of a relative shortage of centrally located jobs,

the growth of jobs located in central cities . . . outpaced the growth of employment. Undoubtedly this reflects people moving to the suburbs but retaining their downtown jobs. Clearly, if central city residents had experienced an increase in employment proportionate to the growth of downtown jobs, there would be a smaller unemployment problem for city residents than there is now.[6]

Independent evidence on the net direction of the intrametropolitan journey-to-work (particularly for the poor) comes from recent experiments in "reverse commuting." Many policy analysts have pressed for programs to transport disadvantaged workers from the urban core out to the suburban fringe where an increasingly large number of the allegedly decent jobs are located. Many specific recommendations have been made, including proposals to reserve parking or breakdown lanes for the unobstructed use of special buses, to extend the subway system (where such a system already exists), and to subsidize car pools. But, even as a short-term expedient, reverse commuting experiments have not met with much success in the municipalities where they have been tried—Boston, Detroit, Washington, D.C., and elsewhere.[7] In the Capital, in fact, there is evidence that special buses running in both directions carry more suburbanites into the city than nonwhite ghetto dwellers out of the city. The figures in Table 23 come

5. Thomas Welch, "Residential Location and Minority Opportunities," unpublished Master's thesis, Department of Urban Studies and Planning, M.I.T., June 1973.
6. Lewis, p. 26.
7. See, for example, Carol S. Greenwald and Richard Styron, "Increasing Job Opportunities in Boston's Urban Core," *New England Economic Review*, Federal Reserve Bank of Boston, January-February, 1969.

TABLE 22
GROWTH OF CENTRAL CITY EMPLOYMENT COMPARED TO GROWTH OF JOBS LOCATED IN CENTRAL CITY: 1953-65

City	Average Annual Rate of Growth of Jobs Located in Central City		Average Annual Rate of Growth of Employment of Central City Residents		Approximate Excess of Average Annual Employment Growth (+) or Job Growth (−)	
	1953-59	1959-65	1953-59	1959-65	1953-59	1959-65
New York	−0.5%	1.0%	−0.3%	−0.6%	7,000	−54,000
Philadelphia	−1.5	−0.1	−0.8	0.0	7,000	1,000
St. Louis	−2.6	0.6	−2.2	−1.7	2,000	− 9,000
Washington, D.C.	2.9	2.8	−0.9	0.2	−13,000	−19,000
Baltimore	−1.1	0.1	−1.0	−0.3	0	− 2,000
Newark	−1.2	1.1	−1.4	−1.5	− 1,000	− 9,000
Atlanta	2.0	4.1	2.7	n.a.	2,000	n.a.
Denver	1.1	2.0	1.4	n.a.	1,000	n.a.
New Orleans	−0.5	2.2	0.1	n.a.	1,000	n.a.
Portland	−0.1	2.8	−0.6	n.a.	− 1,000	n.a.
Paterson-Clifton-Passaic	−1.1	0.4	−1.5	n.a.	0	n.a.
Minneapolis-St. Paul	−0.3	0.7	−1.0	−2.0	− 3,000	−11,000
Chicago	n.a.	0.8	n.a.	−0.7	n.a.	−25,000
San Francisco-Oakland	n.a.	2.0	n.a.	−1.2	n.a.	−17,000

Source: Wilfred Lewis, Table 8.

TABLE 23
AVERAGE NUMBER OF PASSENGERS RIDING CAPITAL FLYER BUSES, WEEK OF MARCH 9-13, 1970

	Per Bus
D.C. OUT to Prince Georges County	7.0
D.C. OUT to Montgomery County	23.5
D.C. OUT to Fairfax County	3.3
Prince Georges County IN to D.C.	23.1
Montgomery County IN to D.C.	19.5
Fairfax County IN to D.C.	28.6

(Full Capacity = 51 Persons)
Source: *The Washington Post*, April 2, 1970, p. F-1.

FIGURE 3

GROWTH OF JOBS LOCATED IN CENTRAL CITIES, COMPARED WITH THE GROWTH OF JOBS HELD BY CENTRAL CITY RESIDENTS, PERCENT CHANGE PER YEAR, 1960-1967

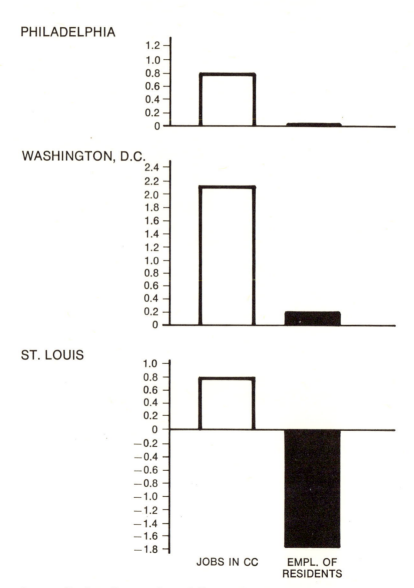

Source: Charlotte Fremon, *Central City and Suburban Employment Growth, 1965-67* (Washington, D.C.: The Urban Institute, 1970), Chart V.

FIGURE 3 Con't.

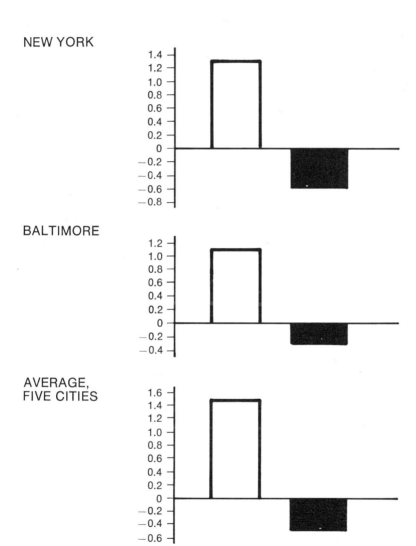

NEW YORK

BALTIMORE

AVERAGE,
FIVE CITIES

from an interim evaluation of a two-year reverse commuting experiment being subsidized by the U.S. Department of Transportation. The only relatively successful run in the table is the ghetto-to-Montgomery-County route, and this is largely attributable to the opening of a Health, Education, and Welfare building in the town of Rockville, Maryland, with virtual door-to-door service.

In a study of the relationship between transportation and central city unemployment in St. Louis, Edward Kalachek and his colleagues at Washington University found evidence of net in-commuting in that metropolitan area. The proportion of ring-to-center commuters of both sexes, all ages and all income levels was greater than the corresponding proportions of center-to-ring commuters. The results are shown in Table 24.

In his Brown University dissertation (in progress), Robert Moffit states the essential implications of this analysis. The decentralization of jobs may

TABLE 24
PERCENTAGE OF AREA RESIDENTS WHO COMMUTE, BY AGE, SEX, AND EARNINGS: ST. LOUIS, 1960

Category	Percent of SMSA Workers Who Live and Work in the:		Percent of SMSA Workers Who Commute to the Ring from the Central City	Percent of SMSA Workers Who Commute to the City from the Ring
	Central City	Ring		
Age and Sex				
Male	40.89%	27.68%	5.40%	16.84%
14–24 years	41.47	31.16	4.93	13.13
25–44 years	38.10	27.80	5.85	18.80
45–64 years	43.55	26.04	5.16	16.33
65 and over	50.43	26.78	3.65	11.13
Female	49.75	25.96	3.74	12.87
14–24 years	49.41	24.51	3.33	13.80
25–44 years	47.66	26.91	4.11	13.95
45–64 years	51.80	25.64	3.63	11.73
65 and over	55.85	25.72	2.75	6.93
Earnings				
Less than $3,000	48.23	31.76	3.47	8.09
$3,000–5,999	47.19	27.41	4.86	12.97
6,000 and over	32.63	30.31	4.43	23.77

Source: Edward D. Kalacheck and John M. Goering, eds., *Transportation and Central City Unemployment* (St. Louis: Institute for Urban and Regional Studies, Washington University, March 1970), Appendix Tables A-3 and A-4.

or may not hurt central city blacks; that depends partly on the extent of the skill mismatch which we will examine in a moment. But suburbanization of white workers potentially helps central city blacks. Certainly orthodox economic analysis would lead one to predict a fall in the supply of central city labor, and a consequent increase in job vacancies (and possibly wage rates) in the core. Commuting, discrimination, and market failure may prevent perfect adjustments, but the tendencies are unmistakable. The conventional view, which considers only the partial effect of *job* decentralization on central city blacks, misses this potentiality entirely.[8]

The Alleged Skill Mismatch

THE SECOND ASSUMPTION WHICH UNDERLIES the widespread belief that suburbanization has directly penalized the inner-city poor is the so-called "mismatch hypothesis." This might (if it were found to be valid) also explain why there are more centrally located jobs than centrally located workers, with the "surplus" jobs going to commuters from the suburbs. There is

an alleged mismatch between the low skill endowments of the central city labor force and the white collar (assumed high-skill) characteristics of those relatively few job classes thought to be still growing . . . in central cities. It should be noted that the data did not exist on which to make such assertions; but this deficiency has not proved a deterrent to their proponents.[9]

One cannot doubt the ubiquity of this assumption in discussions of urban policy or the strength of the conviction with which it is held. Daniel Moynihan, for example, asserts that "it is the low-skilled jobs [which] seem increasingly to be located in the suburban fringe, far from the homes of the central city poor."[10] The prestigious Advisory Commission on Intergovernmental Relations advises congressional and executive agencies that "the new or expanding industries in the city tend to provide white collar jobs with relatively high entrance requirements . . . . The best blue collar job opportunities are moving to suburban and smaller urban areas."[11] And a new undergraduate text book on urban economics informs its readers that "the unskilled and semi-skilled jobs in the manufacturing and service sectors

---

8. Perhaps we need a "filtering theory of employment" to complement the well-known filtering theory of housing. One recent study confirms that (in New York City, at least) whites *are* vacating jobs which are then taken by blacks. William Johnson, *Changing Patterns of Employment in the New York Metropolitan Area* (New York: The New York City Rand Institute, Dec. 1971), R-571-NYC.

9. Fremon, *Occupational Patterns*, p. 1.

10. Daniel P. Moynihan, "Poverty in Cities," in *The Metropolitan Enigma*, ed. James Q. Wilson (Cambridge: Harvard University Press, 1968), p. 348.

11. Advisory Commission on Intergovernmental Relations, *Urban and Rural America: Policies for Future Growth* (Washington, D.C.: U.S. Government Printing Office, 1968), p. 58.

of the economy have become increasingly decentralized and therefore inaccessible [to] low income people in the central cities."[12]

"Dual labor market" studies have repeatedly found evidence of strong demand for low-skilled labor in central cities,[13] while (as already indicated) Kalachek and Goering discovered the opposite to be the case in suburban St. Louis. This, of course, runs directly counter to the mismatch hypothesis. Recently, several of the economists whose work we reviewed earlier began to study the spatial distribution of occupations directly; all who have done so report their inability to find evidence in support of the mismatch hypothesis. Of these various studies, those by Fremon and Kalachek (based, it must be noted, on a very small sample) are the best in that they measure occupation directly, rather than (as in Lewis, Taggart, and Noll) inferring occupational or skill distributions from data on relative wages, a procedure which assumes a degree of allocative efficiency which few urban labor markets actually possess.

Fremon finds that

there is no conclusive evidence at all to support the mismatch hypothesis—or to refute it. There exist no time series data for employment, by occupation, in cities and suburbs. The central hypothesis of the argument—that the jobs growing in central cities are high-skilled ones compared to those growing in suburbs—had only been assumed.[14]

To get at the problem, she has developed intrametropolitan occupational distributions for eight SMSAs. To do this, she took the industry-by-occupation distributions for the (then) 50 percent of national employment monitored by the U.S. Equal Employment Opportunity Commission (EEOC) and used them to translate the Census Bureau's *County Business Patterns* industry distributions for the eight SMSAs into occupational distributions. This procedure makes it necessary to "assume that the total occupational distribution of an industry is similar to that in the reporting firms."[15] Moreover, since her industry data are for 1965 and 1967, while the EEOC occupational data are for 1966, "this method assumes that the occupational distribution of changes in employment is the same as the average in an industry."[16] Finally, public sector data had to be obtained from other sources. Since the most recent of these to give central city and suburban

12.   Arthur F. Schreiber, et al., *Economics of Urban Problems* (Boston: Houghton Mifflin, 1971), p. 13.
13.   Cf. Peter B. Doeringer and Michael J. Piore, *Internal Labor Markets and Manpower Analysis* (Lexington, Mass.: D. C. Heath, 1971); and Bennett Harrison, *Education, Training, and the Urban Ghetto* (Baltimore: Johns Hopkins Press, 1972).
14.   Fremon, *Central City and Suburban Employment Growth*, p. 8.
15.   Fremon, *Occupational Patterns*, p. 4. The EEOC until recently required reports only from firms with over 100 employees.
16.   Ibid., p. 6.

data by occupation was (at the time of writing) the 1960 Census, Fremon's government data correspond to still another point in time.[17]

Fremon groups the nine EEOC occupations into three major categories: officials, managers, professionals, and technicians are classified as *high skilled*; sales, office and clerical workers, craftsmen, and operatives are considered *semiskilled*; and laborers and service workers are *low skilled*.

Figure 4 shows the percentage distribution of additional net employment in the central cities and suburbs of the eight SMSAs. High skilled jobs did grow slightly faster inside the central cities, while semiskilled and low skilled jobs did grow slightly faster in the suburbs over the two-year period. However, about five-sevenths of the net overall central city increases were not in high skilled jobs. Applying that ratio to the remaining central city job growth which took place in the government sector, *some 70 percent of all new jobs in the eight central cities were not highly skilled jobs.* Applying this procedure to the suburban government data yields an estimate of about 75 percent, higher to be sure but only barely so. In any case, the key finding is surely the 3 to 1 ratio of low and semiskilled to high skilled jobs in the core.

Fremon next reintroduces the estimates, reported earlier (see Figure 3), of central city residential unemployment—the labor supply side of the analysis. Her comparisons between the demand for labor of various skill levels and the excess supply of central city labor for the six cities on which all the requisite information is available are displayed in Table 25. In every central city except New York, the extra jobs created between 1965 and 1967 exceeded the number of unemployed persons located within the central city in 1967. Moreover, Fremon's sample is drawn from only the very largest cities. Recalling Cohen and Noll's finding that central city jobs are growing faster in the small-to-medium cities than in the largest cities (see above, pp. 22 ff) and assuming that the occupational patterns are relatively invariant with respect to city size (see footnote 17), then these figures may well understate the extent of the problem. Suburban residents hold a substantial number of low and semiskilled central city jobs, and it is this—as much as the shortage of such jobs assumed by advocates of the mismatch hypothesis—that helps to explain the high unemployment of unskilled central city residents.

---

17. However, "the industry-occupation cross-classification for governmental employment in the 1960 Census of Population . . . reveals great similarity between SMSAs. In all cases, professional and technical categories account for about 32 percent of total government employment, office and clerical for another 33 percent, total blue collar for about 28 percent (with service representing about 19 percent), and the remaining 5-6 percent in the category of officials and managers. It seems likely that the occupational distribution of government employment would remain fairly stable over time," given this very marked cross-section stability, "but there is no way of checking" (ibid., p. 7).

FIGURE 4

PERCENTAGE DISTRIBUTION OF EMPLOYMENT
CHANGE, BY OCCUPATION GROUP: 1965-67

AVERAGE FOR EIGHT CITIES

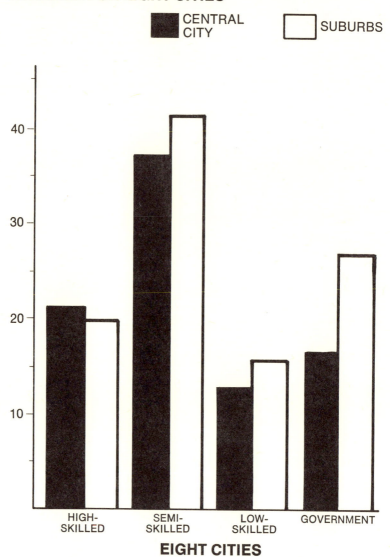

Source: Charlotte Fremon, *Central City and Suburban Employment Growth, 1965-67*, Chart IV-A.

TABLE 25

NUMBER OF UNEMPLOYED CENTRAL CITY RESIDENTS, 1967, COMPARED WITH THE INCREASE OF CENTRAL CITY JOBS, 1965-67, BY OCCUPATION

(numbers in thousands)

Central City	Total Net Job Increase	High-Skilled	Semi-Skilled	Low-Skilled	Govern-ment	Semi-Skilled, Low-Skilled, + 60% of Government[a]	Total Number of Unemployed 1967
Philadelphia	60	13	26	9	12	42	37
San Francisco	48	6	15	10	17	35	30[b]
St. Louis	23	3	10	5	5	18	18
Washington, D.C.	37	9	7	1	20	20	8
Baltimore	31	6	10	4	11	21	21
New York	119	32	47	12	28	76	137
Total, Six Cities	318	69	115	41	93	212	251
Total, without New York	199	37	68	29	65	136	114

[a]See footnote 17, p. 53, for a justification of the 60 percent figure.
[b]Includes Oakland.
Source: Charlotte Fremon, Central City and Suburban Employment Growth, 1965-67, p. 14.

We have referred to Kalachek and Goering's study of the St. Louis labor market, and their finding of net in-commuting for male and female workers of all ages and income classes (Table 24). Table 26 shows a similar pattern for all occupations and industries. Thus, there is somewhat greater reverse commuting for blue-collar than for white-collar workers in St. Louis, both absolutely and relatively. But again, the scale of this commuting must be taken into account. The proportion of SMSA blue-collar workers who commute from the ring into the core is almost three times greater than the proportion of such workers who "reverse commute" from the core out to the ring. The only category of low-skilled labor in which reverse commuting in St. Louis exceeds in-commuting is—not surprisingly—domestic service.[18]

Taggart, after extending a similar analysis for nine cities to 1968, concludes that "the employment opportunities for central city residents were increasing."[19] Working with similar data, Noll also finds that "jobs, particularly for the less skilled, are *easier* to find in the central city."[20]

Adele Massell has pointed out that Kain's hypotheses with respect to suburbanization and the mismatch imply that the nonwhite ghetto unemployment rate can be expected to rise over time.[21] Data on ghetto unemployment are scarce; the only regular time series began in 1967 and were temporarily terminated at the end of 1971. They are graphed in Figure 5. While the relatively short duration of these series precludes the identification of long-term trends, it is clear from Figure 5 that—at least since 1967—ghetto unemployment rates have paralleled national rates.

---

18.   Kalachek addresses the mismatch hypothesis in another way. If there were indeed an excess demand for unskilled labor in the suburbs, as the hypothesis implies, then by implication there must be a shortage of unskilled labor in the suburbs, and suburban employers who use such labor would be interested in importing it from the central city. "Willingness to pay seems an excellent indicator of the seriousness of interest. In our survey of employers in the current destination zone of TEMPO NORTHWEST," write Kalachek and Goering of their St. Louis reverse bus commutation study, "only two firms favorably considered subsidizing the continuation of the bus" after federal financing ceases. "Manufacturers in other parts of the county were also asked. Only nine firms representing six percent of sample employment answered affirmatively." Kalachek and Goering, *Transportation and Central City Unemployment*, p. 5n.
19.   Taggart, unpublished work.
20.   Roger Noll, "Metropolitan Employment and Population Distributions and the Conditions of the Urban Poor," in *Financing the Metropolis*, ed. John P. Crecine (Beverly Hills, Calif.: Sage, 1970), p. 501 (emphasis mine). One especially useful set of data sources used by every student of this subject consists of the papers of Paul O. Flaim (cf. "Jobless Trends in 20 Large Metropolitan Areas," *Monthly Labor Review*, May 1968; "Unemployment in 20 Large Urban Areas," *Employment and Earnings and Monthly Report on the Labor Force*, March 1969; and, by Flaim and P. M. Schwab, "Geographic Aspects of Unemployment in 1969," *Employment and Earnings*, April 1970).
21.   Adele P. Massell, "A Bi-Market Model of Urban Wages and Employment Under Housing Location Constraints," Institute for Public Policy Analysis, Program in Urban Studies, Stanford University, Discussion Paper No. 3 (revised), July 1971, mimeographed, p. 2.

TABLE 26

PERCENTAGE OF AREA RESIDENTS WHO COMMUTE, BY OCCUPATION AND INDUSTRY: ST. LOUIS, 1960

Category	Percent of SMSA Workers Who Live and Work in the:		Percent of SMSA Workers Who Commute to the Ring from the Central City	Percent of SMSA Workers Who Commute to the City from the Ring
	Central City	Ring		
Occupation				
White Collar	46.45%	25.36%	4.16%	18.49%
Professional, techni- cal & kindred	41.38	28.75	5.59	17.62
Managers, officials, and proprietors	43.01	26.06	3.75	20.79
Sales	45.89	25.90	3.02	18.43
Clerical	52.17	22.29	3.84	17.96
Blue Collar	43.38	28.76	6.19	16.05
Craftsmen	38.46	30.16	6.24	19.07
Operatives	46.11	27.55	6.08	14.95
Laborers	48.08	29.18	6.46	10.88
Service Workers	55.80	28.05	4.60	8.33
Domestic Workers	54.46	31.93	5.30	5.10
Others	56.29	26.87	4.41	9.21
Industry				
Construction	37.75	32.36	5.85	16.21
Manufacturing	40.41	28.94	6.98	17.65
Transportation, communi- cations & utilities	48.99	19.96	3.72	20.55
Wholesale & retail trade	49.89	26.01	3.70	16.14
Finance, insurance and real estate	54.45	17.81	1.93	21.34
Business & repair ser- vices	49.63	23.76	3.64	17.95
Personal services	56.68	27.63	4.48	7.97
Entertainment	46.95	28.29	6.95	10.89
Professional	48.80	29.70	4.03	13.21
Government	48.94	23.83	5.80	16.47

Source: Kalachek and Goering (see above, Table 24).

FIGURE 5

UNEMPLOYMENT RATES, URBAN POVERTY AREAS AND THE UNITED STATES: THIRD QUARTER, 1967, TO SECOND QUARTER, 1971[a]

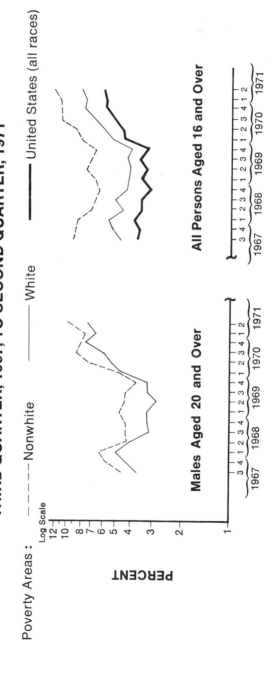

a Includes poverty areas in the 100 SMSAs with populations of at least 250,000. Data for the first six quarters are not seasonally adjusted. In 1971, these 100 sets of poverty areas accounted for about 7.5 percent of the country's population and labor force.

Source: U.S. Department of Labor, News Releases No. 10-017, 10-175, 10-388, 10-560, 71-207, and 71-391.

Conclusion

DONALD CANTY has written

The jobs increasingly are in the suburbs. There is no reason to believe that this trend can be altered to the extent of providing inner-city jobs in numbers anywhere near the scale of need.[22]

But according to Charlotte Fremon,

Measured by job growth, the central cities are not stagnating economically. They have experienced slower growth than have the suburbs, but jobs there have grown, and at an increasing rate.

The growth in central city jobs that has taken place in recent years has not been noticeably skewed in favor of the highly skilled white collar jobs, as has been feared. In fact, there has been sufficient growth in the semi-skilled and lower-skilled jobs to accommodate virtually all of the unemployed in central cities if, in fact, the jobs had gone to them. In short, some of the standard arguments advanced to explain differences in income levels and unemployment rates between central cities and suburbs don't stand up under careful scrutiny.[23]

The policy implications of these findings are exceedingly important.

All of the net increase in jobs in central cities is being absorbed by suburban commuters, and at a time when job opportunities are expanding rapidly in the suburbs. Therefore, we need to develop avenues of access for central city residents to the jobs which are growing in the city.

The high unemployment rates and low incomes of central city residents are not simply a matter of the jobs not being there, or of the jobs being of the wrong type. Therefore, proposed solutions based upon an assumed geographical and skill mismatch will not resolve the employment or income problem.[24]

Like the widespread uncritical emphasis on formal education as an antipoverty instrument,[25] "the mismatch hypothesis has diverted attention effectively, although possibly unintentionally, from the real issues involved."[26]

It looks very much as if we are faced, yet again, with the reality of racial discrimination in hiring and firing. The EEOC has provided ample evidence, in case any was needed, that this is a widespread phenomenon which will require a major national commitment to reverse. And while there is nothing wrong with manpower programs to upgrade the labor force to keep pace with an upward shift in quality of labor demanded, it is perhaps time we focused attention on supervisors and employers as well as the employed.[27]

---

22. Donald Canty, "Perspective: Why Worry About Loosening the Suburban Noose?" *City*, January-February 1971, p. 50.
23. Fremon, *Central City and Suburban Employment Growth*, p. 1.
24. Ibid, p. 15.
25. Cf. Ivar Berg, *Education and Jobs* (N.Y.: Praeger, 1970); Bennett Harrison, "Human Capital, Black Poverty and Radical Economics," *Industrial Relations*, October 1971; Harrison, *Education, Training, and the Urban Ghetto.*
26. Fremon, *Occupational Patterns*, pp. 25–26.
27. Ibid., p. 18.

PART II

SUBURBANIZATION AND MINORITY ECONOMIC OPPORTUNITY

Chapter 4

THE CASE
AGAINST THE CASE
AGAINST GHETTO
DEVELOPMENT

WHATEVER THE PRECISE PAST RATE or future magnitudes of suburbanization, it is clear from the survey we have just completed (and from Census statistics which are far too familiar by now to require recitation here) that poverty and nonwhites are becoming increasingly concentrated in the core of our metropolitan areas. We have learned recently that "there has been an increase in residential segregation in American cities since 1960, in both absolute and relative terms."[1] Moreover, the Census Bureau discloses that, "based upon a preliminary analysis of the 1970 Census, only about 5 percent of the nation's suburban population was found to be black, 'approximately the same proportion as 10 years ago.'"[2]

As the increasingly black and poor residents of the core acquire greater (actual or potential) control over the institutions that govern them, their interest in planned economic redevelopment of the central city will almost certainly grow. But the motivation for black economic development may be more than simply pecuniary:

In the last several years, the twin concepts of political self-determination and economic development have caught the imagination of young blacks (and other minorities) in the urban ghetto. Community self-determination is the political program most often associated with the new spirit of racial identification—"black

---

1.   Bennett Harrison, *Education, Training, and the Urban Ghetto* (Baltimore: Johns Hopkins Press, 1972), p. 164.
2.   Ibid., p. 165.

pride"—in America. The acquisition of economic power is perhaps the only—at any rate, surely the most effective—way for the black community to acquire political influence commensurate with its numerical proportion in the population. And much sociopsychological theory (e.g., the work of Allport and Pettigrew) argues that genuine integration can only take place between groups who are cooperatively dependent on one another, i.e., groups of equal political status.[3]

If Grier, Cobbs, Hampden-Turner, Allport, and Pettigrew are correct that "black power" is a form of group therapy—a "blueprint for psychosocial development"—then progress through affirming black identity is more likely to succeed in a large community in the present ghetto than in the pocket ghettos formed by proposed dispersal. And, of course, there is the "political advantage to be gained from the visibility of large numbers in affecting the allocation of resources toward compensatory education or compensatory investment."[4]

Many liberal economists, however, interpret the movement for black economic development as a retreat from the long-term national agenda of full racial integration. In Kain's words, for example,

Recognition of high rates of Negro unemployment, low incomes and other undesirable conditions found in central city ghettos have led to widespread demands for corrective action. A majority of practical men seem to have concluded that residential integration is either impossible or will take too long. They contend the problems of the urban Negro are current and real and that while residential integration might be desirable as a long-range goal, such a course for the immediate future is uncertain, difficult, and politically dangerous. . . .

Proposals to patch up [or "gild"] the ghetto and make it a better place to live and to create jobs there are heard with increasing frequency.[5]

Kain is one of the leading opponents of "ghetto gilding."[6] One argument he presents is that such programs would reduce political pressure for and interest in racial integration. Another is that the ghetto's capacity to absorb capital is far too small to permit sufficient internal job development to make up the entire deficit. Another and

3.   Thomas Vietorisz and Bennett Harrison, "Ghetto Development, Community Corporations, and Public Policy," *The Review of Black Political Economy*, Autumn 1971, p. 22. A similar argument is made by Joel Bergsman, "Alternatives to the Non-Gilded Ghetto," *Public Policy*, Spring 1971.
4.   Matthew B. Edel, "Development vs. Dispersal: Approaches to Ghetto Poverty," in *Readings in Urban Economics*, eds. Matthew B. Edel and Jerome Rothenberg (New York: Macmillan, 1972), especially pp. 313–14.
5.   John F. Kain, "The Big Cities' Big Problem," *Challenge*, September-October 1966. Reprinted in *Negroes and Jobs*, eds. Louis A. Ferman, et al. (Ann Arbor: University of Michigan Press, 1968), p. 242.
6.   John F. Kain and Joseph J. Persky, "Alternatives to the Gilded Ghetto," *The Public Interest*, Winter 1969.

most telling objection is that such policies might well [aggravate the situation]. There are strong links between Northern ghettos and the still vast pools of rural, Southern Negroes. Ghetto improvement and particularly job-creation programs might well have as their principal result increased migration of Southern Negroes to Northern metropolitan areas. Growth rates of Northern ghettos might increase several fold, greatly aggravating the problems. . . . The distortions of metropolitan growth would be magnified, and the goal of assimilating and integrating the Negro into urban society would be made far more difficult.[7]

Instead, Kain asserts that "there is no alternative but vastly increased suburbanization of Negro populations, if we are to avoid unnecessary economic waste and growing social and political conflict."[8]

We will examine the potential payoff to the ghetto dispersal or minority suburbanization strategy in chapter 5. Here, we will present and evaluate some of the objections to central city redevelopment, particularly with reference to the interpretations of the suburbanization phenomenon which we analyzed earlier.[9]

We will consider four arguments against central city redevelopment: (1) that renewal of the core would, by itself, attract so many more rural migrants that they would swamp any redevelopment effort; (2) that these new migrants would generally be the least able to adjust to urban life without massive social investments; (3) that because of the accelerating suburbanization of jobs—and given the skill mismatch—migrants attracted to the urban core would be locating where there are fewer and fewer jobs which they are capable of filling; and (4) that attracting more blacks to the central city would drive out additional tax-paying middle-class whites and employers.

Ghetto Development and Rural-to-Urban Migration

As WE HAVE MENTIONED, one of the main reasons for opposition to inner city redevelopment is the expectation that it would stimulate increased rural-to-urban migration, and so flood the development effort. Downs, for example, writes:

By making life in central city ghettos more attractive without creating any strong pressures for integration or dispersal of the nonwhite population, [a ghetto development] policy would increase the immigration of nonwhites into central cities.[10]

---

7. Kain, "The Distribution and Movement of Jobs and Industry," in *The Metropolitan Enigma*, ed. James Q. Wilson (Cambridge: Harvard University Press, 1968), pp. 38–39.
8. Kain, "The Big Cities' Big Problem," p. 243.
9. The positive case for ghetto development, as part of a more general program of central city renewal, will be reviewed in chapter 8.
10. Anthony Downs, "Alternative Futures for the American Ghetto," *Daedalus*, Fall 1968, p. 1347.

To Kain and Persky:

The ultimate result of efforts to increase Negro income or reduce Negro unemployment in central city ghettos may be simply to induce a much higher rate of migration of Negroes from Southern rural areas. This will accelerate the already impressive list of urban problems. . . . Indeed, it is possible that more than one migrant would appear in the ghetto for every job created.[11]

We must therefore inquire whether and to what extent black migration is in fact related to differentials in employment opportunities. In a study of the interstate migration behavior of the American population, Cicely Blanco found that "eighty-six percent of the variation in the rate of civilian migration between states during the period 1950 to 1957 can be explained by changes in the level of unemployment and changes in the number of federal military personnel in each state. The first of these factors was found to be by far the most important. The availability of jobs is the principal factor which determines the amount and the direction of interstate migration."[12]

Blanco's conclusion pertains to a period in the 1950s and does not consider race or income class. Using more recent data, Richard Wertheimer found that the net benefits associated with migration from the rural and urban South to the urban North have been highly significant—indeed, greater for nonwhites than for whites.[13] In this study, the benefits of migration are measured by the net differences in the earnings of the head of the household. The net estimated benefits are shown in Table 27.

Samuel Bowles has also made a study of South-to-North migration using the 1960 Census.[14] Bowles, using a somewhat different approach from that of Wertheimer, is interested in testing the human-capital migration decision theory originally suggested by Sjaastad.[15] His dependent variable, therefore,

---

11.   Kain and Persky, "Alternatives to the Gilded Ghetto," pp. 82, 86. It is interesting to observe that this expectation of a high degree of migration sensitivity implicitly assumes a degree of efficiency in the interregional diffusion of job information which is strangely at variance with Kain's own impressions of the inefficiency of the intrametropolitan information system. "Negroes [in the ghetto] may have less information about and less opportunity to learn about [suburban] jobs distant from their place of residence" (John F. Kain, "Housing Segregation, Negro Employment, and Metropolitan Decentralization," *Quarterly Journal of Economics*, May 1968, p. 179).
12.   Cicely Blanco, "The Determinants of Interstate Population Movements," *Journal of Regional Science*, Summer 1963, p. 77.
13.   Richard F. Wertheimer II, *The Monetary Rewards of Migration within the United States* (Washington, D.C.: Urban Institute, 1970).
14.   Samuel Bowles, "Migration As Investment: Empirical Tests of the Human Capital Approach to the Study of Geographical Mobility," *The Review of Economics and Statistics*, November 1970.
15.   Larry A. Sjaastad, "The Cost and Returns of Human Migration," *The Journal of Political Economy*, October 1962 (supplement).

TABLE 27

NET RETURNS TO SOUTH-NORTH MIGRATION FOR MIGRANTS WITH TWELVE OR FEWER YEARS OF SCHOOL, BY RACE

Period following the move	Whites	Nonwhites
	$/year	$/year
First five years	0	800
Next thirty years	1,000	1,000
Thereafter	350	350
Net present value at 10 percent discount rate	6,500	10,000

Source: Wertheimer, *The Monetary Rewards of Migration Within the United States*, pp. 57 and 59.

is not the income or earnings differential, but rather a measure of the actual decision to migrate. Moreover, Bowles deals with aggregate male age-education cohorts; Wertheimer studied microdata. Formally, Bowles' model is specified as:

$$NM = \beta_0 + \beta_1 Y + \beta_2 AY + \beta_3 SY + \beta_4 P + \epsilon$$

where NM = The proportion of a demographic cohort in the three Southern Census regions who migrate to any of the non-Southern Census regions

       Y = the logarithm of the expected net present value of the differentials in lifetime earnings between the location of origin and that of destination

       A = the age of the cohort

       S = years of schooling of the cohort

       P = proportion of the male Southern workers in the age–schooling cohort who earned less than $1,500 in 1959; a proxy for the relative poverty of the cohort.

Fitting the same model to various cohorts, Bowles estimates the following equations (t-statistics are in parentheses):

(1) NM (blacks) = .015 + .018Y − .001AY + .002SY + .197P; $\bar{R}^2 = .64$
            (.77)   (3.97)   (11.75)   (6.42)   (4.53)

(2) NM (whites) = −.035 + .030Y − .001AY + .001SY + .203P; $\bar{R}^2 = .33$
            (4.45) (5.88)   (6.69)   (2.55)   (2.79)

Tests indicate significantly different migration behavior for blacks and whites.

We can draw a crude comparison between the Bowles and Wertheimer studies by solving equations (1) and (2) for Y and computing the differential effect of migration on income ($\partial Y/\partial$ NM). The result,

$$\left[\frac{1}{(.030 - .001A + .001S)}\right]_{\text{Whites}} < \left[\frac{1}{(.018 - .001A + .002S)}\right]_{\text{Blacks}}$$

for migrants with no more than 12 years of school (i.e., $S \leq 12$) is fundamentally the same as that found by Wertheimer: the benefits of South-to-North migration for male workers with at most a high school education is relatively greater for blacks than for whites. Clearly, black migration is strongly related to different employment opportunities as reflected in interregional differences in average earnings.

The possibility remains, nonetheless, that there are other factors pertinent to the migration decision which interact with differentials in earnings in ways as yet unspecified or undiscovered. Considerable research has been devoted to this problem. As Anthony Pascal observes, "A good deal of data now becoming available seem to indicate that migration behavior for the low-skilled and disadvantaged segments of the population is significantly motivated by factors other than employment opportunities."[16] From a review of the literature, Michael Barth concludes that variables "of equal importance" to differences in "income, employment, wages, or job openings" are the "distance between origin and destination, and the existence of friends and relatives . . . in the regions of origin and/or destination."[17] The latter variable seems to be particularly important, and at least one way in which it probably interacts with differential income can be suggested: "[Friends and relatives] at the destination point can both provide information about economic and social conditions to potential immigrants, and ease the financial and social burden of the migrant when he arrives."[18]

This leads to what is known as "chain migration," a frequently observed pattern according to which "prospective migrants learn of opportunities, are provided with transportation and have initial accommodations and employment arranged by means of primary social relationships with previous migrants."[19] Charles Tilly, in a review of the characteristics of black migration to American cities, also concludes that while different economic

16. Anthony H. Pascal, "Manpower Training and Jobs," in *Cities in Trouble: An Agenda for Urban Research,* ed. Pascal (Santa Monica: The RAND Corporation, 1968), p. 71.
17. Michael C. Barth, "Migration and Income Maintenance," in *The President's Commission on Income Maintenance Programs, Technical Studies* (Washington, D.C.: U.S. Government Printing Office, 1970), p. 188.
18. Ibid., p. 189.
19. Ibid., Melvin Lurie and Elton Rayack quoted.

circumstances are undoubtedly correlated with the propensity to migrate, "for people moving without a guarantee of a job, the presence of friends and relatives matters a great deal more than such things as the housing supply or the availability of public assistance."[20] Certainly "the quality of public services does not seem to make much difference to the flow of migrants," nor do the migrants who come place any "exceptional demand on services."[21]

Scholars at the Survey Research Center of the University of Michigan have been engaged in studies of the "factors that condition a person's decision whether or not to move." They found that a migrant's perception of the importance of job-related reasons for moving was positively related to income and educational status. For lower-class migrants, noneconomic reasons were more important, including "family, friends, and community ties." For all of the people in its sample, regardless of class or status, the Center's researchers concluded that "people tend to give more economic rationales for their moves than actually exist. When economic opportunities did influence a move, they motivated those people who already had relative advantages in the labor force."[22] Moreover, "Since 1948, intercounty and interstate moves for the Negro population have been lower than for the white population. . . . The principal impediments to Negro mobility appear to be largely emotional in nature, involving chiefly family ties to a particular place and a general uneasiness about unfamiliar surroundings."[23]

The paths traced by successive generations of interstate migrants are remarkably stable. The principal routes of South-to-North migration—what demographers call "migration trees"—are displayed in Figure 6. The three principal trees and their constituent geographic regions are:

$$\text{South} \begin{cases} \text{South Atlantic} & \longrightarrow \text{Middle Atlantic, New England} \\ \text{East South Central} & \longrightarrow \text{East North Central,} \\ & \qquad\quad \text{West North Central} \\ \text{West South Central} & \longrightarrow \text{Mountain, Pacific} \end{cases}$$

Along the two older trunks (indicated by the thick flows in Figure 6), nonagricultural employment over the period 1947–68 has been growing faster in the Southern "roots" than in the non-Southern "branches," as the following set of average annual percentage rates of growth shows:[24]

20.   Charles Tilly, "Race and Migration to the American City," in *The Metropolitan Enigma*, ed. James Q. Wilson, p. 142.
21.   Ibid., p. 156
22.   Advisory Commission on Intergovernmental Relations, *Urban and Rural America: Policies for Future Growth* (Washington, D.C.: U.S. Government Printing Office, 1968), p. 18.
23.   Ibid., p. 19.
24.   U.S. Department of Labor, *Statistics on Manpower: A Supplement to the 1969 Manpower Report of the President* (Washington, D.C.: U.S. Government Printing Office, 1969), Table D-1.

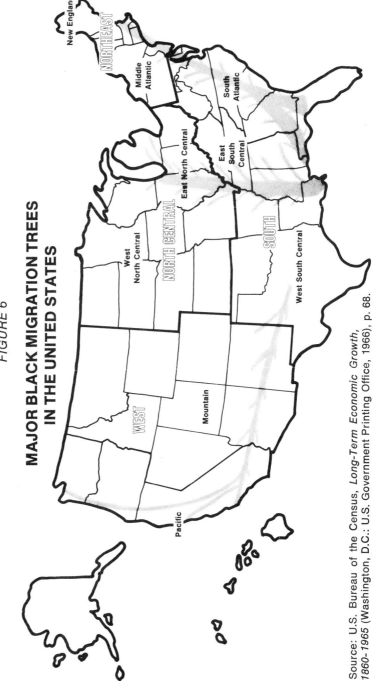

FIGURE 6

**MAJOR BLACK MIGRATION TREES
IN THE UNITED STATES**

Source: U.S. Bureau of the Census, *Long-Term Economic Growth,*
1860-1965 (Washington, D.C.: U.S. Government Printing Office, 1966), p. 68.

(South Atlantic)   2.8 ⟶ 1.0, 1.2 (Middle Atlantic, New England)
(East South Central) 2.3 ⟶ 1.5, 1.9 (East North Central,
                                                                West North Central)
(West South Central) 2.8 ⟶ 3.2, 4.9 (Mountain, Pacific)

Along all three trunks, per capita income between 1947–65 has been growing faster in the Southern roots than in the non-Southern branches:[25]

(South Atlantic)   4.4 ⟶ 3.4, 3.8 (Middle Atlantic, New England)
(East South Central) 4.7 ⟶ 3.7, 3.9 (East North Central,
                                                                West North Central)
(West South Central) 4.2 ⟶ 3.5, 3.4 (Mountain, Pacific)

And yet, despite these very substantial postwar differences in the rates of economic activity in the Southern and non-Southern regions of the United States, black migration from the South continues to the present day.[26] In 1958–59, for example, the percentage of all nonwhite interregional migration going up each of the three trunks was

Middle Atlantic, New England—32 percent
East North Central, West North Central—24 percent
Mountain, Pacific—33 percent

and only 11 percent was intrasouthern or into the South.[27] The most recent published migration figures—preliminary estimates from the 1970 Census—surprised many demographers and political decision makers with the discovery that,

Contrary to widespread assumption, the exodus of Negroes from the South did not slow down significantly during the 1960's. . . .
    Their net migration from Southern states—primarily to California and Northern urban states—was at an annual rate of 140,000, almost the same pace established during the 1940's and 1950's.
    The new Census estimates show that there was a net migration from 16 Southern states of 1.4 million Negroes in the past decade, as compared with approximately 1.5 million in both the 40's and 50's.[28]

25. U.S. Department of Commerce, Bureau of the Census, Long-Term Economic Growth, 1860–1965 (Washington, D.C.: Government Printing Office, 1966), pp. 212–13. This study by the Commerce Department also offers evidence that the North-to-South hourly wage rate gap is closing. Even so, as we shall see shortly, there has been no decline in the rate of South-to-North migration. For an excellent analysis of these North-to-South linkages and migration paths, see John F. Kain and Joseph J. Persky, "The North's Stake in Rural Southern Poverty," in Rural Poverty in the United States, National Advisory Committee on Rural Poverty, U.S. Department of Agriculture, (Washington, D.C.: Government Printing Office, 1968). See also National Advisory Commission on Civil Disorders, U.S. Riot Commission Report (New York: Bantam, 1968), pp. 239–42.
26. The direction of net migration for whites is, however, into the South now. For non-whites, the net direction is still out of the South.
27. Dorothy K. Newman, "The Negro's Journey to the City," Monthly Labor Review, May/June, 1965, p. 505, Table 3.
28. William Chapman, "Southern Negro Exodus Maintains Pace," The Washington Post, March 4, 1971, p. A-5.

And this occurred even though the South grew faster than the North—and has been doing so for over twenty years.

Perhaps the strongest evidence that there are nonincome factors (though correlated with differences in income or employment) involved in an important way in the migration decision is the contrast between postwar variances in interstate employment and income on the one hand, and migration on the other. Over the period, state employment levels varied from 54,000 to 5,518,000 in 1947, and from 139,000 to 6,971,000 in 1968.[29] Per capita incomes by state varied over a similarly broad range: $662 to $1,732 in 1947, and $1,566 to $3,390 in 1968.[30] Yet the annual rate of nonwhite interstate migration over the same period did not vary at all! The average annual percent of nonwhites, aged one and over, making an interstate move between 1948 and 1968 ranged from a low of 1.7 percent per year to a high of 3.1 percent per year.[31] The difference of 1.4 percent is not significantly different from zero. Thus, there has been no statistically significant variation in the annual rate of gross nonwhite interstate migration over the last 21 years!

Other studies have uncovered patterns of behavior which require a more complex theory of migration than that employed by Kain in his critique of the ghetto development strategy. For example, over the decade 1950–60, the percentage change in the nonwhite proportion of municipal populations was found to be *negatively* correlated with the average annual percentage growth in municipal median family income.[32] Between 1960 and 1965, 81 percent of all net migration to U.S. metropolitan areas went to just nine labor market areas[33] (listed in Table 28). I have computed the maximum and minimum average annual unemployment rates in these nine areas and in the other 141 labor market areas, as defined by the Department of Labor. These estimates, shown in Table 28, indicate that the most attractive destinations for recent migrants have been the areas with *above-average* unemployment rates. To the extent that unemployment rates in different labor market areas reflect differentials in employment circumstances, it must follow that factors other than relative income and job possibilities are also at work in the explanation of migration.

Kain's more recent studies of Southern economic development themselves indicate that there is more involved in the migration decision than simply

29.   U.S. Department of Labor, *Statistics on Manpower.*
30.   U.S. Bureau of the Census, *Long-Term Economic Growth.*
31.   U.S. Bureau of the Census, *Current Population Reports*, Series P-20, No. 188, "Mobility of the Population of the United States: March, 1967 to March 1968," (Washington, D.C.: Government Printing Office, 1969), Table 1.
32.   Advisory Commission on Intergovernmental Relations, *Urban and Rural America*, pp. 40–43.
33.   Ibid., pp. 16–17.

TABLE 28
MINIMUM AND MAXIMUM AVERAGE ANNUAL UNEMPLOYMENT RATES IN 150 LABOR MARKET AREAS: 1960-65

Area	Minimum	Maximum
Los Angeles-Orange County	5.5	6.7
New York-Northeastern New Jersey	4.5	5.4
San Francisco-Oakland-San Jose	5.0	5.9
Washington, D.C.	2.2	2.7
Philadelphia	4.3	6.9
Houston	3.2	4.9
Miami-Fort Lauderdale	3.9	9.4
San Bernadino-Riverside	5.9	7.5
Dallas	3.3	4.4
	—	—
Nine-area average	4.2	6.0
(Without Washington)	(4.5)	(6.4)
141 Other Labor Market Areas	3.9	5.6

Source: U.S. Department of Labor, *Statistics on Manpower: A Supplement to the Manpower Report of the President* (Washington, D.C.: U.S. Government Printing Office, 1969), Table D-8.

job-push/job-pull. In a recent paper co-authored with Joseph Persky, he analyzes white and nonwhite outmigration from the 250 nonmetropolitan counties of six states in the Deep South: Alabama, Arkansas, Georgia, Louisiana, Mississippi, and South Carolina. In 1950, blacks constituted 43 percent of the population and 47 percent of the potential male entrants to the decade's labor force (i.e., males aged 10–20 years in 1950). Regression analysis of individual industries disclosed that, for example, "blacks and whites left agriculture at exactly the same rate" between 1950 and 1960.[34] And yet the black outmigration rate was considerably higher than the white outmigration rate. Over the decade, 973,000 blacks moved out of the region, compared with 465,000 whites.[35] In other words, although blacks constituted less than half of the regional population and labor force, and even though they were not displaced from traditional agricultural work any more rapidly than were whites, 68 percent of the decade's outmigrants were

---

34. Joseph J. Persky and John F. Kain, "Migration, Employment, and Race in the Deep South," *Southern Economic Journal*, January 1970, p. 273.
35. Ibid., p. 269.

black.[36] One might wish to conclude from this that blacks have a strong distaste for the Deep South and will leave when given the opportunity—regardless of conditions elsewhere.

I conclude from this review of the literature that we do not yet fully understand the determinants of black migration, and that some circumspection is called for in assuming that differential employment possibilities are dominant in the decision to migrate—and in framing or vetoing antipoverty measures on that assumption. There are obviously factors other than interregional job differences which enter into the migration decision, especially for blacks. We simply do not know how the differential earnings or employment variables interact with these other factors.

The Capacity of Cities to Absorb Migrants

A SECOND FREQUENTLY ENUNCIATED ARGUMENT against ghetto development posits that—to the extent that renewal does stimulate immigration—those who come will impose excessive social service burdens on the destination city. That is, not only will the quantity of migrants be overwhelming, but also the quality of the new migrants will be such as to threaten the success of the very program which first attracted them. Once again, it is Kain who best articulates the conventional wisdom:

Southern blacks . . . are likely to face problems of "assimilation" in metropolitan areas. Often, these problems result in large demands for social services. These costs of migration raise serious questions concerning the desirability of the mass movements involved. To the extent that migration only changes the locale of basic social problems, it represents a wasteful expenditure of individual energies.[37]

Wertheimer disagrees. Black immigrants benefit significantly from moving from the South to the urban non-South. Moreover, they "tend to be drawn from the best qualified and most productive people" in the South, so that—at least up to some point—the destination economy probably

---

36. The authors suggest that the factor which reconciles these figures is the extent of racial discrimination in nonagricultural Southern employment, which they show to be extremely serious; blacks in the region unquestionably hold far less than their proportional share of nonagricultural jobs. Thus, infer the authors, job-push/job-pull *does* explain the observed migration behavior. The problem with this inference is that it is based entirely on ex post observations. If significant numbers of blacks left the region (for whatever reason) immediately after being displaced from agricultural work, this could generate the very same labor force distributions by race on which Kain and Persky report.
37. Persky and Kain, "Migration, Employment, and Race in the Deep South," p. 268. Charles Tilly, as noted earlier, explicitly rejects Kain's assertion that black migration places an exceptional demand on city services.

benefits from their presence.[38] As regards family stability, Tilly finds that, "if anything, the recent migrants are less likely than the rest to have broken families, and this is especially true within the nonwhite population."[39] Moreover,

As for the crime and delinquency so regularly attributed to the newcomers, what evidence there is points the other way: it takes some time in the city for the migrant to catch up with the old residents.[40]

Kain believes that black migration imposes costs on society in the form of "wasted energy." Wertheimer's findings lead him to precisely the opposite conclusion: The cost to the government of stemming migration "would appear to be very high, particularly on a 'per migrant' basis." Providing even just a "substantial fraction of the economic benefits to be derived from migration" to the potential migrant's place of origin "would require massive government expenditures, whether in the form of direct subsidies, subsidies to business and agriculture, or other programs to bolster local economies."[41]

Whatever the capabilities of the new migrants (but especially if they are, as Wertheimer says, "The best qualified and most productive people"), the ghetto development program (which may or may not have attracted them to the city) is potentially capable of inducing institutional change which would improve the city's, and even the ghetto's, ability to absorb migrants. There are historical precedents for such institutional "learning."

The "positive feedback" argument implicitly assumes that ghetto organizations—not to mention city managers—will be no better prepared to absorb and accommodate new immigrants *after* undertaking planned community development than they were beforehand. In other words, those who criticize ghetto development on these grounds must maintain the static view that planned economic change will not be accompanied by political maturation of the agents of

---

38. Wertheimer, *Monetary Rewards of Migration*, p. 76. This finding contradicts earlier assertions by Kain and Persky, as in "The North's Stake in Rural Southern Poverty." In fact, there is evidence that—at least in the late 1950s—"in educational attainment, Negro in-migrants to northern cities were equal to or slightly higher than the resident *white* population" (Karl E. and Alma F. Taeuber, "The Changing Character of Negro Migration," *American Journal of Sociology*, January 1965, p. 429, with emphasis as cited here). A study of the 1970 Census reveals that black South-North migrants had lower poverty incidence, and were less likely to be welfare recipients, than black natives of the destination city. In fact, for the blacks migrating before 1965 their economic status (in terms of these two variables at least) even exceeded that of the native *white* population (Larry H. Long, "Poverty, Status and Receipt of Welfare among Migrants and Nonmigrants in Large Cities," Population Division, U.S. Bureau of the Census, 1973, mimeo).
39. Tilly, "Race and Migration," p. 148.
40. Ibid., p. 149.
41. Wertheimer, *Monetary Rewards of Migration*, p. 76.

change. All the historical experience of the other urban ethnic minorities argues against such an assumption.[42]

The Suburbanization of Jobs and the Skill Mismatch: A Review of the Evidence

THE THIRD ARGUMENT AGAINST GHETTO DEVELOPMENT (that the migrants it would attract to the central city would settle in precisely that part of the metropolitan area which is being deserted by employers) is best addressed by a brief review of the findings of Part I of this monograph. There, we learned that the rate of suburbanization of jobs seems to vary inversely with city size and/or age and with the rate of growth of real Gross National Product. Thus, during periods of strong national aggregate demand, central city job losses are much less severe. Indeed, most cities gained employment during the expansionary period 1963–68. The most rapidly growing sector of the American economy—public service employment—already displays a strong propensity to locate in the core city, and in the future the location of such jobs will be (or can be made to be) to some extent directly subject to government control as an instrument of employment policy. Moreover, the gap between low suburban and high central city land rents, which is thought to have been an important factor in inducing the suburbanization of jobs, may now be closing due to a complex constellation of developments including land speculation in the suburbs. There is, therefore, reason to forecast a *deceleration* of the rate of employment suburbanization in the future—provided we are able and willing to restore an adequate rate of national economic growth.

In Part I, we also found that the majority of those jobs which do remain in the central city do not require extensive skills. Quite the opposite; perhaps 70 percent of the new jobs developed in an admittedly quite small sample of central cities during the mid-1960s were of the unskilled and semiskilled categories. Moreover, central city white populations have suburbanized much more rapidly than central city jobs, so that the excess supply of central city labor is not nearly so great as had been imagined. A major cause of central city unemployment appears to be the competition from suburban residents who commute to the core where they continue to work.

In short, the central city economies appear to be considerably more viable, and the prospects for central city employment (under suitable public policies) considerably brighter, than the critics of ghetto development have assumed. Urban employment and population are indeed undergoing a

---

42.   Thomas Vietorisz and Bennett Harrison, *The Economic Development of Harlem* (New York: Praeger, 1970), p. 65.

process of gradual decentralization. But this now appears to be a normal aspect of mature urban development, rather than a socially pathological phenomenon. Migrants who do come to the central city—whether or not their coming is in response to a program of planned ghetto development—need not be moving into a wasteland.

The Relationship between White Suburbanization and Ghetto Expansion

FOR A CLEAR STATEMENT OF THE FOURTH ARGUMENT in the liberal case against inner-city development, we turn once again to Professor Kain:

> The decline of central cities has been hastened by a conviction in the white community, both individual and corporate, that the ghetto would continue its rapid expansion. . . . The accelerating pace of suburbanization of industry and jobs [is] itself no doubt due partly to the ghetto expansion.[43]

Has the growing concentration of nonwhites in the central city in fact "chased" employers and middle-class citizens to the suburbs? In a private communication, Benjamin Cohen observes that many European cities—where, with the possible exception of London, race is not even at issue—are currently undergoing decentralization. There are, therefore, some grounds for skepticism.

Philip Swan has tested and found no support for the hypothesis that manufacturers' intrametropolitan location was, during the 1950s, a function of minority concentrations in the core. In an analysis of 25 large urban areas, Swan discovered that the percentage growth in central city manufacturing employment over the decade 1950–60 was not significantly tied to the proportion of nonwhites included in the city population, once he had accounted for the effects of the 1960 population density, the age of the city in 1960, and the average wage per production worker in 1958. For manufacturers, the latter was by far the most important "repellent."[44]

While Swan is concerned with the sensitivity of *job* decentralization to changes in central city conditions, several econometric studies have also examined the response of *population* movements to "ghetto expansion." For example, David Bradford and Harry Kelejian find that "for neither the middle class nor the poor does the racial composition of the central city population appear to affect residential location once the other variables have been accounted for."[45] The suburbanization of middle-class families

---

43. Kain and Persky, "Alternatives to the Gilded Ghetto," p. 75.

44. Philip L. Swan, "Metropolitan Decentralization of Manufacturing Employment Opportunities," paper delivered to the Northeastern Meetings of the Regional Science Association, Binghamton, New York, March 19–21, 1971.

45. Bradford and Kelejian, "An Econometric Model of the Flight to the Suburbs," *Journal of Political Economy*, May–June 1973.

(defined by income) during the decade 1950–60 was found to be positively related to median family income in the area (a measure of the ability to move), and inversely related to the "central city middle class fiscal surplus" (a measure of the net dollar value of the central city budget to a middle class family). The authors clearly demonstrate that their variables are not collinear. Sensitivity analyses (including variations in the income-based definition of "middle class") show the results to be robust. The "flight to the suburbs" is a flight from poverty and from the inadequacy of public services oriented toward the middle class—*not* a flight from black or brown neighbors per se. In one simulation, a 75 percent reduction in the number of poor families would, regardless of their racial composition, induce a 23 percent increase in the proportion of metropolitan middle class people living in the core. "The implication appears to be that an effective anti-poverty program would also 'save' the cities!"[46]

A two-wave survey of nearly 1,500 households in forty-three SMSAs, conducted by the National Opinion Research Center in 1966 and again in 1969, was used to study the extent to which concern with crime motivates the migration of central city residents to the suburbs. The researchers at the University of North Carolina asked whether "crime during recent years has been an important factor in suburbanization and a cause of white population losses in central cities." Their conclusions, based upon observation of those who did and did not move, were as follows:

> Perceptions of neighborhood crime and violence have little relationship to . . . changes in residential location. . . . Moves associated with the perception of crime and violence are more likely to result in a new central-city location than in a suburban location [and] the effect of crime and violence on mobility potential is stronger for the poor and black than for high and middle income whites.
> These findings . . . lend little credence to the belief that crime and violence have a strong differential effect on middle class whites, resulting in a massive movement to the suburbs.[47]

If the Bradford-Kelejian model structure continues to be reasonably descriptive of reality in the near future, there is no reason to expect that a central-city/ghetto redevelopment program which successfully reduces poverty would repel additional middle-class whites. If anything, some of them should be drawn back to the central city (just as urban renewal has already begun to attract whites—at least white professionals—back to the core), especially if that redevelopment permits cities to absorb black migrants without increasing the incidence of poverty.

---

46. Ibid., p. 36.
47. Theodore Droettboom, Jr., Ronald J. McAllister, Edward J. Kaiser, and Edgar W. Butler, "Urban Violence and Residential Mobility," *Journal of the American Institute of Planners*, September 1971, p. 324.

Conclusion

IN CONCLUDING THIS DISCUSSION of opposition to inner city economic development because of anticipated migration, it is perhaps worth reminding ourselves that nonwhite migration to the city has constituted one of the largest internal movements of people in the history of the world. Black Americans are now more urbanized than whites.[48] And, as the 1970 Census figures show, this massive redistribution of population continued during the last decade. It is not at all clear how social policy can slow down—let alone reverse these flows. And, as this review has shown, it is perhaps even less clear whether we should *want* to halt or reverse them.

Instead of thinking almost exclusively about reversing the rural-to-urban migration of nonwhite Americans, we should perhaps be giving more attention to the development of policies for helping the cities and their constituent communities to absorb their new immigrants.[49] Moreover, as with the attempt to set national public assistance standards to minimize the interstate benefit differentials which are thought to attract black migrants to higher-benefit areas, one can imagine allocating ghetto development resources in such a way that the interregional growth differentials associated with ghetto development might also be minimized.[50] At the very least, decision makers must become more familiar with the recent findings of researchers studying migration. These are summarized by Charles Tilly:

As for problems directly produced by migration, my main message has been that they have been seriously misunderstood and exaggerated. Migrants as a group do not notably disturb public order, their arrival does not lower the quality of the city's population, they place no extraordinary demands on public services, and they do not arrive exceptionally burdened with personal problems. These things happen to them later. The difficulties faced by inhabitants of ghettos and by cities containing them are not to any large degree products merely of migration.[51]

---

48. "Fifty-six percent of all Negroes now [1968] live in the central cities of metropolitan areas, while only about one-fourth of the white population of the United States now live in these cities." Advisory Commission on Intergovernmental Relations, *Urban and Rural America*, p. 5.

49. The theme of this paragraph is elaborated in an excellent review of two books on regional planning by Niles Hansen (see Gary Gappert, "Can We Help Our Cities by Leaving Them?" *The New Republic*, May 29, 1971).

50. That is to say, it *could* be done this way. But it is by no means certain that interstate differentials in welfare levels contribute to migration. See the discussion of the results of studies on New York, California, and Maryland in Barth, "Migration and Income Maintenance," p. 190.

51. Tilly, "Race and Migration," p. 155.

Chapter 5

THE POTENTIAL
PAYOFF TO
GHETTO DISPERSAL

The popular view of suburbanization as a manifestation of the decline of central city economies has led those who oppose inner city development to advocate the large-scale suburbanization of central city minorities. This is the so-called "ghetto dispersal" strategy.

A fundamental assumption underlying the demand for dispersal is that suburban residence is a crucial requisite for minority employment gains. Thus, efforts to attack discrimination in suburban housing are seen as the means by which the upgrading of minority employment can be attained. "The ghetto has isolated the Negro economically as well as socially [through] inadequate access to the job market."[1] "If [ghetto] residents were to move to suburban areas, they would have a far better chance of getting decent employment."[2] According to the Kerner Commission:

Future jobs are being created primarily in the suburbs, but the chronically unemployed population is increasingly concentrated in the ghetto. This separation will make it more and more difficult for Negroes to achieve anything like full employment in decent jobs. But if, over time, these residents began to find housing outside central cities, they would be exposed to more knowledge of job opportunities. They would have a far better chance of securing employment on a self-sustaining basis.[3]

---

1. John F. Kain and Joseph J. Persky, "Alternatives to the Gilded Ghetto," *The Public Interest*, Winter 1969, p. 77.
2. Anthony Downs, "Alternative Futures for the American Ghetto," *Daedalus*, Fall 1968, p. 1364.
3. National Advisory Commission on Civil Disorder, *U.S. Riot Commission Report* (New York: Bantam Books, 1968), p. 406.

The idea that discrimination in suburban housing is responsible for the high rates of nonwhite unemployment in SMSAs has been promoted most aggressively by John F. Kain.[4] It is to his seminal study that we turn first.

Suburbanization, Segregation, and Black Employment

THE CENTRAL HYPOTHESIS OF KAIN'S PAPER is that the black share of total employment in any part of the metropolis is directly related to the black residential density in that part.[5] Because of suburban housing discrimination, the black share of all SMSA jobs should decrease with distance from the core city ghetto. This hypothesis is tested with data from Detroit (1952) and Chicago (1956), using 98 workplace zones. The basic results are as follows[6] (t-ratios are in parenthesis):

Chicago:

$$W_i = \begin{array}{c} 9.18 \\ (16.7) \end{array} + \begin{array}{c} 0.458R_i \\ (15.6) \end{array} - \begin{array}{c} 0.521d_i^n \\ (4.3) \end{array} \qquad\qquad ; R^2 = .780$$

$$W_i = \begin{array}{c} 9.28 \\ (10.5) \end{array} + \begin{array}{c} 0.456R_i \\ (15.4) \end{array} \qquad\qquad - \begin{array}{c} 0.409d_i^m; \\ (4.2) \end{array} R^2 = .782$$

$$W_i = \begin{array}{c} 9.36 \\ (10.6) \end{array} \quad \begin{array}{c} 0.455R_i \\ (15.4) \end{array} - \begin{array}{c} 0.324d_i^n \\ (1.2) \end{array} - \begin{array}{c} 0.176d_i^m; \\ (0.8) \end{array} R^2 = .785$$

Detroit:

$$W_i = 12.78 + \begin{array}{c} 0.091R_i \\ (2.9) \end{array} - \begin{array}{c} 1.141d_i^n \\ (4.4) \end{array} \qquad\qquad ; R^2 = .359$$

$$W_i = 12.64 + \begin{array}{c} 0.100R_i \\ (2.9) \end{array} \qquad\qquad - \begin{array}{c} 0.758d_i^m \\ (4.7) \end{array} ; R^2 = .382$$

---

4. John F. Kain, "Housing Segregation, Negro Employment and Metropolitan Decentralization," *Quarterly Journal of Economics*, May 1968.
5. "The Negro percentage of population residing in each of the 98 workplace zones is a proxy for the employers' propensity to discriminate in favor or [sic] against nonwhite workers because of real or imagined attitudes of the resident population toward the employment of Negroes" (ibid., p. 180). Many students of the economics of poverty and discrimination believe this kind of behavior to be relatively less serious than "statistical discrimination," according to which "employment decisions are generally made on the basis of a few readily (and hence inexpensively) assessed traits such as race, demeanor, accent, educational attainment, test scores, and the like. Such traits tend to be statistically correlated with job performance but not necessarily (and probably not usually) causally related to it. Hence, a number of candidates who are rejected because they do not possess these traits are actually qualified for the job" (Michael J. Piore, "The Dual Labor Market: Theory and Implications," in *Problems in Political Economy: An Urban Perspective*, ed. David M. Gordon [Lexington, Mass.: D.C. Heath, 1971], p. 91). If this process of statistical discrimination is at work, then increased black residential suburbanization need not lead to any significant increase in suburban black employment.
6. Kain, "Housing Segregation," pp. 181–82.

$$W_i = 13.45 + 0.082R_i - 0.563d_i^n - 0.520d_i^m; \ R^2 = .400$$
$$\quad\quad\quad\quad (2.3) \quad\quad (1.7) \quad\quad (2.5)$$

where $W_i = \left(\dfrac{\text{Negro workers employed in zone i}}{\text{All workers employed in zone i}}\right) \times 100$

$\qquad R_i = \left(\dfrac{\text{Negro workers residing in zone i}}{\text{All workers residing in zone i}}\right) \times 100$

$\quad d_i^n =$ Airline distance in miles from zone i to the nearest boundary point of the nearest predominantly Negro residence area.

$\quad d_i^m =$ Airline distance in miles to the nearest boundary point of the *major* black ghetto.[7]

Clearly, black residential density *is* a highly significant correlate of black job density. Evaluated at the means, "a 1 percent increase in the number of Negro workers living in a Chicago residence area is associated with nearly a .5 percent increase in Negro employment."[8] For Detroit, this "residence elasticity of employment" is .1.

Kain also examines the relationship between black residential and employment densities for individual industries and occupations in Chicago. The residence elasticities, derived from regressions using the centroid of the major ghetto as the distance variable, are given in Table 29. All are statistically significant.

It is clear from these estimates that the residence elasticities are greatest for the white-collar occupations, some of which—professional and managerial in particular—entail substantial skills. If we accept the causal interpretation offered by Kain, then the greatest gains which blacks will make through suburbanization will be in the highest-paying occupations.

Kain estimates the aggregate employment impact of residential integration in Chicago and Detroit by assuming an even spatial distribution of blacks (the most extreme form of zero segregation) over all 98 zones (i.e., $R_1 = R_2 = \cdots = R_{98} = R_{SMSA}$). The actual value of R_{SMSA} is substituted into each estimated equation, permitting the calculation of "expected black employment" in each zone. The differences between expected and actual black employment are summed over all zones to achieve the two widely-discussed estimates of job loss attributable to residential segregation—22,000 to 25,000 for Chicago (depending on which equation is used), and 4,000 to 9,000 for Detroit. The specificity (not to

---

7. It is obvious from the high t-values for the distance variables in the first two Chicago equations and the low t-values in the third Chicago equation that the nearest black area and the major black area are often the same for any particular zone i. Kain infers from this that Chicago blacks are more highly segregated than are Detroit blacks.
8. Kain, "Housing Segregation," p. 183.

TABLE 29
RESIDENCE ELASTICITIES FROM THE
KAIN MODEL FOR CHICAGO: 1956

Category	$\frac{\% \Delta W}{\% \Delta R}$
Occupation	
Professional	0.8
Managerial	1.0
Clerical	0.8
Sales	1.1
Craftsmen	0.4
Operatives	0.3
Service	0.3
Laborers	0.1
Industry	
Durable Manufacturing	0.3
Nondurable Manufacturing	0.3
Transportation	0.4
Retailing	0.7
Finance, Insurance, Real Estate	0.6
Wholesaling	0.5
Business Services	0.3
Government	0.4
Total	0.4

Source: Kain, "Housing Segregation," p. 188.

mention the magnitude) of these numbers has lent an enormous credibility, especially in government circles, to the inference that residential desegregation is a sufficient condition for reducing minority unemployment.

The difficulty of drawing causal inferences from such a simplistic model has been dramatically demonstrated by two published commentaries on the original paper. Offner and Saks show that Kain's results are highly sensitive to the form of the regression used to estimate the residence elasticities.[9] Using exactly the same data and a quadratic specification of R, they find that the residence coefficients are much smaller than those estimated by Kain. For example, with respect to Chicago, Kain's estimate is

$$W = \quad 9.18 + \quad 0.46R \qquad\qquad - 0.52d^n$$
$$(10.7) \quad (15.6) \qquad\qquad\qquad (4.3)$$

<hr>

9. Paul Offner and Daniel H. Saks, "A Note on John Kain's 'Housing Segregation, Negro Employment, and Metropolitan Decentralization,'" *Quarterly Journal of Economics*, February 1971.

while those of Offner and Saks are

$$W = 10.84 + 0.049R + 0.005R^2 - 0.67d^n$$
$$(12.8) \quad (0.6) \qquad (4.8) \qquad (5.9)$$

$$W = 11.08 \qquad\qquad + 0.006R^2 - 0.69d^n$$
$$(15.4) \qquad\qquad\qquad (18.0) \qquad (6.5)$$

When they fit their quadratic model to the occupational data for Chicago used by Kain, the authors report:

We have found that a redistribution of Negroes throughout the population would result in relatively large Negro job *losses* . . . in those occupations [sales, managers, officials, proprietors, clerical, professional, technical] where discrimination is most important. In contrast . . . Kain's regressions show Negroes gaining jobs in several of these occupations.

Our results for total employment do not prove or disprove Kain's contention that Negroes suffer a job loss as a result of residential segregation. Our point was simply to emphasize the sensitivity of such estimates to the manner in which the relationship is specified.[10]

The second commentary on Kain's original study is contained in a paper by the late Joseph Mooney.[11] Mooney specifies a completely different relationship, with a sample of 25 SMSAs (institutionally more representative than Kain's sample of 2), using 1960 Census data. His dependent variable (E/P) is the product of the labor force participation rate (labor force/population) and the employment rate (employment/labor force) for those central city census tracts in which nonwhites constitute more than 50 percent of the population and in which median family income is less than two-thirds of the SMSA-wide median. The variables which "explain" the intercity variation in "ghetto" employment include

U_i = 1960 unemployment rate in the ith SMSA

$\left(\dfrac{E_{cc}}{E_{SMSA}}\right)$ = ratio of jobs in wholesale trade, selected services, retail trade, and manufacturing in the central city to all jobs in the four sectors in the ith SMSA in 1960

$\left(\dfrac{M_{cc}}{M_{SMSA}}\right)_i$ = ratio of manufacturing jobs in the central city to all manufacturing jobs in the ith SMSA in 1960

$\left(\dfrac{R}{cc}\right)_i$ = all nonwhites over age 14 who worked in the ring but lived in the central city, divided by all nonwhites over age 14 who lived in the central city in 1960.

---

10. Ibid., p. 156, emphasis mine.
11. Joseph D. Mooney, "Housing Segregation, Negro Employment and Metropolitan Decentralization: An Alternative Perspective," *Quarterly Journal of Economics*, May 1969.

Mooney's results for males in the $i = 1, 2, \ldots, 25$ SMSAs follow (again, t-ratios are in parentheses):

$$\left(\frac{E}{P}\right)_i = .63 \quad -2.86U_i \quad +.19\left(\frac{E_{cc}}{E_{SMSA}}\right)_i \quad +.24\left(\frac{R}{cc}\right)_i \; ; R^2 = .95$$

$$(12.11) \quad (5.11) \quad (3.17) \qquad\qquad (4.00)$$

$$\left(\frac{E}{Y}\right)_i = .68 \quad -3.08U + .14\left(\frac{M_{cc}}{M_{SMSA}}\right)_i \quad +.24\left(\frac{R}{cc}\right)_i \; ; R^2 = .94$$

$$(13.60) \quad (5.3) \quad (2.80) \qquad\qquad (4.00)$$

Ghetto employment is directly related to the centrality of SMSA employment and "the accessibility of the fringe areas to the central city ghetto residents."[12] This is certainly consistent with the spirit of Kain's work although not the letter, since Mooney's model does not attempt to relate suburban nonwhite residential and employment densities. Nevertheless, Mooney warns us that

the reader should not lose sight of the fact that the size of the coefficient of the unemployment rate is substantially higher than the size of the coefficients for either of the other variables. Thus . . . relative to aggregate demand conditions in a particular metropolitan area (as represented by the unemployment rates), the factor of geographic separation does not seem to be too important.[13]

The implication of this rather detailed review is that Kain's models for Chicago and Detroit are misspecified since they ignore the macroeconomic determinants of local conditions. This is much the same criticism as was made by Cohen and Noll and examined earlier in connection with the measurement of postwar employment decentralization.[14]

I have used the results of these two commentaries on Kain to point out some of the weaknesses in the *form* of his models. However, it is probably more important to emphasize the absence of a firm causal hypothesis in his segregation-decentralization paper. One can explain his results with a

---

12. Ibid., p. 306.
13. Ibid., p. 308. The accessibility variable (R/CC) also had the lowest beta coefficient.
14. See pp. 24–25 above. It may be argued in rebuttal that a cross-sectional model like Kain's (with only two cities) cannot possibly "catch" variations in macroeconomic or labor market conditions. But that in itself underscores the nature of the misspecification. It might be added that Mooney's "accessibility" variable is itself somewhat ambiguous. It is possible that the central city nonwhites who are working in the ring are *not* from the ghetto, but rather from non-ghetto central city neighborhoods. My own results on twelve SMSA's strongly support such a possibility; as will be seen below (pp. 87–101), the unemployment rates of nonpoverty area central city nonwhites in 1966 were somewhat lower than the rates for nonwhite central city poverty area residents. In any case, Mooney's model also tells us nothing about causality.

theory most uncongenial to the proposition that access via proximate residence determines employment. Our knowledge of the relevant technologies suggests that suburban manufacturing and wholesaling establishments (the sectors which most intensively employ blue-collar workers) will tend to locate in low-density areas, where land rents are low. Indeed, that is presumably one of the reasons why they "suburbanized" in the first place. Firms whose labor demands are relatively more skill-intensive (retail, finance, real estate, etc.) will, on the other hand, tend to locate in high-density, largely residential suburban areas. If these assumptions are correct (and there is as yet little evidence on the matter), then—in any of Kain's suburban "zones"—population density is very apt to be positively related to white-collar employment density and negatively related to blue-collar employment density. Kain's regressions show that the more blacks there are living in a zone, the higher will be the incidence of black white-collar employment. I would suggest that the more *people* there are in a zone, the higher will be the incidence of white-collar employment. Kain's results only confirm what many location theorists predict: that blue-collar-intensive plants are highly clustered ("undispersed"), even within the suburbs. They do *not* prove that suburbanization of blacks will increase black suburban employment.

The newest contribution to the burgeoning literature on the Kain hypothesis is an impressive study by Stanley Friedlander. Using Census data for 1960 and the unpublished results of a 1966 Labor Department survey, Friedlander sought to test the Kain hypothesis that the decentralization of jobs and the confinement of blacks to segregated areas in the urban core exacerbate black unemployment. For a sample of thirty metropolitan areas, Friedlander regressed various unemployment rates (central city as a whole, central city nonwhites, ghetto residents, and ghetto teenagers) on the ratio of suburban to SMSA jobs (overall and in manufacturing) and on the Duncan index of residential segregation,[15] controlling (in different regressions) for a host of demographic and structural variables thought to vary across cities. In thirty-eight attempts, the job decentralization variable was statistically significant only twice (with the expected positive sign). In eighteen "runs," the segregation index was significant six times (with a *negative* sign, imply-

---

15. "The value of the index [developed by Alma and Karl Taeuber] may be interpreted as showing the minimum percentage of nonwhites who would have to change the block on which they live in order to produce an unsegregated distribution—one in which the percentage of nonwhites living on each block is the same throughout the city" (Stanley Friedlander, *Unemployment in the Urban Core* [New York: Praeger, 1972], p. 35).

ing that the existence of the ghetto *reduces* inner city black unemployment, presumably by reducing the competition from white workers).[16]

Suburban Wages for Ghetto Commuters

APART FROM PRESUMING THAT residential suburbanization of minorities will reduce their unemployment, advocates of ghetto dispersal seem to expect it to produce an altogether independent, positive effect on income (the "good" jobs are in the suburbs). Earlier we had occasion to refer to a number of experiments in reverse commuting, most of which have been rather unsuccessful. It has been shown that one of the causes of the meager demand by central city ghetto residents for seats on the suburban-bound buses is the very low wages offered by those surburban employers willing to hire ghetto workers. There may be jobs in the ring, but they are not necessarily jobs that will raise the ghetto dweller's standard of living.

In their St. Louis study, for example, Kalachek and his colleagues concluded that "most unemployed Negro central city residents . . . will not be tempted to an expensive and time consuming journey unless jobs in the far suburbs are appreciably better than more proximate jobs. However, . . . our survey of St. Louis County manufacturers found no relationship between the distance of an establishment from the ghetto and its pay scale."[17] A survey in Los Angeles found suburban jobs paying two dollars or less an hour, with transportation costs equaling as much as a third of daily earnings.[18] With respect to the Boston experiment cited earlier, "One reason the 'Employment Express' attracted few riders was that there was already fairly good transportation connecting Roxbury with downtown Boston and Cambridge, and the wages offered in the suburbs [were] not sufficiently higher than wages downtown to compensate for the increased

---

16. Ibid., Appendix tables 1–32. Friedlander also regressed unemployment on inner city population density, a measure (he argues) of the difficulty of accommodating industry (and therefore jobs) in the central city. Unemployment and population density *were* positively correlated in multiple regressions (not shown in the book); "this finding tends to support the view that cities without the capacity to expand physically or cities in which the costs of plant location are high will have less employment growth and fewer employment opportunities for their labor force" (ibid., p. 44). For a survey of new technological developments in the creation of industrial space in dense inner cities, see chapter 7 below.
17. Edward D. Kalachek and John M. Goering, eds., *Transportation and Central City Unemployment* (St. Louis: Washington University, Institute for Urban and Regional Studies, March 1970), p. 12.
18. This study, conducted by the California State Business and Transportation Agency, is described in the U.S. Department of Labor's *1971 Manpower Report of the President* (Washington, D.C.: U.S. Government Printing Office, 1971) p. 96.

commuting time."[19] Overall, the results of these various experiments conducted under the auspices of the Departments of Transportation and Housing and Urban Development have been mixed:

As might be expected, it was found that the demand for transportation from slum areas to outlying employment centers depends on the job opportunities available to ghetto workers. Improved transit will reduce unemployment only when there are job openings for the potential users of the service at wages high enough to cover commuting expenses. Transportation is part of a larger problem and needs to be handled as such. The experiments were valuable in reaffirming this concept and in leading to a number of broad conclusions.

One of the most important of these conclusions was that transportation arrangements, when geared to slum residents, should be subsidiary to a job development and placement program.[20]

These experimental results do not strengthen the argument that suburban jobs—even if accessible—would materially improve the welfare of ghetto residents.

The Economic Welfare of Suburban Nonwhites

IT IS NOW POSSIBLE TO DIRECTLY OBSERVE a substantial sample of nonwhites (about 93 percent of whom are black) *already living* in the suburbs of the twelve largest metropolitan areas in March 1966, and to compare their economic welfare with that of nonwhites living inside the central city.[21] Such a cross-sectional view is admittedly limited in its policy applications; it tells us nothing directly about the benefit to the nonwhite household which actually changes its residence. Indeed, since the data are by place of residence, we do not know but that some of the suburban nonwhites in the sample are actually working inside the central city. Moreover, simple residence in the ring does not constitute a very satisfactory control for access to suburban jobs; resegregation into peripheral ghettos located far from the new industrial parks is quite consistent with observed suburbanization of blacks. Moreover, suburban areas tend to have even poorer public

---

19.   Wilfred Lewis, Jr., "Urban Growth and Suburbanization of Employment: Some New Data," (Washington, D.C.: The Brookings Institution, 1969), unpublished manuscript, p. 33.
20.   *1971 Manpower Report of the President*, p. 104.
21.   Pages 89–101 below are heavily dependent on both the text and the illustrative material in chapter 4 of Bennett Harrison, *Education, Training, and the Urban Ghetto* (Baltimore: The Johns Hopkins Press, 1972), pp. 98–109. Thus, Figures 11–19 and Table 12 of the Johns Hopkins Press volume appear below as Figures 7–15 and Table 30. With respect to textual borrowing, I have tried to avoid disconcerting the reader with excessive punctuation and so have quoted myself verbatim at times, without quotation marks or explicit attributions to *Education, Training, and the Urban Ghetto*. This material is used with the kind permission of The Johns Hopkins Press.

transportation than central cities.[22] Nevertheless, this study provides us with the only available portrait of nonwhites who have already suburbanized, or who have moved directly to the ring from outside the SMSA.

The sample, drawn from the U.S. Office of Economic Opportunity's *1966 Survey of Economic Opportunity*, consists of 6,797 white and nonwhite males aged 14 and older who lived in one of the nation's twelve largest SMSAs in March 1966, were no longer in school at that time, and had been in the labor force for at least 13 weeks in 1965. Three residential zones are distinguished—the central city poverty areas, the rest of the central city, and the suburban ring. To determine economic well-being, the study uses four measures:

1. weekly individual earnings in March 1966,
2. annual individual unemployment,
3. occupational status, measured by a scoring procedure which assigns an ordinal rank of 0–100 to each of the 308 Census occupational titles on the SEO tapes,[23]
4. the share of gross annual family income contributed by the male family head, if present. The latter constitutes an additional check on the adequacy (in terms of support) of the job or jobs which the suburban family head holds.

The weekly male earnings distributions are displayed in Figures 7 and 8. The distribution for central city white males outside of the poverty areas clearly lies to the right of the ghetto distribution, and the suburban white distribution shows a still greater frequency of high incomes (and a smaller frequency of low incomes). At the modes, weekly earnings rise from $95 to $105 to $200. In Figure 8, the three curves are clearly distinct and widely spaced; this is confirmed by pairwise chi-square significance tests. White earnings (for males, at least) are highly sensitive to the intrametropolitan residential location of the worker. For nonwhite men, this is clearly *not* the case. The three curves in Figure 7 are clustered much more closely together than was the case for whites; there is only a 5 percent chance that these distributions could have been drawn from different populations. Moreover, the largest frequency of relatively high earnings (i.e., above approximately

22.   Despite these serious qualifications, Kain and Persky assert that even "re-ghettoized suburbanization" is likely to improve minority economic welfare. "Many of the disadvantages of massive, central ghettos would be overcome if they were replaced or even augmented by smaller, dispersed Negro communities. Such a pattern would remove the limitations on Negro employment opportunities attributable to the geography of the ghetto" ("Alternatives to the Gilded Ghetto," p. 80).

23.   The procedure was developed by the National Opinion Research Corporation and Otis Dudley Duncan; see Duncan, "A Socioeconomic Index for All Occupations," in *Occupations and Social Status*, Albert J. Reiss, et al. (New York: The Free Press, Division of Macmillan, 1962).

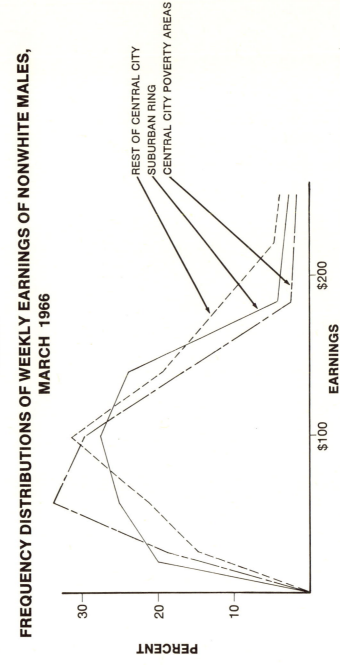

FIGURE 7

FREQUENCY DISTRIBUTIONS OF WEEKLY EARNINGS OF NONWHITE MALES, MARCH 1966

Source: Bennett Harrison, *Education, Training, and the Urban Ghetto* (Baltimore: The Johns Hopkins Press, 1972), Figure 11.

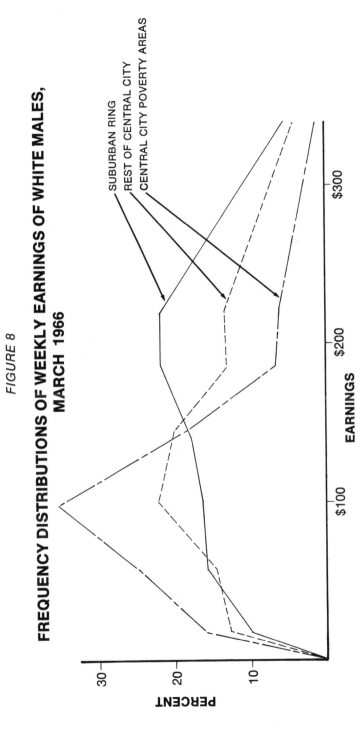

FIGURE 8

FREQUENCY DISTRIBUTIONS OF WEEKLY EARNINGS OF WHITE MALES,
MARCH 1966

Source: Bennett Harrison, *Education, Training, and the Urban Ghetto*, Figure 12.

$160 per week in Figure 7) occurs, not in the suburbs, but in the rest of the central city, while both of these distributions have the same mode. There is much less dispersion among nonwhite than among white earnings, in every part of the metropolis. Employment opportunities are highly variegated for whites. But the constraints on the opportunities for nonwhites are such that most find themselves in much the same situation vis-à-vis the urban labor market.

A similar pattern was found for the unemployment variable. In Figure 9, the unemployment rates associated with the three frequency distributions fall as our attention moves from the central city poverty areas to the suburban ring. Again, the three curves are fairly distinct; white unemployment is sensitive to residential location within the SMSA. However, the nonwhite curves in Figure 10 do not share these attributes. In fact, median nonwhite unemployment in the suburbs exceeds the rate for the nonpoverty areas of the central city.

The results of mapping the 308 SEO occupational titles into the 100 Duncan-N.O.R.C. prestige scores are shown in Figures 11 and 12. The pattern for white males is precisely what the suburbanization literature would lead us to expect: suburban residents have a higher probability of being in "high status" jobs than do central city nonpoverty area residents, and the latter in turn face higher expectations of "success" (in terms of status) than do the white male ghetto dwellers. While the distribution for the latter group is clearly skewed left, the suburban white distribution is much more nearly rectangular, indicating that suburban whites are distributed more or less uniformly throughout the range of occupations, from very low status to very high status positions. For nonwhites all three distributions are sharply skewed left and are virtually undistinguisable. Over half of the nonwhite males in the sample (including those living in the suburbs) are—to employ Barbara Bergmann's term—"crowded" into the lowest fifth of the occupations, in terms of status.

The central tendencies of these distributions are displayed in the bar charts of Figures 13–15. When 95 percent confidence intervals are constructed about these means and medians, employment opportunity for whites definitely rises (or at least does not fall) with distance from the ghetto. For nonwhites, however, the three descriptions of employment opportunity show relatively little sensitivity to intrametropolitan residential location. Nonwhite earnings are significantly higher outside the ghetto than inside, but—once outside—there is no significant difference between the average levels associated with central city and suburban residence. Nonwhite unemployment rates in the ghetto and in the suburbs are not statistically different, and are only slightly lower in the nonpoverty central city. Finally, the indicator of occupational status for nonwhite men is completely insensitive to residential location.

FIGURE 9

FREQUENCY DISTRIBUTIONS OF ANNUAL UNEMPLOYMENT: WHITE MALES, 1965

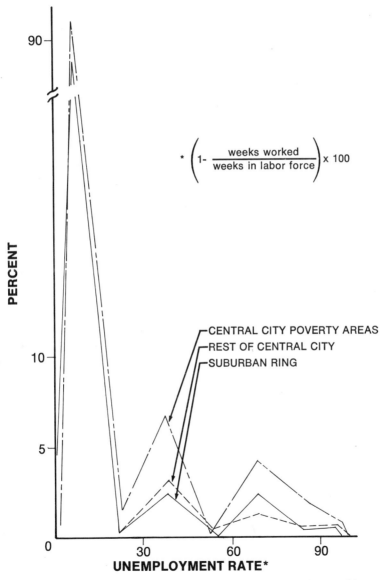

$$* \left(1 - \frac{\text{weeks worked}}{\text{weeks in labor force}}\right) \times 100$$

CENTRAL CITY POVERTY AREAS
REST OF CENTRAL CITY
SUBURBAN RING

Source: Bennett Harrison, *Education, Training, and the Urban Ghetto*, Figure 13.

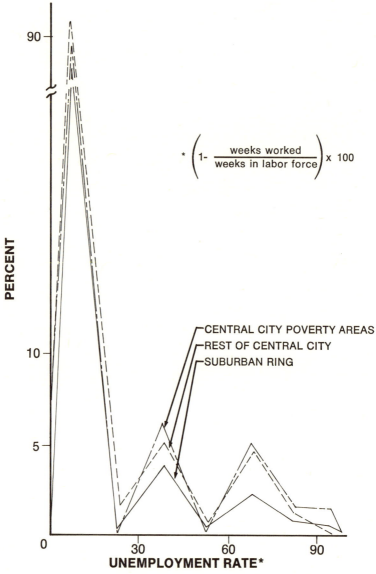

FIGURE 10

FREQUENCY DISTRIBUTIONS OF ANNUAL
UNEMPLOYMENT: NONWHITE MALES, 1965

$$* \left(1 - \frac{\text{weeks worked}}{\text{weeks in labor force}}\right) \times 100$$

CENTRAL CITY POVERTY AREAS
REST OF CENTRAL CITY
SUBURBAN RING

Source: Bennett Harrison, *Education, Training, and the Urban Ghetto*, Figure 14.

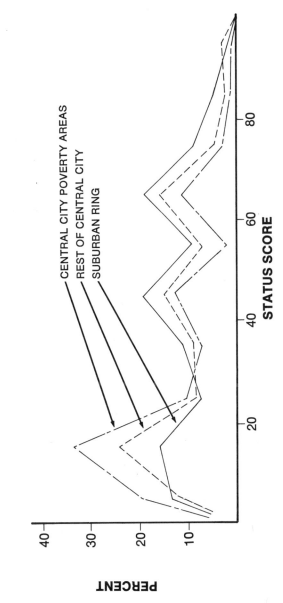

FIGURE 11

FREQUENCY DISTRIBUTIONS OF OCCUPATIONAL STATUS:
WHITE MALES, MARCH 1966

Source: Bennett Harrison, *Education, Training, and the Urban Ghetto*, Figure 15.

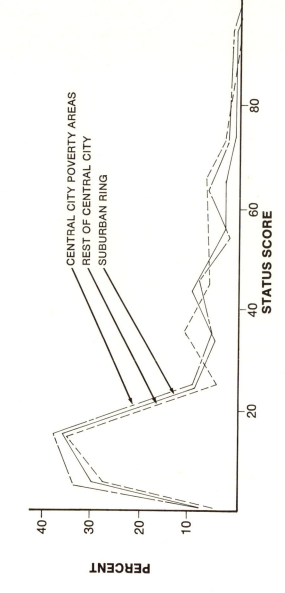

FIGURE 12

FREQUENCY DISTRIBUTIONS OF OCCUPATIONAL STATUS: NONWHITE MALES, MARCH 1966

Source: Bennett Harrison, *Education, Training, and the Urban Ghetto,* Figure 16.

FIGURE 13

MEDIAN MALE EARNINGS* BY
INTRAMETROPOLITAN RESIDENTIAL LOCATION

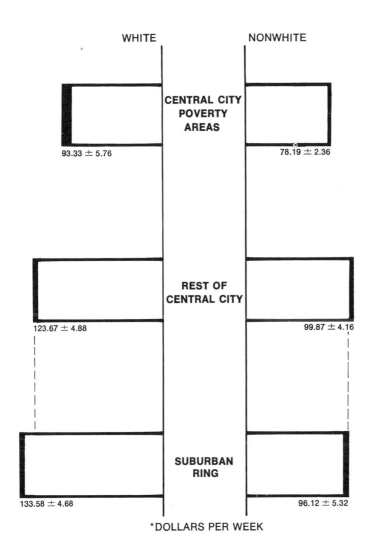

WHITE   NONWHITE

CENTRAL CITY
POVERTY
AREAS

93.33 ± 5.76   78.19 ± 2.36

REST OF
CENTRAL CITY

123.67 ± 4.88   99.87 ± 4.16

SUBURBAN
RING

133.58 ± 4.68   96.12 ± 5.32

*DOLLARS PER WEEK

NOTE: Black Bands Represent 95% Confidence Intervals

Source: Bennett Harrison, *Education, Training, and the Urban Ghetto*, Table 17.

MEAN MALE UNEMPLOYMENT RATES* BY INTRAMETROPOLITAN RESIDENTIAL LOCATION

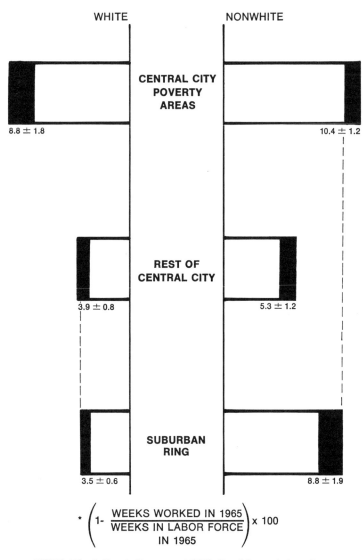

NOTE: Black Bands Represent 95% Confidence Intervals

Source: Bennett Harrison, *Education, Training, and the Urban Ghetto*, Table 18.

FIGURE 15

MEDIAN MALE OCCUPATIONAL STATUS* BY INTRAMETROPOLITAN RESIDENTIAL LOCATION

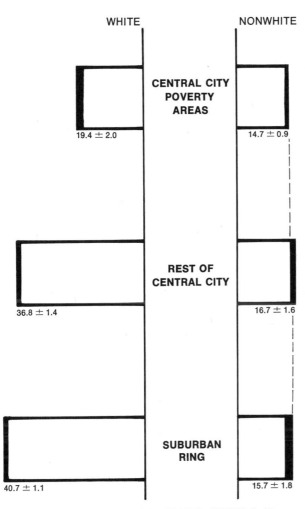

★DUNCAN STATUS SCORE, 0–96

NOTE: Black Bands Represent 95% Confidence Intervals

Source: Bennett Harrison, *Education, Training, and the Urban Ghetto,* Table 19.

We turn now to examination of the fourth and final indicator of economic well-being: the contribution of the male family head to the total income of the family. This indicator has especially important implications for the stability of family structure. Underemployment of the male head—sporadic work at substandard wages in low-status occupations or jobs to which the worker has only a loose attachment—forces the other family members to resort to additional means of acquiring income, many of which are illegal or, even when within the law, are inherently exploitative of other persons in the community. Young children may have to go to work. The family may enroll for public assistance, although in many cities this could require the father to leave (or to pretend to leave) the home. As a composite measure of economic well-being, the share of gross family income contributed by the male head is an important indicator.

Table 30 shows the relevant estimates for the six Survey of Economic Opportunity subsamples. On the average, the head of the white ghetto family contributes 46 percent of the family's gross annual income. At the means, a 1 percent increase in family income is associated with only a .65 percent increase in the male head's earnings. Across the three residence zones, the relative importance of the white head increases with distance from the ghetto. But the relative importance of the nonwhite head to *his* family *diminishes* with distance from the ghetto; nonwhite men contribute a smaller share of family income in the suburbs than in the central city ghetto![24]

These results may be summarized as follows: nonwhite underemployment, in all of its many manifestations, is pervasive *throughout* the metropolitan area. On the average, central city men living in nonpoverty neighborhoods (i.e., outside the "ghetto" but inside the city limits), appear to enjoy a slight advantage over other urban nonwhites. They receive somewhat higher earnings, are unemployed less often, find their way into slightly higher status occupations, and enjoy higher family incomes than either ghetto or suburban nonwhites. However, when the statistical variation about these average indicators of employment opportunity is taken into account, we find that nonwhite male underemployment is rather insensitive to intrametropolitan residential location, the conventional wisdom notwithstanding.

In another comparison of the economic well-being of blacks in the

---

24.   Duran Bell has also found that black suburban women are relatively more important contributors to the incomes of their families than are white women, even though they find it more difficult to find work in the suburbs than in the nonpoverty central city (Duran Bell, Jr., "Residential Location, Minority Opportunity, and Public Employment," in *Patterns of Racial Discrimination*, ed. George M. von Furstenberg, et al. [Lexington, Mass.: Heath-Lexington Books, 1974]).

TABLE 30
CONTRIBUTION OF THE MALE FAMILY HEAD TO 1965 FAMILY INCOME, BY INTRAMETROPOLITAN RESIDENTIAL LOCATION AND RACE

	1965 Means		Average Importance of the Head $(\overline{W}/\overline{Y})$	Marginal Importance of the Head $(\Delta W/\Delta Y)$		Relative Importance of the Head $\left[\dfrac{\% \Delta W}{\% \Delta Y}\right]^{a}$
	Gross Family Income $(\overline{Y})$	Earnings of the Head $(\overline{W})$				
Central City Poverty Areas						
White Families	$ 8,120	$3,815	0.46	0.30	(.09)	0.65
Nonwhite Families	5,995	3,102	0.52	0.29	(.05)	0.56
Rest of the Central City						
White Families	10,468	5,234	0.50	0.33	(.05)	0.66
Nonwhite Families	8,458	4,080	0.48	0.26	(.08)	0.54
Suburban Ring						
White Families	10,839	5,710	0.53	0.36	(.07)	0.68
Nonwhite Families	7,285	3,520	0.48	0.25	(.12)	0.52

[a] Elasticity $= \widehat{B}\left[\dfrac{\overline{Y}}{\overline{W}}\right]$ where $\widehat{B}$ is an estimate of the slope in the regression $W = B_0 + B_1 Y$.

Note: standard errors are shown in parentheses.
Source: Bennett Harrison, *Education, Training, and the Urban Ghetto*, p. 108.

ghettos and suburbs, George M. von Furstenberg examines whether the black occupants of segregated suburban housing projects in Detroit earn more than the black occupants of segregated central city projects.[25] In an excellent econometric analysis which takes into account (as so many other studies of racial family income differences do not) intrafamily labor force participation, von Furstenberg finds that the suburban families average $826 more in annual family income than central city families, about a sixth of mean central city family income (n = 1232 families). Unfortunately, von Furstenberg's data do not allow him to distinguish between gross family income and individual earnings; and only the latter variable unambiguously reflects labor market access. Moreover, he does not examine comparative unemployment rates or occupational status.

Bernard Frieden has analyzed the aggregate statistics collected annually in the Current Population Survey of the Census Bureau. Referring to the same period as that of my own studies—the mid-1960s—Frieden writes:

These data, fragmentary as they are, show little support for the belief that suburban residence is the key to better jobs and higher incomes. They suggest instead that residential location in itself is only one factor of many that contribute to racial inequalities in jobs and incomes, and that other factors may be more important singly or certainly in combination. Conceivably even living in the suburbs, closer to the centers of new job growth, does not suffice to bring black people into good communication with the job market. If public transportation between central-city locations and the new industrial parks is poor, it is probably no better in the suburbs. The worker without a dependable car is probably equally disadvantaged in both places. Or perhaps living in suburbs does help people cope with problems of communication or transportation, but it does not provide workers with new job skills nor does it deal with discrimination in hiring or in the selection of people for manpower training programs. Opening more suburban housing to the black poor may be helpful in terms of employment, but the evidence suggests that it is not decisive.[26]

Moreover, it is by no means clear that low skilled, low income ghetto blacks would enjoy greater *real* consumption in the suburbs than in their present neighborhoods. While per capita educational expenditures do tend to be greater outside than inside the city (although there is much interarea variation within the suburbs), "expenditures on other public services suggest that their other needs may be met better in the central cities. Noneducational expenditures of local governments, on a per capita basis, are consistently higher in the central cities. In the thirty-seven largest metropolitan areas as of 1966–1967 there were no exceptions to this pattern. . . . The

25.   George M. von Furstenberg, "Place of Residence and Employment Opportunities within a Metropolitan Area," *Journal of Economic Issues*, June 1971.
26.   Bernard J. Frieden, "Blacks in Suburbia: The Myth of Better Opportunities," in Lowdon Wingo, ed., *Minority Perspectives* (Baltimore: Johns Hopkins Press, 1972), pp. 38–39.

black family moving from an average central city to an average suburb, then, is likely to find a different mix of public services which is not uniformly better."[27]

Earlier, we cited Kain's assertion of the relative superiority for blacks of "pocket ghettos" on the urban fringe, especially in terms of accessibility to jobs. In a case study of the Pittsburgh SMSA, Peter Hutchinson worked with pocket ghettos that were unambiguously located outside of the central city.[28] He found that the adverse effect of residential segregation on the conditional probability of black employment was significantly greater in these suburban ghettos than in the central city, *especially for black teenagers*, and that the marginal effect of education on black employment was greater for centrally-located than for peripherally-located blacks. Both findings seem (to me, at any rate) to seriously qualify Kain's claim that even the pocket ghettoization of "suburbanized" blacks would be better than no suburbanization at all.

Conclusion

DAVID BIRCH, IN HIS PREVIOUSLY CITED STUDY of metropolitan form, concludes that "by most social and economic measures, suburban blacks are increasingly better off than their central city counterparts."[29] He presents no evidence in support of this conclusion, and the evidence which we have been able to marshal can certainly not be considered favorable to Birch's position. The econometric analyses conducted by Kain (on extremely old data with a sample of two SMSAs) are subject to multiple causal interpretations, the implications of which are not always consistent. In short, the empirical basis for the widespread expectation that minority suburbanization, or ghetto dispersal, will improve at least the labor market standing of the dispersed is not well-founded.

---

27. Ibid.
28. Peter Hutchinson, "The Effects of Accessibility and Segregation on the Employment of the Urban Poor," *Patterns of Racial Discrimination*, ed. George M. von Furstenberg, et al.
29. David Birch, *The Economic Future of City and Suburb* (New York: Committee for Economic Development, 1970), pp. 30, 32.

PART III

THE VIABILITY
OF THE
CENTRAL CITY

Chapter 6

THE FISCAL CRISIS OF THE CENTRAL CITY

THE LARGE BODY OF LITERATURE we have reviewed in the previous chapters suggests, more than anything else, that one should not jump to conclusions about the viability of the economy of the central city. In particular, recommendations that public investment should concentrate on suburban jurisdictions and the relatively less dense areas between the large cities, and that minority equal opportunity and economic improvement programs should focus on the suburbs, are seen to have been based on a relatively superficial reading of the data describing the modern history of American cities. Scholars, like political decision makers, have a right to their value judgments; indeed, it is often value judgments that determine which questions we ask. Nevertheless, we have a responsibility to inform these judgments through careful scientific study.

Further research will help to determine whether or not such phenomena as the skill mismatch really exist, and (if they do) the extent to which they explain the disadvantage of low income residents (especially nonwhite) of the central city. Studies of the relationship between business cycles and the rate of job decentralization will tell us where and how we may have gone wrong in our previous thinking by ignoring the possible effects of such a macroeconomic relationship. The research agenda for urban economists is rich and exciting. For the present (which, as Keynes reminded us, is the temporal state in which most of us are forced to live), the evidence of the previous chapters strongly suggests that urban poverty should be subjected to a policy analysis which is based on the working assumption that the central city *is* (at least in principle) a viable *locale* for public investment.

What can statecraft do to perpetuate that economic vitality? How do the alternative policy approaches to the restructuring of urban government and the urban economy affect the minorities whose economic well-being is a central concern of this study? Those are the questions which we address in this and the following chapters.

Annexation

SEVERAL TIMES IN THIS ESSAY, we have suggested that the decentralization of employment and population is a normal manifestation of urban growth with no intrinsically pathological implications.

Yet the "urban crisis"—consisting at least in part of the concentration of poverty in cities which are increasingly less able to support themselves or to invest in their own economic futures—is a tangible phenomenon; it is no academician's fantasy. To the extent that the economic vitality of central cities is being sapped by the suburbanization of productive activity—i.e., by the city's loss of jurisdiction over decentralizing activities—it becomes that much more difficult to increase the economic opportunities of central city minorities. How can we reconcile these two seemingly contradictory aspects of urban economic growth?

Part of the answer seems to lie in the process of *annexation*. Since their initial incorporation, most American cities have had the legal power (with the blessing of their state governments) to annex peripheral areas, thus enabling them to internalize the benefits of decentralization. As long as annexation was possible, the tendency for productive economic activity to locate near the edge of the city did not penalize the central city tax base and the many services which were financed almost exclusively by it.

Even as long as thirty years ago, it appears that central city economic growth was closely associated with geographic growth. Using what may well be the only available data source, I have estimated the correlation between the rates of central city growth of employment and land area over the period 1938–61 (see Table 31).[1] The simple correlation coefficient between the average annual rates of growth of manufacturing jobs and area was .67 (significantly different from zero at the .05 level).[2] Cities that have not in the past been able to annex much area have also tended to display

---

1.   John H. Niedercorn and Edward F. R. Hearle, *Recent Land-Use Trends in Forty-Eight Large American Cities* (Santa Monica: The RAND Corporation, September 1963). One could well wish for better or at least temporally comparable data, since the base and terminal years differ for different cities, as Table 31 shows.
2.   The correlation between the growth of commercial employment and area was only .09, not significantly different from zero even at the .10 level. This is not a surprising result, since commercial employment tends to be more concentrated in and around the central business district (CBD).

TABLE 31

EMPLOYMENT AND AREA EXPANSION
IN SELECTED CENTRAL CITIES: 1938–61

City and State	Period	Average Annual Percent Growth Rates		
		Manufac-turing Employment	Commercial Employment	Area
Boston, Massachusetts	1950–58	−1.4	−0.1	0.0
Buffalo, New York	1940–58	1.4	1.5	−0.2
Chicago, Illinois	1941–61	1.7	1.9	0.2
Cincinnati, Ohio	1948–60	−1.7	0.2	0.0
Cleveland, Ohio	1950–58	−2.2	0.2	0.0
Dallas, Texas	1950–60	5.3	3.7	3.1
Detroit, Michigan	1943–54	−1.9	0.0	0.0
Los Angeles, California	1940–60	6.7	2.4	0.4
Minneapolis, Minnesota	1948–58	−0.3	0.1	0.0
New York, New York	1938–59	1.8	0.3	0.2
Newark, New Jersey	1947–60	−3.0	−0.1	−0.2
Pittsburgh, Pennsylvania	1940–59	2.2	0.4	0.3
St. Louis, Missouri	1940–50	1.9	0.6	0.0
San Antonio, Texas	1951–56	4.6	4.0	9.9
San Francisco, California	1938–48	4.2	0.2	0.9
Seattle, Washington	1938–53	6.4	0.8	2.0

Source: Niedercorn and Hearle, *Recent Land-Use Trends in Forty-Eight Large American Cities*, Tables 6 and 12.

slow manufacturing job growth. As long as the central cities were able to annex the gradually decentralizing tax base[3] they could continue to grow. It is, therefore, not decentralization per se which threatens the growth of central city jobs, but certain constraints which force cities to forego the revenue growth usually accompanying annexation. These constraints take the form of increasingly vocal and powerful demands by the peripheral communities for local control—precisely the same force which has sparked the more visible movement for community control of ghetto institutions by *their* residents. State governments have supported this declaration of

---

3. Peripheral growth centers and industrial complexes contribute more than taxes to the vitality of the city. They attract secondary and tertiary activities—such as service shops, cultural amenities, entertainment facilities—which often make their environs desirable places in which to live, work, and shop, even despite such negative externalities as noise, smoke, and congestion. Even where they employ nonresidents of the city, such peripheral centers benefit the city economy by providing a substantial export market for local producers of goods and services. For city residents employed in these centers, the income streams generated by their payrolls contribute directly to central city economic growth.

political independence by suburban communities, but neither they nor the federal government have developed new institutional arrangements to compensate the central cities for their attendant losses in income and wealth.[4]

Is There Really a Fiscal Crisis in the Central City?

THERE IS NO QUESTION THAT MANY CENTRAL CITIES—especially the older ones in the northeastern and midwestern regions of the country—have larger budget deficits than the suburban jurisdictions which surround them. This is verified in Table 32, based upon a study of 37 large urban areas in 1966–67. Age of city is an important background variable in this analysis; except in regions with a small share of old cities, such as the South and the West, central city deficits exceed suburban deficits (and this is true even in the relatively young West if the costs of educational programs are excluded).

It has been suggested that this predicament is primarily the result of inadequate local tax effort. Banfield, for example, expresses the opinion that

what a mayor means when he says that his city *must* have state or federal aid to finance some improvements is (1) the taxpayers of the city (or some important group of them) would rather go without the improvement than pay for it themselves; or (2) although they would pay for it themselves if they had to, they would much prefer to have some other taxpayers pay for it. . . . In short, the "revenue crisis" mainly reflects the fact that people hate to pay taxes and that they think that by crying poverty they can shift some of the bill to someone else.[5]

Melville Ulmer's critique of general revenue-sharing is based upon evidence that the state governments, at least, operate with substantial excess fiscal capacity.[6] Data for the first half of 1972 indicate that state governments did indeed record large budget surpluses in that period.[7]

But city governments are not state governments, and there is considerable evidence against the proposition that central city governments and citizens

4.   As this book goes to press, Seymour Sachs of Syracuse University informs me that a great deal of annexation took place between 1960 and 1970—all of it outside the Northeast—and that, as in the early period, this contributes significantly to the statistical explanation of central city job growth in the 1960s. The "crunch" that I am predicting will therefore probably be delayed (especially in the Southwest).

5.   Edward C. Banfield, "The Unheavenly City," in *Readings in Urban Economics*, eds. Matthew B. Edel and Jerome Rothenberg (New York: Macmillan, 1972), p. 586.

6.   Melville J. Ulmer, "The Limitations of Revenue-Sharing," *The Annals of the American Academy of Political and Social Science*, September 1971.

7.   Edwin L. Dale, Jr., "Record Funds Reported in States on the Eve of Revenue Sharing," *The New York Times*, November 10, 1972, p. 1.

TABLE 32
PER CAPITA EXPENDITURES, TAXES,
AND INTERGOVERNMENTAL TRANSFERS
IN THIRTY-SEVEN SMSAs: 1966-67
(regional averages)

Region and item	Education		Other	
	central city	ring	central city	ring
Northeast (11 SMSAs)				
per capita municipal expenditures	$126	$160	$282	$145
per capita municipal taxes	61	105	159	79
per capita intergovernmental aid	46	64	86	34
net per capita surplus (+) or deficit (−)	−19	+9	−37	−32
suburban-central city gap		+28		+5
Midwest (11 SMSAs)				
per capita municipal expenditures	137	159	211	126
per capita municipal taxes	75	89	113	56
per capita intergovernmental aid	35	54	54	35
net per capita surplus (+) or deficit (−)	−27	−16	−44	−35
suburban-central city gap		+11		+9
South (8 SMSAs)				
per capita municipal expenditures	113	155	158	116
per capita municipal taxes	45	52	90	52
per capita intergovernmental aid	47	74	18	13
net per capita surplus (+) or deficit (−)	−21	−29	−50	−51
suburban-central city gap		−8		−1
West (7 SMSAs)				
per capita municipal expenditures	149	199	257	169
per capita municipal taxes	95	91	135	83
per capita intergovernmental aid	59	78	76	55
net per capita surplus (+) or deficit (−)	+5	−30	−46	−31
suburban-central city gap		−35		+15
Unweighted average (37 SMSAs)				
per capita municipal expenditures	136	170	230	138
per capita municipal taxes	69	84	126	66
per capita intergovernmental aid	45	66	60	33
net per capita surplus (+) or deficit (−)	−22	−20	−44	−39
suburban-central city gap		+2		+5

Source: Advisory Commission on Intergovernmental Relations, *Information Bulletin No. 70-1* (Washington, D.C.: January 1970), Tables 8-10.

have been unwilling to tax themselves adequately—especially relative to their suburbs.

In the first place, central cities have significantly less taxable property per capita than do their suburbs. During the period 1957–61, the ratio of suburban to core per capita taxable property value averaged well above unity in a sample of large urban areas.[8] Moreover, the center's share has been shrinking. Between 1961 and 1966, the suburban proportion of total SMSA property values rose from 57 percent to 62 percent in the Northeast, from 51 to 59 percent in the Midwest, from 38 to 52 percent in the South, and from 50 to 56 percent in the West.[9]

The central cities' share of federal and state tranfers to metropolitan areas is also less than proportional to their population, certainly for education and possibly for the noneducation categories other than welfare as well. In 1966–67, per capita intergovernmental aid to the 37 cities in the Advisory Commission on Intergovernmental Relations (ACIR) sample averaged $48 for education and $80 for other categories. The suburban per capita averages were $64 and $36 respectively.[10] Clearly, education aid goes where it is least needed. Moreover, the bulk of the noneducation central city aid consists of welfare transfers; if that category could be excluded, we might discover a similar core-ring imbalance for the remaining categories of public expenditure.

Table 33 shows quite clearly that central city tax rates compare favorably with those in neighboring suburban jurisdictions. In all but three of the 37 areas sampled (Providence, Houston, and San Diego), taxes as a percentage of personal income were higher inside than outside the city limits. Since personal incomes are much higher in the suburbs,[11] it seems fair to infer that suburban jurisdictions exert relatively less tax effort than the core municipalities.

On the average, about 80 percent of city tax income derives from property. There are, to be sure, a number of tax instruments (particularly the income tax) which many central city governments have not used. But this may be at least partly outside their control. Cities are legal creatures of the states, and ever since the end of the Civil War state legislatures have systematically restricted their cities' freedom to deal with emerging problems.

In this period between the mid-1870s and the turn of the century . . . many states went through a wave of constitution remodeling. . . . One of the cardinal rules followed in this period was that government must be run efficiently and along

---

8. Dick Netzer, *Economics of the Property Tax* (Washington, D.C.: The Brookings Institution, 1966), Tables 5–7. In the old northeast cities of New York, Philadelphia, and Newark, the ratios were 1.31, 1.46, and 1.58 respectively.

9. Advisory Commission on Intergovernmental Relations (ACIR), *Information Bulletin No. 70–1* (Washington, D.C.: 1970), Table 11.

10. Ibid., Table 10.

11. In the 37 sample areas, there were 1.45 times as many families in the suburbs with incomes above $10,000 as in the core, and only .7 as many with less than $5,000 (ibid., Table 6).

TABLE 33

TAXES AS A PERCENTAGE OF PERSONAL INCOME IN THIRTY-SEVEN LARGE METROPOLITAN AREAS (CENTRAL CITY AND SUBURBS): 1966–67

Metro. Area	Taxes (local) as a % of Personal Income	
	Central City	Outside Central City
Washington	9.1%	4.4%
Baltimore	7.2	3.5
Boston	8.4	4.0
Newark	8.8	5.5
Patterson—Clifton	6.4	6.2
Buffalo	7.7	5.2
New York	8.0	5.6
Rochester	6.4	4.8
Philadelphia	6.2	4.0
Pittsburgh	5.8	3.9
Providence .	5.4	5.6
Northeast	7.2	4.8
Chicago	5.2	3.9
Indianapolis	5.3	3.9
Detroit	4.9	4.2
Minneapolis—St. Paul	5.1	4.8
Kansas City	6.3	3.4
St. Louis	7.0	3.8
Cincinnati	6.3	3.5
Cleveland	6.4	4.2
Columbus	4.8	3.9
Dayton	6.8	3.2
Milwaukee	6.4	3.9
Midwest	5.9	3.9
Miami	6.7	4.6
Tampa—St. Petersburg	5.3	4.2
Atlanta	5.1	2.9
Louisville	4.6	3.2
New Orleans	3.7	2.1
Dallas	4.5	3.3
Houston	4.0	5.3
San Antonio	3.3	1.0
South	4.7	3.3
Los Angeles—Long Beach	6.3	6.3
San Bernardino—Riverside	8.2	8.0
San Diego	5.2	6.1
San Francisco	7.1	5.7
Denver	6.5	5.0
Portland	5.9	4.2
Seattle	3.7	3.5
West	6.1	5.5
Total	6.1	4.3

Source: Advisory Commission on Intergovernmental Relations, *Information Bulletin No. 70-1*, Table 12.

business lines. . . . State constitutions decreed balanced budgets, minimal government costs, and the avoidance of debt. . . . To prevent municipalities from taxing
business operations, tax powers were withdrawn or so reduced by legal limitations
on the rates as to render them largely ineffectual. State legislative approval would
be needed for any new tax powers, or for going beyond any of those low limits.
. . . Power, authority, and responsibility were taken away. These basics are still
missing in the majority of our cities.[12]

Municipal revenue powers have been expanded in this century, of course,
but "just enough to cover the new public assistance and welfare requirements that the post-Depression national commitment to these needs imposed upon them."[13] As a result of their "tradition of negativism," says
Reeves, the states have become "the fiddler on the roof."

The Exploitation Hypothesis

IF MANY CENTRAL CITIES HAVE A RELATIVELY greater budget deficit than
the jurisdictions which surround them, then one cause may be their "exploitation" by suburban residents, especially commuters. Exploitation is said
to occur if the benefits which central city governments provide to nonresidents are not fully offset by such direct means as user charges and
nonresident payroll taxes, and by such indirect effects as the economies
of scale which centrally located activities can achieve precisely because
of the existence of a wider metropolitan market.[14]

The exporting of central city services to suburban residents is substantial:

Increases in suburban populations have created a large demand for many . . .
central city services. For example, the suburban population makes regular use
of central city streets, parks, zoos, museums, and other public facilities; its routine
presence in the central city increases problems of the sanitation department and

---

12.   David N. Alloway and Francesco Cordasco, *Minorities and the American City* (New
York: McKay, 1970), pp. 31–32. Chapters 2–4 present an excellent historical analysis of the
traditional anti-urban bias in American politics, and the ways in which this bias—through
the actions of state legislatures—combined with technological and demographic forces
to reduce the competitive advantage of central city governments vis-à-vis other jurisdictions. For a similar analysis with an even longer perspective, see H. Clyde Reeves, "Have
State Policies Produced the Current Urban Problems?" *Public Administration Review*,
March/April 1970.
13.   Alloway and Cordasco, p. 36.
14.   The market price of a private good centrally produced and sold to (say) a commuter
would, under competitive conditions, just offset the benefit which has been "exported."
However, if the existence of the export market permits centrally located producers to achieve
scale economies, then the savings in unit production costs constitute an additional, or
"external," offset.

contributes to the costs of fire protection; the daily movement in and out of the central city of the large commuting population requires services that constitute a large proportion of the operating budget of both the police and highway departments. These are only some of the costs experienced by central city governments as a result of services they provide to their suburban neighbors.[15]

Whether this results in the exploitation of the core depends upon whether the core receives full payment for services rendered to suburbanites and full compensation for the external diseconomies (e.g., traffic congestion and pollution) imposed on the core by suburbanites, less the external benefits conferred upon the former by the latter.

The author of a recent study of 168 metropolitan areas concluded that in 1970 the suburban population level explained 44 times as much of the intercity variance in central city public service expenditures as did the level of the central city population. When changes in population over the decade 1960–70 were specified, the suburban change was 20 times as important as change in the core. Among individual public service sectors, suburban population growth was 17 times as important as central city growth in explaining variation in central city police expenditures, while for fire and sanitation the factors were 10 and 13 respectively. These differences were reduced only marginally by adjusting the data for annexation, age of the city, personal income of city residents, and racial composition of the central city population.[16] These magnitudes suggest—although they are insufficient to prove—that a great deal of exploitation *has* taken place, since, with the possible exception of sanitation and some recreation activities, all of these functions in the 168 cities are financed out of general taxation (so suburban users are surely undercharged).

An extraordinarily detailed cost-benefit analysis of Detroit and the six towns that surround it has been conducted for the fiscal year 1966 by William Neenan, who concludes that "the exploitation thesis is indeed verified in the Detroit SMSA."

Six suburban communities in the Detroit SMSA enjoy a considerable welfare gain through the public sector from Detroit. For a family of four this welfare gain ranges from over $4.00 to nearly $22.00 a year. . . . These are minimal estimates [since] many incidental services, supplied by Detroit to its suburban area, have not been included in the values estimated. . . . Suburban residents seem to be enjoying a welfare gain at the expense of the metropolitan core. Thus the one obvious prescription that emerges from this analysis is that the relative tax burdens

---

15. John D. Kasarda, "The Impact of Suburban Population Growth on Central City Service Functions," *American Journal of Sociology*, May 1972, pp. 1116–17.
16. Ibid.

on residents in suburbia, taken as a whole, be increased to compensate for benefits they are currently receiving from central cities.[17]

Financing Urban Government

THE EXPLOITATION HYPOTHESIS CONCENTRATES on net fiscal flows in the public sector. We must also look at private sector transactions between suburban consumers and centrally located producers to appreciate the extent of interdependence among the areas that make up a metropolis.

According to Kasarda's study of the relative impact of suburban and central city population levels (1960, 1970) and changes (1960–70) on central city retail, wholesale, and private service sales,

with the exception of wholesale trade at the former point in time, suburban population has a larger direct [positive] effect on every category of central city service function than does central city population.[18]

A comparison with statistical estimates for the previous decade 1950–60 shows that this relative importance of suburban consumers to central city sales is decreasing over time, but that it is still quite substantial.

This part of Kasarda's study has important implications for the design of policy for financing urban government. Whether or not (but especially if) exploitation exists, efficiency in the supply of public goods and services

---

17.   William B. Neenan, *The Political Economy of Urban Areas* (Chicago: Markham, 1972), pp. 137–38. For each function analyzed (including tax exempt colleges and hospitals, with the exemption treated as an income flow), Neenan allocates the total cost of production and distribution among the seven municipalities on the basis of use surveys, expressing the results as proportions of central city population. The portion financed by Detroit residents is obtained by multiplying the per capita figures by the incidence of Detroit taxes—i.e., the proportion of total Detroit revenues which Detroit residents actually pay. The application of specific assumptions to official data yields an incidence estimate of 52 percent for Detroit. The figures resulting from this multiplication (which, he admits, are still measures of *cost* rather than of *output*) are then transformed into benefit indices by a technique which assumes that the marginal utility of public services increases with income at a rate which is constant across all incomes, individuals, and the seven jurisdictions. Under this assumption, and using Detroit as *numéraire*, he multiplies each of the previous figures by the ratio of median family income in the corresponding jurisdiction to the median family income of Detroit. "In other words, willingness to pay for the same public service is 34 percent higher in Dearborn than in Detroit because Dearborn's income level is 34 percent higher than Detroit's" (p. 108). Finally, he estimates the magnitude of compensatory income transfers from suburbanites to Detroit residents through state sales and other taxes and via the Detroit tax on nonresident incomes. Subtraction of this set of compensatory payments from the "willingness-to-pay" benefits yields the results reported in the text. They are extremely sensitive to the utility-benefit transformation; without this routine, two of the six suburbs become net subsidizers of the city, and—among the remaining four suburbs which are subsidized by Detroit—the net transfers fall to $1.64-14.60 for a family of four. A related examination of Washington, D.C., and its suburbs, with a strong emphasis on methodological refinement and extension, is presented in Kenneth V. Greene, William B. Neenan, and Claudia D. Scott, *Fiscal Interactions in a Metropolitan Area* (Lexington, Mass.: Heath-Lexington, summer 1974).
18.   Kasarda, "Impact of Suburban Population Growth," p. 1115.

can theoretically be increased by the broader implementation of user charges,[19] especially for suburban visitors and commuters. However, commuters also confer substantial benefits upon central city residents through their market purchases. User charges, to the extent that they induce suburbanites to substitute suburban for central city shopping trips, can easily reduce central city welfare even further. They must, therefore, be used very cautiously, given the present fragmented jurisdictional structure of most metropolitan areas.

In developing a system for financing urban government, a minimum objective should be neutrality with respect to the welfare of the central city poor. There may be some room for higher property, sales, and income taxes—assuming the state governments will cooperate—especially for those presently exempt institutions which are least likely to move away as a result (e.g., large universities and churches). Nevertheless, the risk of accelerating the suburbanization process is always present. This is an example of Gunnar Myrdal's "cumulative causation" with a vengeance.

The answer would therefore appear to rest with a wholesale reorganization of the intergovernmental fiscal system; there is little that central cities can do on their own. Ulmer is surely correct in arguing that this should begin with federal pressure on, coupled with incentives for, the states to increase *their* taxes (especially through the income tax) and share the proceeds more generously with their cities. At the federal level, the central policy issue seems to concern the trade-offs between categorical federal transfers to cities (the present grant-in-aid program) and untied (or only partly tied) transfers (revenue sharing). Many criteria may be suggested in terms of which to debate the issue. Only one of these is central to this monograph: the criterion of impact upon the poor, especially the residents of the urban ghetto. We must ask whether local governments will in fact allocate *to* the poor untied transfers intended by Congress *for* the poor.

A series of studies of the Model Cities Program calls for some skepticism on this score.[20] Both in 1969 (when the program was just underway) and again in 1971 (by which time it was employing some 25,000 people across the country), fewer than half of the salaried workers in Model Cities were residents of the target inner city areas, in violation of both legislative and administrative intentions. At stake was an income flow of over $200 million a year in wages, salaries, and fringe benefits. The cities which allocated the smallest share of their Model Cities jobs to "model neighborhood" residents were those whose personnel systems extensively used educational

---

19.   Cf. Selma J. Mushkin, ed., *Public Prices for Public Products* (Washington, D.C.: The Urban Institute, 1972).
20.   Bennett Harrison, "The Participation of Ghetto Residents in the Model Cities Program," *Journal of the American Institute of Planners*, January 1973; and "Ghetto Employment and the Model Cities Program," *Journal of Political Economy*, March/April 1974.

credentials and police records as screening devices (even for unskilled jobs), those with powerful mayors (as measured by their veto authority and number of terms in office), and those which did not have to deal with actual or latent "black power" (as measured by the level and growth of the black population, and whether or not the city experienced a "civil disorder" during the summer of 1967). Moreover, it was found that target area residents received about $1,500–1,900 per year less in salaries than non-neighborhood residents with the same age, race, sex, education, civil service coverage, occupation, and (public) employer. The two-year study concluded that,

Once again, the urban poor have not received as large a share as might have been possible of the benefits associated with a government program ostensibly directed to improving their welfare. This "leakage" of public antipoverty resources into the hands of individuals at least some of whom are of doubtful standing as proper recipients has characterized other federal programs. . . . The research . . . suggests . . . that local governments with the political power to do so . . . can and will distort the equity objectives of federal programs.[21]

The Advisory Commission on Intergovernmental Relations (ACIR) issued a statement in 1970 in which a comprehensive reform of the intergovernmental fiscal system was proposed. A $5 billion annual revenue sharing program was outlined, with an interstate allocation formula based on population and tax effort, and containing a mandatory "pass-through" formula to guarantee a share for city governments. In addition, the Commission called for the "nationalization" of all welfare and medicaid costs, thus saving the states an estimated $5 billion per year. In return, the states would have to assume all nonfederal elementary and secondary education costs from their constituent localities—a shift of some $12 billion. Then, states would be induced to introduce their own income taxes by the creation of a Federal tax credit for state residents, to cost the national treasury $4–6 billion per year in foregone revenues. Finally, the states were urged to "revise their distribution formulas for such programs as public health, hospitals, and highways" in order to reduce intrastate fiscal imbalances such as those between central cities and their suburbs.[22]

Unfortunately, the ACIR recommendations do not directly address problems of distributive justice *within* jurisdictions, such as those associated with the Model Cities Program. Nevertheless, given that it seeks to operate totally within the existing intergovernmental system (a constraint which the following chapter recommends relaxing), the ACIR proposal embodies an important agenda for wide political debate.

---

21.   Harrison, "Ghetto Employment and the Model Cities Program."
22.   ACIR, *Information Bulletin*, pp. 12–14.

Conclusion

RESOLUTION OF THE FISCAL CRISIS of the central city is crucial to the welfare
of the urban poor. That the flight to the suburbs may not be irreversibly
related to race has already been suggested by Bradford and Kelejian (see
pp. 77–78 above). It is poverty and the shortage of central city public
services which repel the middle class and exacerbate the central city fiscal
crisis, not race per se. Central city poverty, of course, can be ameliorated
to only a limited extent by manipulating public instruments in the control
of local governments. There is need for a major national effort addressed to
job development, income maintenance, enforcement of antidiscrimination
laws, and reduction of labor market segmentation (this interpretation
assumes that housing and employment discrimination *can* be eliminated
or at least neutralized by public policy).

On the other hand, the difficulties being experienced by such European
cities as Stockholm indicate that the deterioration of American cities is
not entirely a matter of inadequate financial resources. This suggests that
we must look beyond public finance to the structure of the central city
economic system itself.

Chapter 7

THE FEASIBILITY OF CENTRAL CITY ECONOMIC DEVELOPMENT

In the last chapter, we examined a number of issues concerning the financing of public activity in cities. However, the public finance question may be of secondary importance. Until we decide what it is that we want the public sector to do in urban areas, and until we have examined alternative substantive programs, we are in no position to judge whether or not it would be worthwhile to reorganize the intergovernmental fiscal system.

One of the things which some people would like the public sector to pursue actively is the economic redevelopment of the central city. Our earlier findings suggest that the urban sector of the economy is still viable and that it offers urbanized black and poor workers their best—perhaps their only effective short-run—opportunity for increased economic well-being. But there are other considerations as well. To what extent are there still *regional* amenities which central areas are uniquely capable of providing? Are these of value to the residents of the metropolis? Do businesses still exist (especially small ones) which are aided by agglomeration economies? Will the pace of innovation continue to be related (as Jane Jacobs believes it to be) to the frequency and intensity of human interaction? And are there people who still *enjoy* central city life and want to continue that mode of existence? To the extent that these questions are answered in the affirmative, central city redevelopment is a useful and sensible goal for the public sector to pursue.

A comprehensive feasibility analysis of central city redevelopment would have many dimensions. For example, whether (and how) the cooperation of whites might be elicited in improving the quality of an environment which is becoming increasingly black would have to be explored. Such an analysis would surely question the sufficiency of any urban development program in the absence of a fundamental transformation of the American income distribution and of the key factors which seem to determine its shape: segmented labor markets, corporate power, and the asymmetry between income derived from work and income derived from the ownership of private property. Finally, a host of technical questions would have to be raised about the potential "capital-absorption capacity" of central cities, the availability of the kinds of production and distribution technologies necessary in a high-density environment, and the ability of existing or proposed government institutions to manage such redevelopment.

Consideration of such a range of issues is clearly beyond the scope of the present monograph.[1] In the following pages, we will confine ourselves to the technical and government-reorganization aspects of the matter.

The Availability of Vacant and Unutilized or Underutilized Space

ONE OF THE MOST COMMON OBJECTIONS to proposals for central city economic development concerns the alleged "critical shortage" of urban land. Even if the usable supply of this two-dimensional resource were as scarce as some assert, it would still be possible to exploit what Irving Hoch calls "three-dimensional urban space" through the use of air rights, subterranean construction, and high rise development. Moreover, much space ostensibly in current use may be seriously underutilized or even abandoned, as is the case with deserted apartment buildings and old railyards.

In fact, the myth of "no more central city land" is just that—a myth. We now have access to a major land use study based upon data first compiled by the National Commission on Urban Problems and then updated by its author through personal correspondence with each of the cities in the sample.[2] For various years between 1960 and 1970 (mainly 1968–70), in a sample of 86 of the 130 American cities with populations of more than

---

1. For discussions of some of the questions, cf. David M. Gordon, *Theories of Poverty and Underemployment* (Lexington, Mass.: D.C. Heath, 1972); Bennett Harrison, *Education, Training, and the Urban Ghetto* (Baltimore: Johns Hopkins Press, 1972), chaps. 5–7; William Spring, Bennett Harrison, and Thomas Vietorisz, "Crisis of the Underemployed," *The N.Y. Times Magazine*, November 5, 1972; and Thomas Vietorisz, "Income Redistribution via Earned Family Incomes," testimony delivered to the Democratic Party Platform Committee Hearings, New York City, June 22, 1972, published under the title "We Need a $3.50 Minimum Wage" in *Challenge*, May/June 1973.
2. Ray M. Northam, "Vacant Urban Land in the American City," *Land Economics*, November 1971.

100,000, there were an estimated 1,349,041 acres of vacant land, 25 percent of the total acreage of these cities. As one would expect, the per capita volume of vacant land decreases at an increasing rate with population; the densest cities (in New England and the Middle Atlantic states) have only a fifth as much vacant land per capita as the least dense cities of the Southwest and Pacific states. In 33 of Oregon's 222 cities smaller than 50,000 population, the average vacancy rate is 38 percent (a result based upon a separate sample).[3]

Among the 86 large cities, 78 percent of the vacant area was considered buildable by local experts. "The cities of Buffalo, Corpus Christi, Fresno, Jersey City, Kansas City (Kansas), Los Angeles, Miami, Norfolk, and St. Petersburg report that *all* their vacant land is buildable."[4]

If the 86 cities in Northam's study are treated as a representative sample, then there may be as many as ([.78 × 1.3 × 130]/86 =) 1.53 million acres of buildable vacant land in the 130 largest cities in the country.

During the operation of the Harlem Development Project in 1967–68,[5] a systematic search for usable industrial space was undertaken. The search led to a large industrial area adjacent to the old South Bronx yards belonging to the New Haven Railroad. City Planning Commission land use maps indicated that this area was still in active industrial use. A "windshield" survey clearly indicated, however, that much of it was deserted. Indeed, the deteriorating, boarded-up buildings had become a haven for drug addicts and derelicts. Young children were playing in the rubble of old factories. A few small companies were still operating in this environment but it was not difficult to forecast their futures. All together, at least 20 city blocks zoned for industry and officially alleged to be in active use were either underutilized or not used at all. Private corporate planners would, of course, argue that this is hardly prime industrial space and that the diseconomies imposed on any developer by the neighborhood would ensure the unprofitability of such development. But that of course constitutes one of the more widely accepted justifications for public development.[6]

---

3. Ibid., Table 1.
4. Ibid., p. 354. The criteria for buildability used by the local officials seem conservative. Most, for example, said that slopes of greater than 10 percent would be considered unbuildable. Yet some cities routinely build on land which is much steeper than this. In Pittsburgh, for example, "we've considered slopes up to and including 25 percent as buildable. Some land at 30 percent is being used for multi-unit development" (p. 350). Moreover, much of the vacant land is classified as unbuildable because the parcels into which it is divided fall short of the minimum lot sizes prescribed by local zoning ordinances. Such laws hardly constitute *technical* barriers to the use of these parcels.
5. Bennett Harrison, "A Pilot Project in Economic Development Planning for American Urban Slums," *International Development Review*, March 1968, reprinted in *Black Business Enterprise*, ed. Ronald E. Bailey (New York: Basic Books, 1971).
6. Cf. Otto Davis, "Economics and Urban Renewal: Market Intervention," in *Financing the Metropolis*, ed. John P. Crecine (Los Angeles: Sage Publications, 1970).

It is the third dimension which is most seriously underutilized in cities, according to many planners.[7] Skyscrapers are the most well-known, but hardly the only, application of the principle of "vertical-intensity" in urban design. Some companies have begun to purchase "air rights" to build over urban highways with structures supported by stilts (this can be seen, for example, along the Boston extension of the Massachusetts Turnpike). Imaginative plans for building under and around as well as over such already elevated structures as commuter rail lines have been published.[8] Elevated decks constructed over large facilities, like railroad yards, would effectively double the supply of buildable space within such areas. The Housing Act of 1964, and the Demonstration Model Cities Act of 1966, specifically authorize federal grants-in-aid for air-rights site preparation for industrial development.

"New towns in-town" could be or are being (as in the case of New York City's Battery Park City and Jersey City's Liberty Harbor) constructed on the edges of existing coastal cities, out over or on the water. In the John Hancock Center tower building in Chicago, apartments, offices, and shops are all combined, making it possible to commute by elevator. Other mixed use, three-dimensional projects include an apartment house built over a three-story school in the Bronx, a housing development built on the air rights over a Bedford-Stuyvesant day care center, and the mixed commercial-residential Martin Luther King Center in the Hough ghetto of Cleveland.

Development is also feasible in a downward direction. Thus, for example,

The Chase Manhattan Bank has a six-level development below ground [with] a cafeteria, bank facilities, building services, and vaults at rock level. . . . In 100 Russian cities, 35 percent or more of investment in structures is underground. . . . Sweden has one of Europe's great aircraft plants located 200 feet underground [and] a number of other manufacturing operations and sewage disposal plants. . . . Rockefeller Center pioneered in the use of the first basement level of all its buildings as an underground pedestrian thoroughfare and shopping arcade. . . . The Rockefeller Center underground network links about 17 acres of buildings. A much larger area [is] served by an underground system in Montreal. . . . Particular levels are devoted to subway transit, passenger trains, garages, pedestrian concourses and shopping, and to surface traffic. . . . Foot traffic at major inter-

---

7. Irving Hoch, "The Three-Dimensional City" in *The Quality of the Urban Environment,* ed. Harvey S. Perloff (Baltimore: Johns Hopkins Press, 1969); and Harrison, *Education, Training, and the Urban Ghetto,* pp. 199–204.

8. Cf. a Columbia University proposal for the upper Park Avenue railroad line, which, among other things, would create a traffic-free pedestrian boulevard, supporting shops, restaurants, theatres, and schools, with mixed-income housing above the train tracks (which would be enclosed in a well-ventilated and brightly lighted vault), with parking below (Department of Architecture, Columbia University, *The New City: Architecture and Urban Renewal* [N.Y.: Museum of Modern Art, 1967]).

sections above ground has fallen by roughly 70 percent. . . . A master plan for Philadelphia exhibits similar features.[9]

A project already underway in Honolulu (a working model is now in place) is developing a "space-saving floating city," which "will embrace the high-density, three-dimensional approach with apartments clustered and rising high into the sky, each with a view." The project will include shops, electric-powered mass transit, and an internal communications system.[10] Hawaiians have already constructed the Ala Moana Center in Honolulu, a fifty-acre, three-dimensional complex with malls, gardens, offices, medical centers, and stores employing nearly five thousand workers. "The renewed center of Stockholm . . . represents the same combined approach to transportation and buildings, with internal circulation by pedestrian walkway. Transit, rail lines, and parking are all underground, below the pedestrian mall [which] contains stores, theatres, and restaurants, and . . . five eighteen-story office buildings. The connecting subway carries passengers between the center and the outlying new towns."[11]

Urban economists define as "vital" those economies which are capable of responding to major shocks by developing new activities to substitute for those which have, for one reason or another, been eliminated. By the early 1960s, one of the major components of Chicago's economic base—meat-packing—had almost completely disappeared, the victim of the rapid post-war substitution of truck for rail shipment and the introduction of improved chemical means for preserving meat (developments which permitted the regional decentralization of the packing industry). The old stockyards and the adjacent railroad yards are now being converted into a modern light industrial park as part of the Mid-Chicago Economic Development Project. The core area, Stockyards-Packingtown, contains 77 acres of buildable land.[12]

In New York City, the closing of the U.S. Naval Shipyard in Brooklyn in 1966, in eliminating one source of income and employment, has created

9.   Hoch, "The Three-Dimensional City," pp. 119–23.
10.   William Helton, "Floating City—a Space Saver," *Maine Sunday Telegram*, August 13, 1972, p. D-12. A similar project is being considered for the Baltimore harbor. Architects frequently associated with such three-dimensional "urban clusters" are Moshe Safdi (of "Habitat" fame), Paolo Soleri, and Buckminster Fuller (who several years ago embarked on feasibility studies for an atomic-powered floating city whose modular construction would permit part of the city with its population to be moved across the oceans to other parts of the world where certain types of skills might be in short supply).
11.   Wilfred Owen, *The Accessible City* (Washington, D.C.: The Brookings Institution, 1972), pp. 59–60.
12.   Mayor's Committee on Economic and Cultural Development, *Mid-Chicago Economic Development Project* (Washington, D.C.: U.S. Economic Development Administration, May 1970).

the impetus for the development of a new source. Under the direction of the city's Economic Development Administration, a new industrial park is under construction on the site of the old navy yard. By utilizing high density structures (as with the Chicago project) and giving priority to labor-intensive industries, the city hopes to create at least 15,000 jobs in the 266-acre complex. Development is underway on and over the water, as well as out along some of the old piers.[13]

New Developments in Urban Technology

THE UNEXPECTED AVAILABILITY OF URBAN SPACE which we have just reviewed is being matched by the development of new technologies for exploiting urban space.

One important use of underground space is for the installation of subterranean utility lines, which releases additional quantities of surface space for other uses. Coordinated installation of all utility lines in a single network of trenches in Oakland cut costs from $1,000 per household to only $225. Continuous tunnel borers ("mechanical moles") are now in use, and laser-techniques for splitting rock are under active study.[14]

Industrial engineers have produced designs for high-rise industrial buildings, which permit vertical handling of materials. One variant—being used in the Mid-Chicago Development Project—provides truck access to every floor via graded roadways which circle the building, and subterranean parking and loading areas.[15] Similar structures will be built in the Brooklyn Navy Yard industrial park, where at least some old loft buildings will be rehabilitated and converted to the modern technologies:

---

13. Institute for Urban Studies, Fordham University, *The Brooklyn Navy Yard: A Plan for Redevelopment* (Washington, D.C.: U.S. Economic Development Administration, May 1968). The Chicago project is much more balanced—and ambitious—than the effort in New York. The Chicago development is intended to retain existing manufacturers within the city, to attract some new manufacturers from the outside, to reduce local income leakages in the surrounding black ghettos by expanding the number of locally-owned commercial establishments (especially by white-to-black ownership transfers), and to coordinate extensive manpower training programs with the actual industries that locate in the area.

14. Hoch, *"The Three-Dimensional City,"* pp. 122–24. Since present excavation costs constitute as much as a third of total subway construction costs, the potential impact on urban development might be considerable. The Minnesota Experimental City project plans not only to bury its utility lines, but to employ "a common utility trench serving piped and wired traffic of all kinds [e.g., cable television signals], and perhaps furnishing belt-line movement of freight as well. . . . It would be possible by video surveillance to detect breakdowns and service interruptions, and to make repairs at minimum cost" (Wilfred Owen, *The Accessible City*, p. 103).

15. John H. Alschuler and Irving M. Footlik, "Industry Can Cut Costs With Multi-Story Buildings," in Mayor's Committee for Economic and Cultural Development, *The Mid-Chicago Development Study* (Washington, D.C.: U.S. Economic Development Administration, 1966), Vol. I.

The techniques of materials handling in a combined horizontal and vertical system are constantly being improved. Stacking trucks, elevators and "lowerators," sloping conveyors, hoists, belts, ramps, pallets, and trays—are now all in use. Even the most delicate material and procedure can be handled with care by modern equipment. . . . By providing additional space on a new mezzanine served by automatic conveyors and lifts, a factory or warehouse can add substantially to its usable area.[16]

Many building codes have become obsolete; a good example is the widespread provision against plastic tubing—generally used for water pipes—as an alleged fire hazard. This has prevented greater use of modular construction techniques for building mass-produced housing. Obsolete codes have also made it difficult for cities to experiment with high-rise industrial structures, in which, for example, "Free movement vertically and horizontally is aided by the easy interchange of partitions and floor plates." City fire and building codes often prohibit such construction—although the permission of authorities in Chicago made it possible for vertical conveyors to be employed in the industrial redevelopment project there.[17]

In March 1972, the first high-rise industrial condominium was opened in New York City. The modern, eleven-story $2.5 million building, initially purchased and redeveloped by the New York State Urban Development Corporation, is owned entirely by its occupants (currently several firms in the printing and publishing industry). Normal loft operations, even when technically satisfactory, become difficult for small urban businesses because landlords can so easily raise rents to capture some of the profits of their more successful tenants. The condominium strategy is designed to relieve that pressure. Moreover, as owners, the firms are free to reallocate internal space as their relative needs change, a flexibility facilitated by the use of modular design.[18]

The Reorganization of Urban Government

VIRTUALLY ALL RECENT ATTEMPTS by one or another "government" to significantly improve the economic viability of central cities have fallen far short of material success. Many trace this to the growing lack of

---

16.   Institute for Urban Studies, *The Brooklyn Navy Yard*, p. 174.
17.   Ibid., pp. 174–75.
18.   Will Lissner, "Industrial Condominium Opens as Experiment Here," *The New York Times*, March 6, 1972, p. 1. The Urban Development Corporation is currently engaged in research and development work on building technologies for high density areas. Just as new technologies are being developed for exploiting urban space, so engineers are beginning to give some attention to the design of more efficient high-density-oriented processes for producing and distributing such public services as sanitation, fire-fighting, and traffic control. Cf. *The Struggle to Bring Technology to Cities* (Washington, D.C.: The Urban Institute, 1971).

consensus on appropriate delivery systems. In other words, which government or governments should be (or are capable of being) in charge of a comprehensive urban economic development program? Economic and political forces seem to be pulling in opposite directions at once, outward toward metropolitan or regional government on the one hand, and inward toward "community control" on the other. Unless this tension is resolved, urban redevelopment may be politically infeasible, even if it is technologically obtainable.

Friesema gives three general arguments in favor of expanding effective control over the urban region from the municipal to the metropolitan level.[19] The first concerns the increasing interdependence of economic activity across jurisdictional lines. This is perhaps most obvious in the case of air and water pollution, which physically diffuses from the location where it is generated to adjacent areas. But there are many other examples of such "spillover effects." Moreover, the externalities are by no means always negative. Will a particular jurisdiction develop a park that benefits neighboring areas as well? Efficient fire protection in one neighborhood benefits adjacent areas by reducing the probability that fires will spread to the latter. It is a fundamental theorem of welfare economics that, where such external economies are present, public goods and services will be underproduced.[20]

One way to rectify this situation is to negotiate with neighboring communities, but the problems of noncentralized information gathering and negotiations costs (including those to be imputed to a delay in decision making) are likely to make this an inefficient way of rationalizing the provision of these services. An alternative solution is to internalize the externalities by forming a higher level territorial system which will be better able to provide the service in question.[21]

A second argument for "metropolitanism" is based upon the public finance issues raised earlier in Chapter 6. To the extent that local expenditures continue to depend mainly on a local revenue base, that base must necessarily be equal to the task. The revenue base of many existing central cities is not. Thus, it is proposed that regional governments be created which are capable of financing their own public sector activities. Indeed, advocates of metropolitanism often posit internal self-sufficiency in balanc-

19.   H. Paul Friesema, "The Metropolis and the Maze of Local Governments," in *The New Urbanization*, eds. Scott Greer, et al. (New York: St. Martin's, 1968).
20.   Cf. Mancur Olson, *The Logic of Collective Action* (Cambridge, Mass.: Harvard University Press, 1965); and Burton A. Weisbrod, "Geographic Spillover Effects and the Allocation of Resources to Education," in *The Public Economy of Urban Communities*, ed. Julius Margolis (Baltimore: Johns Hopkins Press, 1965).
21.   David Harvey, "Social Processes, Spatial Form, and the Redistribution of Real Income in an Urban System," *Symposium of the Colston Research Society* (London, Butterworth's Scientific Publications, 1970), vol. 22, p. 297.

ing taxes and expenditures as a formal criterion for identifying the boundaries of the "optimal urban region."

The third argument for metropolitanism is technical. If the production and distribution of public services display economies of scale, if the activity level consistent with minimum average cost warrants a scale of production which exceeds normal consumer demand within a given jurisdiction, and if production and distribution are organized on a jurisdictional basis, then gross production in the region will be socially inefficient—i.e., cost savings which could be used elsewhere will be foregone. This creates a situation similar to that discussed above. Jurisdictions could arrange to specialize in different services, exporting to one another in order to increase the size of their markets. As before, however, this is likely to be logistically difficult, if not impossible. Thus, the desire to exploit economies of scale constitutes another rationale for metropolitan government.

These arguments are not without their critics. The estimation of public service cost functions is by no means an easy matter, and different competent researchers have produced different estimates of the optimal scale of production.[22] Moreover, these estimates are very sensitive to variations in local sociopolitical institutions (an obvious example is the difficulty with which police and fire services are delivered in many black ghettos, because of racial tensions). Besides, it may well be that the potential savings which would flow from the attainment of scale economies are worth foregoing. It is impossible to say, without first examining the potentially offsetting advantages of preserving—and even strengthening—decentralized government. Just as private resource allocation decisions require balancing benefits against costs, so, too, a public policy prescription based solely on costs is seriously incomplete. Another technical criticism argues that there is no longer any level of government short of the nation itself which would be capable of financing all of its public services entirely out of revenues generated within its jurisdiction. If so, then one of the few unambiguous criteria for identifying an optimal scale for regional government loses its precision.

One of the more recent—and emotional—criticisms of metropolitanism comes from, or on behalf of, members of the black community.

As central city populations have changed and the number of black citizens has increased, metropolitan merger increasingly has been visualized as an attempt to cheat black Americans out of their growing political power in the city. Whatever the logical merits of such attitudes, they not only exist, but they reinforce

---

22. For a survey of some of these studies, see Werner Z. Hirsch, *The Economics of State and Local Government* (New York: McGraw-Hill, 1970), pp. 178–84.

the political inertia of the existing constitutional and statutory arrangement of urban governance.[23]

Where metropolitan reform proposals have been put to the voters (as in Cleveland, St. Louis, Nashville, and Miami), blacks have consistently voted no. In fact, "The attitudes of Negro wards became more negative to metropolitan reorganization as the number of predominantly Negro wards increased in Cleveland. As power grew, Negroes apparently felt they had more to lose from metropolitan reform."[24]

Blacks would surely be an electoral minority in any metropolitan government based on existing SMSAs. Why the suburban communities which currently make up the "white noose" would be any more responsive to the needs of black central cities within a formal regional apparatus than without one is not at all clear. The black mayors of large American cities have had little enough success in acquiring outside resources. Would their relative power be any greater in the councils of a metropolitan government?

At the other extreme in the ongoing debate over optimal urban government is the demand for community control.

According to [Mancur] Olson's analysis, the smaller the group the more willing it is likely to be to provide itself voluntarily with collective goods. The smaller the group, the more it is likely to achieve some collective aim. This has important economic implications, for it indicates the possibility of higher motivation in small community settings than in large—a quality which [Harvey] Leibenstein calls "X-efficiency," as opposed to the usual economic measures of efficiency. . . . It has also been argued on more doctrinaire grounds that the only way to achieve a genuine democracy is through community control based on local neighborhood units—only then, it is argued, will it be possible to ensure that everyone has a voice in decisions.[25]

Community control of specific public functions (especially in the sensitive areas of police and education services) has been advocated by a wide range

23.   Royce Hanson, "Toward a New Urban Democracy: Metropolitan Consolidation and Decentralization," *The Georgetown Law Journal*, March-May 1970, p. 871. See also Frances Fox Piven and Richard A. Cloward, "Black Control of Cities," *The New Republic*, September 30, 1967 and October 7, 1967; and U.S. Commission on Civil Rights, "Metropolitanism: A Minority Report," *Civil Rights Digest*, Winter 1969. In his case studies of existing metropolitan governments, Melvin Mogulof recognizes the legitimacy of these black fears but offers in rebuttal the powerful observation that black control of existing central cities may be a "hollow prize," not only (or so much) because of fiscal insolvency as because so many areas of city life are increasingly coming under the control of politically independent special jurisdictions, which would be especially resistant and offensive to new black mayors (see Melvin B. Mogulof, *Five Metropolitan Governments* [Washington, D.C.: The Urban Institute, 1972]), pp. 115–20.
24.   Dale Rogers Marshall, "Metropolitan Government: Views of Minorities," in *Minority Perspectives*, ed. Lowdon Wingo (Baltimore: Johns Hopkins Press, 1972), p. 15.
25.   David Harvey, "Social Processes, Spatial Form, and the Redistribution of Real Income," p. 296.

of political writers of all races,[26] and considerable experimentation along these lines is underway.[27] A much smaller number of writer-organizers have advocated the extension of selective functional control to wholesale community self-government.

The concept of community is more complex than many advocates of decentralized urban government may have realized. Royce Hanson's strong criticism is not atypical of the orthodox response to the demand for neighborhood government:

[It] rests upon the assumption that a clear and distinct local community of interest, peculiar to the local community, or even a neighborhood can be found and articulated politically. . . . In this context, according to cant, the citizen can become familiar with his communal government and, through the shared experience of the community, learn the ropes of politics and become a full member of the larger body politic. Moreover, he also can "control" his own destiny jointly, with his neighbors.

This quaint and bucolic idea, however, is somewhat in conflict with the economic, physical, psychological, and political facts of urban life. . . . The neighborhood is only one politically significant basis for the organization of interest, citizen participation, and shared political experience. Work place, professional or occupational groupings, ethnic characteristics, ideology, or economic interests may serve equally or better as the organizational base of a "community."[28]

On the other hand, it is possible that many of these different communities converge in the case of urban blacks, due to the pervasiveness of racial discrimination in housing, education, and employment, in which case the geographic neighborhood may indeed have the significance that proponents of decentralized black government claim for it.[29] In any case, this disagreement over management of selective public service functions versus comprehensive neighborhood government permeates the community control movement, preventing, thus far, the emergence of a powerful united front which might bargain for changes in city political structures.[30]

---

26. Cf. Roy Innis, "Separatist Economics: A New Social Contract," in *Black Economic Development*, eds. William F. Haddad and G. Douglas Pugh (Englewood Cliffs, N.J.: Prentice-Hall, 1969); Gerson Green and Geoffrey Faux, "The Social Utility of Black Enterprise," also in the Haddad and Pugh volume; and Nathan Glazer, "For White and Black, Community Control Is the Issue," *New York Times Magazine*, April 27, 1969.

27.   Cf. Howard Hallman, *Neighborhood Control of Public Programs: Community Corporations and Neighborhood Boards* (New York: Praeger, 1970); and George J. Washnis, *Municipal Decentralization and Neighborhood Resources: Case Studies of Twelve Cities* (New York: Praeger, 1972). We will examine some of these experiments in Chapter 8.

28.   Hanson, "Toward a New Urban Democracy," pp. 874–75.

29.   Alan Altshuler, *Community Control* (New York: Pegasus, 1970), pp. 124–29.

30.   Thomas M. Gannon, "Plato, Aristotle, and Neighborhood Government," *America*, March 20, 1971.

Out of this confusion and disagreement between the advocates of centralization and those who call for radical decentralization is emerging—perhaps not surprisingly—something of a synthesis. Political scientists refer to it as "multi-level government." So far, the attempts to actually implement "a territorial organization which is hierarchical in nature and which allows maximum local participation while at the same time ensuring a closer to optimal provision of general urban services"[31] have been modest; perhaps the best-known is the recent consolidation of Indianapolis and some of the adjacent jurisdictions into a new regional government call Unigov. Nevertheless, a number of rather daring proposals have been proffered, and we shall conclude this section by reviewing some of them.

One plan proposed by the Committee for Economic Development (CED) builds on the work of Alan Campbell and the actual experience of the city of Toronto.[32] In 1954, the Ontario legislature created a federation out of the 13 jurisdictions which make up the Toronto region. Later, these were consolidated into six boroughs. The CED-Campbell model would create similar federations, except that the existing central cities would not necessarily be retained as legal or political entities. Rather, the city boundaries would be extended "to encompass the entire metropolitan area, while simultaneously creating at the local level a series of community governments to protect the interests and concerns about their own immediate needs."[33]

Richard Burton's "metropolitan state" would also consist of a regional-neighborhood mix of governmental institutions, with no role for the existing municipalities.[34] Here, however, the new entities would actually receive statehood status; their constituent neighborhoods would thus assume the status of legislative districts. This novel approach would make large urban areas directly eligible for a panoply of federal assistance programs presently monopolized by the existing state governments.

Other urbanists are frankly skeptical about these "fantastic" schemes. "Redesign will take time," writes Donald Canty, "and meanwhile we must get on with the job. . . . We need a new areawide instrument now."[35] These

---

31.   Harvey, "Social Processes, Spatial Form, and the Redistribution of Real Income," p. 297.
32.   Committee for Economic Development, *Reshaping Government in Metropolitan Areas* (New York: CED, 1970).
33.   Quoted by Donald Canty, "Metropolity," *City*, March/April 1972, p. 39. See also Joseph F. Zimmerman, *The Federated City: Community Control in Large Cities* (New York: St. Martin's, 1972).
34.   Richard P. Burton, *The Metropolitan State* (Washington, D.C.: The Urban Institute, 1970).
35.   Canty, "Metropolity," p. 19.

individuals would embed existing city governments in a larger institutional matrix. Albert Mayer would create a second tier of neighborhood governments under the existing city in order to "declutter" City Hall. His model is fashioned after London and its constituent boroughs, whose populations of 100,000 to 300,000 elect their own councils and control many local functions. Mayer explicitly rejects as "painfully extended gradualism" the introduction in New York City and Boston of "little city halls," or New York's "'community planning advisory boards' which have no power and, since they are appointive, represent nobody in particular."[36] Royce Hanson would add a third tier to the Mayer scheme: the regional super-government itself.

> In creating the metropolitan governments on this tier, the state . . . could provide certain express powers to be exercised by the metropolitan tier. . . . Insofar as possible, special purpose regional authorities should be reorganized in the general government of the metropolitan tier.[37]

Perhaps the most impatient of the urban reformers is Donald Canty. Rather than wait for a formal restructuring of urban government to promote economic development, he would create an "interim instrument" to do the job now: the Metropolitan Development Agency (MDA). This would consist of "population-equal community districts smaller than the central cities, and larger than the smallest suburbs. Each district would elect its own governing board and officers. And these . . . would choose delegates to form the areawide MDA governing board. Officers of the MDA would be chosen in an areawide general election."[38] The MDA itself would be federally financed, and granted the powers of eminent domain and supercession of local building and land-use regulations (powers possessed until recently by the New York State Urban Development Corporation). Specified powers would be reserved to the "communities." The principal objective of the MDA would be "the widening of options and opportunities for the poor and minorities."

Cities would participate in the MDA (it is not clear how). The superagencies themselves would not be general-purpose governments, but Canty hopes that such governments would grow "naturally" around the activities of the MDA. In anticipation of this organic growth of regional governments, Canty proposes that the enabling legislation outfit the MDAs with "self-

---

36. Albert Mayer, "A New Level of Local Government Is Struggling to Be Born," *City*, March/April 1971.
37. Hanson, "Toward a New Urban Democracy," p. 897.
38. Canty, "Metropolity," p. 19.

destruct" mechanisms, to avoid their becoming yet another special purpose district like the N.Y. Port Authority.[39]

The federal sponsorship of the MDA provides an important ingredient missing from all of the other proposals. In any metropolitan government for the foreseeable future, the majority of constituent "districts" or "neighborhoods" (whatever they are called, and however their boundaries are selected) will be neither black nor poor. How will the minority of low-income districts fare in the legislative competition? Extrapolation from historical experience does not offer an optimistic forecast. Federal intervention may be necessary in order to protect the interests of these black districts from their white neighbors. To be sure, the federal administrators, including the White House, may not care to provide such protection—recall the earlier analysis of the Model Cities Program. But the point is that the federal administrators may provide that support and reinforcement if they wish.

To recognize the desirability of maintaining supportive linkages between black and brown neighborhoods and the federal government certainly does not preclude the forging of new links with the white ethnic neighborhoods that lie next door. It is simply a recognition that racism exists, that it is likely to continue to do so for some time, and that black urban organizers must continue to protect their own group interests. In this sense, Canty's model is pragmatic.[40]

Public Control of Urban Land

ONE OF THE MAJOR ACTIVITIES of any reorganized urban government will—according to a growing number of analysts—have to be the nationalization and public deployment of substantial quantities of urban land. From "radical geographers" through conservative architects to urban historians (notably Mumford), there is a widespread interest in planning public land use.

39. If federal dollars for economic development flow directly to the MDAs rather than through—let alone to—the cities, it is difficult to see how the latter can remain viable, and it is even harder to imagine the MDAs gracefully closing their books in response to the appearance of a more "legitimate" metropolitan federation. Burton writes: "Can anyone . . . seriously doubt the notorious propensity of organizations not to 'wither away,' but to maintain themselves long after their purpose has been served (like many of our state and city governments)?" Richard P. Burton, "Letter," City, Summer 1972, p. 42.
40. This review of the literature on the reorganization of urban government has explicitly excluded truly radical proposals, which integrate plans for political decentralization with a fundamental transformation of the entire economic system. These proposals require much more detailed attention than they could possibly be given in this already lengthy manuscript. For an especially thoughtful example, see Gar Alperowitz, "Socialism as a Pluralist Commonwealth," in The Capitalist System, ed. Richard C. Edwards, et al. (Englewood Cliffs, N.J.: Prentice-Hall, 1971).

Canty is particularly explicit on this matter:

Almost the entire American development experience has proved in a negative way, and the experience of other Western democracies in a positive way, that only public ownership of land at some point in the process of development can assure that the results will serve, rather than obstruct, public purposes.[41]

Public ownership of land under public development would mean that increases in value created by that development would accrue to the public, rather than to private speculators. The MDA, acting as a "land banker," could "undercut the ruinous speculation that consistently destroys the economic feasibility of low- and moderate-income housing in the inner city."[42] In a new book, Robert Wood also advocates "public ownership and public planning" in order to achieve "genuine land reform" in American cities. "Only a general plan with [public] land ownership and control being the decisive forces in critical areas can do the job."[43]

In a major National Policy Task Force Statement issued in early 1972, the American Institute of Architects formally called for public control of urban land, in order to rationalize the development process and (as Faux pointed out) make low-income housing construction feasible.

We are convinced that an effective national growth policy requires that land development increasingly be brought under public control. . . . *We favor public acquisition and preparation of land in advance of development.* We believe that the appreciating value of urbanizing land should be recycled into the costs of developing, serving, and maintaining it. [Emphasis in the original.][44]

In 1969, in connection with the Harvard University Program on Technology and Society, economist Robin Marris concluded that one of the most significant types of "market failure" impeding private sector efforts to deal effectively with urban poverty occurs in the land market. His analysis led him to recommend that "the business community perhaps needs to consider whether the tradition of a free market in land and other natural resources (including riparian rights), only relatively qualified by government powers, is in the best interests of the nation or for that matter of the business community itself. . . . It is becoming increasingly apparent that the basic

---

41. Canty, "Metropolity," p. 42.
42. Geoffrey Faux, "CDCs in the Cities' Future," *Center for Community Economic Development Newsletter*, July 15, 1972, p. 13.
43. Robert Wood, *The Necessary Majority* (New York: Columbia University Press, 1972).
44. "Memo," *Newsletter of the American Institute of Architects*, January 1972 Special Issue, p. 4. For a similar recommendation from an ideologically opposite position, see David Harvey, "Revolutionary and Counter-Revolutionary Theory in Geography, and the Problem of Ghetto Formation," in *Perspectives in Geography* (DeKalb, Ill.: Northern Illinois University Press, 1972), vol. II.

cause of the trouble is the custom of private ownership of urban land. However much we may dislike this fact, we cannot escape it."[45]

While the emergence of a significant political movement organized around the demand to substitute public for private ownership of urban land seems far off, there has been some activity in recent years addressed toward increasing public control over private land use decisions.[46] Until 1922, the states controlled most local zoning. As part of its thrust toward greater home rule, the "good government" movement urged decentralization of zoning power. In 1922, an advisory committee organized by (then) Secretary of Commerce Herbert Hoover recommended such decentralization. This was promulgated by the Department of Commerce as the Standard State Zoning Enabling Act of 1922, according to which states would cede to their local governments the police power to regulate, through appropriate zones, the uses of private land.

Locally-controlled zoning has not worked out well. Spillover effects, land assembly requirements that sometimes cross jurisdictional boundaries, and the fundamentally regional nature of air and water resource management problems impose upon localities the demonstrably impossible task of co-operating in the use of their individual authorities. When the incentive to cooperate conflicts with short-term gain (e.g., through the acquisition of ratables), the usual result is a series of beggar-thy-neighbor decisions on the part of each individual jurisdiction. Powerful interest groups have also found it easier to deal with atomistic jurisdictions; and once a major land use decision has been forced in one place, it often becomes next to impossible for neighboring jurisdictions to refuse to follow suit.

The Housing Act of 1954 recognized these difficulties, and authorized a program of "Urban Planning Assistance." The so-called "701 Program" encouraged comprehensive land use planning on a regional basis, provided financial support for the new metropolitan-wide councils of government, and financed the graduate training of a generation of city and regional planners. Subsequent administrative regulations by executive agencies, especially in the 1960s (and especially in HUD), "edged steadily towards encouragement of interlocal cooperation, regional coordination and metropolitan government." Highway and infrastructure (e.g., airport, water and sewer, waste treatment) projects were no longer to be approved without

---

45. Robin Marris, "Business, Economics, and Society," in *Social Innovation in the City*, eds. Richard S. Rosenbloom and Robin Marris (Cambridge: Harvard University Press, 1969), pp. 26, 42.
46. This discussion draws heavily on an excellent unpublished Urban Institute manuscript by William K. Reilly. For some case studies of recent state programs of land use control, see Fred Bosselman and David Callies, *The Quiet Revolution in Land Use Control* (Washington, D.C.: Council on Environmental Quality, 1971).

the filing of statements showing their relationship to a general plan of development. In 1969 the Office of Management and Budget (OMB) published Circular A-95, which defines the federal programs subject to such a procedure for obtaining clearance (that is, through public hearings).

Still, land use planning is a technical matter, and citizens have found it difficult to articulate their objections to particular land use decisions (when they have been sufficiently motivated to organize around these issues at all). And as long as local jurisdictions held policing power with respect to zoning, they were able to resist pressures for real citizens' participation in land use decisions, as well as attempts by professional planners and others to base such decisions on regional interests. In recent years, housing and federal construction have been added to the OMB circular's list of covered activities. Jurisdictions are now required to produce statements on civil rights (racial employment) as well as on economic development.

Still, the circular has not in itself been sufficient to produce truly public control over land use, nor has it been able to impose a regional perspective on land use planning:

Something, clearly, has not worked out. Comments are made, paper generated and circulars and regulations complied with, yet close observers of the process do not believe that planning in most areas is particularly comprehensive, local development activity well distributed from a regional or metropolitan point of view, or federal agency activity coordinated. One could cite examples from around the country of local actions taken, many with federal financial support, in disregard of local comprehensive plans, and without any concern for regional impact. [We face] the continued predominance of the public works planners over the comprehensive planners, the local boosters over the regional planners, the immediate and local economic advantage over the longer run and metropolitan interest.[47]

The federal government may have begun to break the logjam with a series of pieces of new legislation. The National Environmental Policy Act of 1970 (and the Environmental Protection Agency which it created) require jurisdictions to file "anticipated environmental impact statements," which must be debated in open public hearings (with *all* records open to public—including media—inquiry) and before federal agencies and congressional committees. Perhaps the most important long-run effect of NEPA will be to expose to public consideration the competing criteria by which local land use decisions are guided.

The Land Use Policy and Planning Assistance Act of 1972, which passed the Senate by a 60-18 vote but failed of passage in the House, would go much further by inducing state governments to take back their power over land use zoning through a major new grant-in-aid program. The hope is that the states would be in a better position to make and enforce land

47.   William K. Reilly, unpublished notes.

allocation decisions that internalize the external effects of local land use decisions. State control would in principle also make it easier to plan the preservation of air and water sheds and other regional resources.

Whether these attempts at exerting public control over private land use will work remains to be seen. Whether anything short of actual nationalization of urban land will be sufficient is a major unresolved—indeed, hardly even mentioned—issue. In any case, the analysis contained in the earlier pages of this chapter strongly suggests that the feasibility of central city economic development may be dependent to a great extent on our ability to negotiate a rather fundamental change in a basic American institution: the private ownership of urban land. Other Western countries have succeeded in doing so; indeed, the Swedes maintained public ownership of the land in and around Stockholm well into the nineteenth century to prevent private speculation from interfering with the development process.[48] This is probably a much more immediate problem than the reorganization of urban government, although both could benefit from coordinated implementation.

Economists can contribute to this ground swell by estimating the impact of public control of urban land on such key variables as housing costs and the number of expected starts, on the reinvestable surplus (or monopoly rent) which land development might generate for public treasuries, and indeed on the cost of living itself.

Owen's "Accessible City"

AFTER MANY YEARS OF STUDY AND WRITING on problems of urban transportation and urban form, Wilfred Owen recently published a monograph advocating the replacement of market-organized cities by planned polynuclear clusters of mixed densities. Public control of land is the central institutional change which makes this kind of urban planning possible.

According to Owen, "The great advantages of the city, diversity and choice, are being thwarted by immobility and lack of access."[49] The conventional remedy is increased public and private investment in transportation. "The trouble with much of the urban transport effort is that the improvements being made either help to crowd more people into inadequate space or encourage a kind of spread-out city that denies people the satisfactions of being part of a community. Both have resulted in environmental deterioration and in the neglect of housing and infrastructure and services. . . . The only remedy is to recognize that anything is techni-

---

48. Goran Sidenbladh, "Stockholm: A Planned City," in *Cities: A Scientific American Book* (New York: Alfred A. Knopf, 1968).
49. Owen, *The Accessible City*, p. 9.

cally possible and to choose the kind of environment to be sought. The laissez-faire city is likely to end in disaster."[50]

A great and growing variety of urban transport systems are becoming economically and technically feasible: express-routed buses (highly successful in experiments in Northern Virginia), taxis, demand-activated taxi-bus combinations, subways and other rapid-transit modes, sunken auto roadways, and so-called "dual-mode" systems using private cars which are personally controlled in low density suburbs and exurbs and computer-overridden inside the high density core (passenger capsules are available for those who don't own cars, making them a kind of horizontal elevator service). But it would be inefficient to plan the deployment of these new or modified systems without simultaneously planning—and changing, if necessary—the locations of trip origins and destinations as well. Under market allocation, job and residential locations are determined under a variety of debilitating "market failures." The public sector is then expected to come to the rescue by connecting these disparate locations (or subsidizing private efforts to connect them) "at minimum cost." Such cost-minimizing transportation "plans" are therefore necessarily second best, their alleged optimality undermined by the inefficient way the market allocates the locations of origins and destinations.

Such partial planning of transportation systems can easily generate positive feedbacks which exacerbate initial conditions. For example, a subway oriented to the central business district and designed to relieve congestion in the core may attract such a large number of new shoppers that congestion actually increases.

The root of the problem is that location decisions are based on the economic feasibility of individual structures, and not on the total costs incurred by the community. A building constructed on a new subway line can be a sound investment for the owner, while a series of such investments may create so many demands on municipal services that collectively they prove to be an economic disaster. This is why a community design establishing the densities and locations of urban activity and relating them to whatever transportation capacity will be available is necessary. *Without public control over how urban land is to be used,* transportation needs are likely to be miscalculated, both for automobiles and for transit [italics added].[51]

Control over land use permits the development of articulated activity in space. Present American cities lack even the degree of articulation found within a modern hospital:

Hospitals are composed of wards, operating rooms, kitchens, and laboratories, and related activities are grouped together to reduce unnecessary movement and avoid

---

50. Ibid., p. 50.
51. Ibid., p. 49.

through traffic where it has no reason to be. But if the building were badly designed so that food had to be wheeled through the operating room, it would be impossible to carry out the goals for which the structure was planned. Similarly, a house built with the kitchen at one end and the dining room at the other is bound to create excessive traffic and loss of efficiency.[52]

Private development generates urban sprawl, because the market leads developers to be most profligate with that resource—land—which *appears* to be (and is in fact to them, although not to society) cheapest. Sprawl creates the need for excessive investments in transportation. As an alternative, Owen would manipulate job location, household location, and transport simultaneously.[53] With all three as instrumental variables, he argues, the optimal design—or at any rate a design well worth investigating—is the "polynuclear city," a cluster of several high-density central places embedded in lower-density interstices, the whole surrounded by extremely low-density countryside. Common resources (air, water, waste removal) might be regionally planned, while individual central places would regulate their own local public services. A prototype exists in Stockholm, where "a combined attack has been launched on congestion by a combination of central city renewal and the creation of urban satellites about ten miles out to contain the displaced population and provide for growth." Since the turn of the century, "an important ingredient of Swedish urban development has been the policy of purchasing land within and outside the city at an early stage to guide urban growth and to reap part of the financial rewards from the resulting increment in land value. Public ownership of urban land has permitted the municipality, rather than the land owner and real estate developer, to benefit from the urbanization process, and this has been an important measure for avoiding the financial difficulties that confront so many cities around the world."[54]

In this and other examples offered by Owen (Belgrade, Rome, and a number of smaller French cities), further density in the largest cities is replaced, not by market-induced sprawl, but by planned clusters of central places of mixed densities, the "polynuclear accessible city" which "offers a compromise between undesirably high density and the destructive side effects of indiscriminate sprawl."[55]

---

52. Ibid., p. 58.
53. Thomas Vietorisz's research on new town planning for New York State has led him to the conclusion that industry is becoming rapidly more "footloose." If so, this makes the manipulation of industrial location even easier, in the sense that the opportunity costs to a firm of any particular location (measured in terms of foregone profit) are reduced. See Vietorisz, et al., *The Design and Evaluation of Alternative Patterns of New Town Development for the State of New York* (Ithaca: Center for Urban Development Research, Cornell University, 1971).
54. Owen, *The Accessible City*, p. 67.
55. Ibid., p. 112.

Owen summarizes his argument with a check-list of the criteria for the development of polynuclear accessible cities:

—good housing *close to employment*
—environmentally "clean" industrial parks
—public services and amenities near the housing
—underground freight delivery at major shopping and neighborhood centers
—high-quality public transit with low or no fares
—major highways and transit systems connecting the clusters
—pedestrian-oriented clusters with circulation systems of elevators, escalators, moving sidewalks, electric cars, minibuses, and underground terminals and parking
—open space surrounding the clusters
—landscaping of city streets and control of commercial encroachments.

Underlying all of these recommended aims, and in a sense the necessary condition for achieving any of them, is public land acquisition to permit large-scale development and eventual recoupment from increased land values to help finance low-cost housing and community services.[56]

Conclusion

REDEVELOPMENT OF THE CENTRAL CITY as a site for economic activity appears to be technically and—with suitable institutional changes—politically feasible.

Whether we should want to revive the central city economy is a value judgment. One such judgment might be made on the basis of efficiency (Kain has said, "I know of no good reason for trying to reverse the trend toward dispersal"). Others, who base their choices on essentially noneconomic or nonpecuniary factors, take the position that efficiency should not be the only—or even the major—consideration, but that economic feasibility *is* a relevant constraint. It is the latter issue with which this chapter has been concerned.

Within the issue of central city redevelopment is embedded the (if anything, even more politically divisive) issue of ghetto (or "inner city") economic development. It is to this subject that we turn our attention in the next chapter.

---

56. Ibid., p. 115.

Chapter 8

APPROACHES TO REBUILDING THE GHETTO ECONOMY

RECOGNITION THAT CENTRAL CITY SLUMS were socially undesirable (whether because they were "bad for business" or "morally insupportable") first became reflected in federal policy in the urban renewal program that followed World War II. Concern for the problem dwindled and very nearly disappeared in the fifties. The civil disorders which erupted in one central city after another during the period 1965–68 reawakened public interest in ghetto problems and led directly to a host of programs ostensibly designed to ameliorate the conditions which had led to the riots.

Prominent among these endeavors—all but one of which has involved at most only minimal institutional change—were the urban renewal program, public encouragement (with modest subsidization) for private corporations to locate plants inside the ghetto, creation of the Model Cities Program to "plan and coordinate" social and economic investments within the ghetto, an expansion of the number of individual "black capitalists" doing business both inside and outside (but especially inside) the black community, and the more institutionally innovative program referred to as "community economic development."

The Theory and Record of Urban Renewal

URBAN RENEWAL IS ONE OF A NUMBER of public policies necessitated by the failure of private markets—in this case, the real estate market—to allocate resources efficiently or equitably.

For an abbreviated version of this chapter, together with a survey of research on the structure of the ghetto economy, see Bennett Harrison, "Ghetto Economic Development," *Journal of Economic Literature*, April 1974.

The result of this market failure in urban real estate is a "prisoner's dilemma": i.e., a situation in which "the best result, which could be achieved by unified action, is not attained because it is too risky for any individual to attempt to achieve it if he is not sure others will follow him."[1] Thus, each individual decides according to his own private interest, with the collective result that each individual is worse off than before. The paradox is perhaps best captured in James Buchanan's well-known dictum: "The selfish pursuit of private good leads instead to the achievement of public bad." Adam Smith's Invisible Hand—his argument that the confluence of many individual decisions, each made on the basis of self-interest, results in public good—is inoperative where prisoners' dilemmas are present.

That so much of the inner city land which developers would like to purchase for new uses is "ghetto turf" creates a major problem. A developer would have great difficulty selling an isolated unit—however sumptuous—to a middle or upper class corporate or household buyer because of the external diseconomies which the surrounding ghetto would impose on the unit.

Another problem derives from the spatial indivisibility associated with an increasing number of industrial and residential projects. Developers who must assemble large tracts of urban land to accommodate modern plants, office buildings, and apartment houses, are confronted by the fact that

> most urban land is held in small parcels. A government study of urban renewal acquisitions during 1962–63 showed the average parcel was 0.17 acres in size; in Baltimore the average was as low as 0.04 acres. If it is known that a developer is planning a large project, it is rational for each of the many small landowners to hold back his parcels of land, hoping to be the last to sell, and to capture a disproportionate share of the increase in value.[2]

Each owner would benefit by selling, and the developer himself would benefit. Yet each owner, acting in self-interest, holds out for the premium. The result is that *no* sales are made, and *all* parties are worse off (in this model, nonowners do not count). Thus the prisoner's dilemma.

This leaves two possible approaches. Those large corporations with the power to do so may attempt to acquire adjacent properties over time through dummy purchasers, or front men. The second approach a developer may take is to "convince" the local government to use its power of eminent domain to take the necessary land on the grounds of "higher social use,"

---

1. Matthew B. Edel, "Development or Dispersal? Approaches to Ghetto Poverty," in *Readings in Urban Economics*, eds. Matthew B. Edel and Jerome Rothenberg (New York: Macmillan, 1972), p. 312.

2. Matthew B. Edel, "Planning, Market, or Welfare?—Recent Land Use Conflict in American Cities," in *Readings in Urban Economics*, eds. Edel and Rothenberg, p. 141.

and then sell it back (often at a considerable discount) to the developer. This is the urban renewal approach.[3]

In theory, local governments perceive the existence of slums, and use urban renewal as an instrument for eliminating the blight which slums create—the diseconomies they impose on the rest of the city. Again in theory, the improvement of the living conditions of the slum dwellers is a major *raison d'être* for renewal. The relationship between public agencies and private developers is based on mutual interest and convenience; governments help (or work through) developers because the normal, profit-oriented activities of the latter promote the "general welfare."[4]

In practice, the processes by which urban renewal programs in American cities are instituted are very different. During the twentieth century, as their incomes increased, many white families who had originally resided in the urban core moved farther out, in search of open space and large housing lots. The city neighborhoods which they evacuated were gradually occupied by working class blacks and whites. In many of these neighborhoods, deterioration of both physical and human capital progressed to the point where they could be described as ghettos. Since World War II, however, and especially since the early 1960s,

> Once commuting distances became great enough, and incomes high enough, the income elasticity of demand for proximity to work and to cultural institutions . . . [became] greater than that for space. This is true at least for families without young children. Rehabilitated townhouses, large apartments, and luxury high-rise condominiums . . . yield as much satisfaction as larger tracts of cheaper suburban land. The bid-price curves of the wealthy and upper middle class are thus likely to [become kinked]. Very close to the center of the city, there will be the steepest bid-price curves, and in a market situation, purchasers of these luxury dwellings will be able to bid land at the urban core away from the poor. . . . The changing pattern of land uses suggested by this model may be accentuated by the expansion of downtown financial districts and cultural institutions, both of which are likely to grow as urban population and the wealth of middle- and upper-income groups increase. . . . A further factor in the battle over downtown space has, in many cases, been university [expansion].[5]

Because of the prisoner's dilemma, however, the market cannot efficiently engineer this reconversion of inner city land uses. Consequently, private developers anxious to exploit the new demands of the nonpoor for central

---

3.   On the record of urban renewal, cf. Martin B. Andersen, *The Federal Bulldozer* (Cambridge: MIT Press, 1964); and Jane Jacobs, *The Death and Life of Great American Cities* (New York: Random House, 1961).
4.   This is the standard "liberal" view of the intent of the Housing Act of 1949, which established the Urban Renewal Program. For an alternative interpretation, according to which no significant antipoverty orientation was ever intended by Congress, see Julie Vitullo-Martin, "Liberals and the Myths òf Urban Renewal," *Public Policy*, Spring 1971.
5.   Edel, "Planning, Market, or Welfare?" pp. 139–41, 147.

city space exert pressure on local governments to resort to urban renewal for the desired reconversion. Indeed, it is not unusual to find developers and others associated with the real estate industry themselves occupying permanent or advisory positions in such strategic local governmental offices as the planning commission and the budget bureau.

All too often, professional planners support this class-biased use of urban renewal (however inadvertently) through their elitist conception of what constitutes a slum. Given the expanded white demand for central city space, it is still necessary to select specific areas for renewal. While politicians are likely to focus on neighborhoods with the least political power, planners are disposed toward a more "scientific" criterion—namely, whether or not a neighborhood is a slum, often defined operationally as an area where "housing inventory is old, densities are high, and mixed land uses are prevalent."[6] To the residents of these neighborhoods—and this seems especially true of white ethnics—none of these characteristics are necessarily undesirable. Older housing is generally less expensive and often roomier, high densities do not automatically imply congestion (which *is* undesirable), and mixed land uses afford residents convenience to their workplaces and an intensity of street life which appears to be a highly successful deterrent to crime (with spatially segregated land uses, nonresidential zones are usually deserted after dark, which facilitates crime, while in mixed-use neighborhoods, there are always—to use Jane Jacobs' apt expression—"eyes that watch the streets"). The development of a social policy orientation in many university planning departments is a welcome and important event. Yet,

Although city planners have begun to appreciate the systemic relationship among social, economic, and physical inputs into their designs, this new sensitivity is not reflected in the programs, either public or private, which are intended to restore our urban centers.[7]

In sharp contrast to the theory, urban renewal programs almost invariably *reduce* the welfare of the poor, who are displaced from the center of the city, find it almost impossible to afford the new housing constructed on the old sites, and—because of racial and class segregation in the non-ghetto housing market—find it difficult to obtain housing elsewhere to replace what they have lost.[8] As a result, they move in with friends and

---

6. Richard Krickus, "White Ethnic Neighborhoods: Ripe for the Bulldozer?" National Project on Ethnic America, American Jewish Committee, no date, pp. 3–4.
7. Ibid., p. 20.
8. In 1970, the General Accounting Office reported that the Urban Renewal Program destroyed about 3.5 units for each new one built. Cited in Arthur I. Blaustein and Geoffrey Faux, *The Star-Spangled Hustle: White Power and Black Capitalism* (New York: Doubleday, 1972), p. 260.

relatives elsewhere in the ghetto, increasing congestion and consequent pathologies even further. When housing does open up outside the ghetto, the mass relocation forced by urban renewal creates a flood of potential new movers which frightens whites in the destination zone and feeds the panic psychology which underlies such real estate practices as blockbusting. Thus, the possibility of integration is replaced by ghetto expansion—the new neighborhood becomes an extension of the older ghetto.

Actually, this process by which government policies simply shift the ghetto around is nothing new. In 1872, Engels observed a similar phenomenon in the cities of England:

This method is called "Haussmann" [and entails] making breaches in the working class quarters of our big towns, and particularly in those which are centrally situated, quite apart from whether this is done from considerations of public health and for beautifying the town, or owing to traffic requirements. . . . No matter how different the reasons may be, the result is everywhere the same; the scandalous alleys disappear to the accompaniment of lavish self-praise from the bourgeoisie on account of this tremendous success, but they appear again immediately somewhere else and often in the immediate neighborhood! The breeding places of disease, the infamous holes and cellars in which the capitalist mode of production confines our workers night after night, are not abolished; they are merely *shifted elsewhere!*[9]

The damage done by urban renewal goes beyond the forcible eviction of households, although it is surely because of this that the disadvantaged (especially blacks) have a low opinion of urban renewal (hence the cynical expression, "Urban renewal means Negro removal"). The uprooted residents are seldom adequately compensated for their property. Moreover, small businesses are also uprooted, as are political-cultural institutions such as churches and community centers—the "glue" of the neighborhood. These commercial and institutional linkages are especially fragile and difficult to reproduce in the new areas into which the dislocated citizens are forced. Finally, by increasing land values in the renewal area (indeed, speculators have been known to pay enormous bribes to city officials for advance information on the location of future renewal sites), spillovers are generated which may worsen the economic welfare of ghetto residents living *outside* the renewal area. To protect values within the original renewal zone, there is pressure to bring its borders under renewal as well. Thus, for example, in San Francisco,

Six thousand blacks used to live in the first Fillmore renewal area. After redevelopment . . . only three black families were able to move back into the area. . . . In 1964, the Redevelopment Agency began to make its move into adjacent areas in the Fillmore ghetto. Over fourteen thousand people, 70 percent of whom are

---

9. Frederick Engels, *The Housing Question* (N.Y.: International Publishers, 1935), pp. 76–77.

black, have been and will be affected by this thrust. The basic reason given for the expansion of Fillmore renewal was to protect high land valuations in the first renewal area.[10]

The Housing Act of 1968 introduced a number of new provisions ostensibly to mitigate the negative impact of urban renewal on ghetto and white working-class neighborhoods. Projects in predominantly residential areas must allocate at least 20 percent of their new housing to low income families. Relocation subsidies are expanded, and neighborhoods not yet under the bulldozer are offered rehabilitation grants and loans which—if actually delivered—might reduce the probability that an area will be designated a renewal zone.

Yet the same Act offsets these modest reforms by actually expanding the scope of Negro removal programs. Funds are authorized to reduce the delay in implementing urban renewal projects, which would make it even more difficult for the poor (who are understandably slower at such things than trained professionals and entrenched politicians) to study renewal proposals and organize their communities for participation or resistance. A new so-called "Neighborhood Development Program" makes it financially easier to expand renewal activities in contiguous areas than before.

In any case, congressional appropriations fell so far short of authorizations as to doom any chance of real reform.

The Congress was requested to provide $15 million for tenant services under public housing programs. None was appropriated. $75 million was requested for the one percent interest rate housing programs (sales housing), and only $25 million was appropriated. Exactly the same request and exactly the same appropriation occurred for the rental-housing segment under that subsidized interest-rate provision.[11]

More fundamental solutions than compensating those who are dislocated are clearly needed. Radicals would supplant competitive bidding by a socially controlled urban land market and a socialized control of the housing sector.[12]

In any case, urban renewal programs have succeeded only in perpetuating the ghetto by relocating it. They have certainly not helped to rebuild the ghetto and transform it into a viable social sector of the metropolis.

---

10. Danny Beagle, Al Haber, and David Wellman, "Creative Capitalism and Urban Redevelopment," in *Problems in Political Economy: An Urban Perspective*, ed. David M. Gordon (Lexington, Mass.: D. C. Heath, 1971), p. 404.
11. William L. Henderson and Larry C. Ledebur, *Economic Disparity* (New York: The Free Press, 1970), p. 202.
12. David Harvey, "Revolutionary and Counter-Revolutionary Theory in Geography, and the Problem of Ghetto Formation," *Perspectives in Geography* (DeKalb, Illinois: Northern Illinois University Press, 1972), p. 19.

The Location of Corporate Branch Plants in the Ghetto

A SMALL NUMBER OF MAJOR CORPORATIONS HAVE, since 1966, experimented with the location of branch plants within the urban ghetto, an undertaking for which a few senators and congressmen, led by the late Senator Robert F. Kennedy, have encouraged federal support.

These investments were not intended as charity but were expected by all concerned to show a profit. On the other hand, since greater profits were available in other locations, any large-scale program would surely require the government to apply political leverage and extend financial incentives. Without such inducements, voluntary corporate efforts would inevitably remain fragmentary.

Nevertheless, even the modest branch-planting investments of 1966–70 (there has been virtually no new investment since the 1970 recession) were expected to produce benefits for the ghetto. Jobs and earned incomes would be created both directly and (through purchases of intermediate products and services) indirectly. New plants would stimulate the sales of adjacent small businesses such as coffee shops. The facilities would permit the companies to engage in the training of both line workers and—perhaps more important in the long run—new managers. Through so-called "turn-key" programs, according to which companies set up subsidiaries intended to be spun off for eventual ownership by community groups, the ghetto would eventually acquire control over profits and the capital stock itself. In short, it was hoped that the expansion of the ghetto's industrial base through absentee-owned corporations operating in national (and even international) markets would catalyze black economic development.[13]

The Watts riots of 1965 caused the White House to seek help from the corporate community in dealing with the situation. Hubert Humphrey, then Vice President, was instrumental in assembling a group of Los Angeles industrialists led by the chairman of Aerojet-General Corporation. It was decided to use federal subsidies from the Small Business Administration, the Manpower Administration, and the Economic Development Administration to support the location by these companies of branch plants inside Watts and other "impacted areas." The first such ghetto-based facility was the Watts Manufacturing Company, designed to employ about 500 people producing postal equipment and housewares.[14]

---

13. For more detail on the experiences of individual companies and communities, see The Conference Board, *Business and the Development of Ghetto Enterprise*, New York, 1971, 2 volumes; and Sar Levitan, Garth Mangum, and Robert A. Taggart III, *Economic Opportunity in the Ghetto: The Partnership of Government and Business*, (Baltimore: Johns Hopkins Press, 1970).
14. Jules Cohn, "Private Industry and the Disadvantaged," in *Problems in Political Economy*, ed. David M. Gordon, p. 134.

A series of meetings culminated in the so-called Test Program of Job Development which, during the period 1967–68, administered corporate branch-planting activities in five cities: Boston, Washington, Chicago, San Antonio, and Los Angeles. The companies involved were Aerojet-General, General Dynamics, Lockheed, Thiokol, Avco, North American Rockwell, General Electric, and Fairchild Hiller—all major defense and space contractors.[15] With such federal assistance as labor training subsidies, low-interest loans, and procurement contracts, the program proceeded through the election of 1968. After that,

with the Republican victory in November 1968, its major champions left Washington and the books were closed on what had been an expensive and highly political product that yielded few positive results. According to a former official who was with the program from the beginning, "It suffered from a lack of empathy for the people we were supposed to serve. Our clients were assumed to be the firms rather than the people they were serving."[16]

At the same time (1967–68), the Department of Labor launched its Special Impact Program (SIP).[17] Three firms which moved into the Brooklyn ghettos "received more than $3.5 million to hire and train 1,200 people for at least six months at low-wage unskilled jobs; at the end of two years all three firms had closed down the ghetto sites and between them had managed to employ only 300 people for more than six months." SIP's activities in East Los Angeles were even more disastrous. Five firms received a subsidy of $5 million to locate in the Chicano barrio and employ about 1,600 residents.

One of the firms moved closer to East Los Angeles than it had been before, three of them located about the same distance away [as before] and one firm took the Labor Department's money and moved farther out. Three of the firms eventually ended up some twenty miles from East Los Angeles.[18]

By 1969, according to an evaluation of SIP conducted by the Westinghouse Learning Corporation, two of the companies were in bankruptcy and a third had "lost interest in the program."

What kinds of companies engaged in ghetto branch-planting? A study by McKinsey and Company concluded that "the greatest percentage of

15. Geoffrey Faux, *CDCs: New Hope for the Inner City* (New York: The Twentieth Century Fund, 1971), p. 39.
16. Ibid., p. 40.
17. This Department of Labor program to subsidize private corporate branch-planting in the ghetto should not be confused with the OEO program of the same name. Created under Title I-D of the amendments to the Economic Opportunity Act, OEO's SIP is the principal source of federal assistance to the indigenous ghetto development corporations which we will study later.
18. Faux, *CDCs: New Hope*, p. 39.

participants is found in aerospace companies. . . . The president of a new conglomerate [told us], 'Aerospace has to go out of its way to be a good citizen in order to keep the government money flowing.' " [19] Those central city industries which are the least "footloose"—insurance companies and public utilities—also tended to participate to cool down what they considered a threat to the safety of their enormously expensive facilities.

The McKinsey survey was not sanguine about the general results of the branch-plant strategy. According to McKinsey consultant Jules Cohn:

> Of the 247 companies in my study, only 11 set up subsidiaries. And the number of employees and trainees participating in them is small. A total of only about 1,000 disadvantaged workers are reported involved in the programs I studied. Upgrading had been achieved . . . for 125 employees, but few of these were transferred to jobs in parent companies.[20]

As for the turnkey operations, they, too, quickly ran into trouble. By May of 1969, and despite Labor and Defense Department subsidies and contracts totaling well over $4 million, the Watts Manufacturing Company had lost several hundred thousand dollars and employment had been cut back to two hundred workers. In 1970, the Aerojet-General subsidiary was sold to the Chase Manhattan Capital Corporation. EG & G's metal fabrication plant in Roxbury "failed before it could be spun off to the community." Overall, according to Sar Levitan and his colleagues, "The experience generally has not been favorable."[21]

Federal Support: The Kennedy Plan

THE SAME URBAN RIOTS WHICH LED to the inauguration of the Test and Special Impact Programs and unaffiliated corporate investments in the ghetto also had their effect on the Congress:

> In the summer of 1967, separate but similar bills to create incentives in the form of tax credits and deductions for businesses that located in the ghettos were introduced in the Senate, one by Senator Jacob Javits and the other jointly by Senators Robert F. Kennedy and James Pearson.[22]

The most widely discussed of these and related pieces of legislation has been the so-called "Kennedy Plan."[23] In fact, the plan included not only support for outside companies constructing plants within the ghetto, but also substantial assistance for indigenous businesses (including direct and

---

19. Jules Cohn, p. 128.
20. Ibid., p. 135.
21. Levitan, Mangum, and Taggart, *Economic Opportunity in the Ghetto*, p. 62.
22. Faux, *CDCs: New Hope*, p. 39.
23. Reprinted from the *Congressional Record* as Robert F. Kennedy, "A Business Development Program for Our Poverty Areas," in *The Ghetto Marketplace*, ed. Frederick D. Sturdivant (New York: The Free Press, 1969).

guaranteed loans, interest subsidies, short-term capital aids, government contracts to purchase locally produced goods and services, and technical assistance for prevocational and on-the-job training). Nevertheless, it is the branch-planting aspects of the Kennedy Plan which have received most attention.

A firm wishing to avail itself of the subsidies provided under the plan would request certification from the Secretary of Housing and Urban Development. To qualify, the firm would have to commit itself to hire at least fifty workers in its ghetto plant, two-thirds of whom would have to be unemployed or underemployed residents of the area; to pay the higher of the federal minimum wage or the local "prevailing wage for similar work"; and to have no pre-existing facilities in the poverty area in which it intended to locate the new plant.

A certified firm would be eligible for many subsidies, including the following: a seven percent tax credit on construction or leasing of a plant, a ten percent tax credit on the purchase of machinery and equipment, a three-year carryback credit, a credit carryover of ten taxable years, a net operating loss carryover of the same duration, accelerated depreciation of $66\frac{2}{3}$ percent, a wage bill subsidy in the form of a tax deduction of 25 percent of the salaries of all low income resident workers hired, and training allowances.

Could such a strategy attract new plants to the ghetto? (The question is deliberately conjectural, for neither Kennedy-Pearson nor other legislation with similar aims has ever passed Congress.) There is considerable evidence—as from the earlier Area Redevelopment Administration Programs to develop rural depressed areas—that "efforts to overcome with financial incentives the preference of company officials for one area over another have not been very successful."[24] A review of the literature dating from the 1940's concluded that "government financial incentives to industry . . . are not of significant value in attracting new industry to an area or encouraging expansion of already existing industry in an area."[25]

Assuming that new economic activities were induced by the Kennedy Plan, what kinds of firms would such incentives be most likely to attract to the ghetto? Here, there seems to be considerable agreement among analysts. A study by the U.S. Department of Commerce predicted that most of the firms who would find the program financially attractive would already be doing business in the ghetto (and therefore be ineligible for

---

24. Faux, *CDCs: New Hope*, p. 38.
25. William C. Lewis, "Tax Concession and Industrial Location," *Reviews in Urban Economics*, Fall 1968, p. 44. See also William J. Stober and Laurence H. Falk "The Effect of Financial Inducements on the Location of Firms, *Southern Economic Journal*, July 1969.

assistance). Most would be low-wage, labor-intensive firms; the expected wage (based on previous experience) would be only about $3,000 a year.[26] Subsidies would often accrue to firms that would have expanded operations even in the absence of help.[27] "The firms most likely to respond would be those for whom the subsidies would make the greatest difference; these tend to be low-margin firms producing standardized products in highly competitive markets, paying relatively low wages."[28] In order to attract better firms to the program, according to William Tabb, the government will have to change the factors such as inadequate public services and excessive congestion which make central city locations inferior to suburban sites. But the Kennedy Plan makes no significant provision for such *public* investment in the ghetto.

Would the firms which did respond to the Kennedy incentives make a profit? Again, the analysts seem to concur in their pessimism. John Garrity's hypothetical profit-and-loss analysis led him to conclude that the only firms which could take full advantage of all the incentives in the Kennedy Plan would be those capable of earning a pretax annual profit of about half a million dollars. Only one percent of American corporations earn this much. Less profitable companies, according to Garrity, would not be able to survive in the ghetto, despite help from the government.[29] This stark forecast is contingent upon Garrity's rather harsh (and, as it turns out, unrealistic) assumptions about the likely quality and behavior of the ghetto labor force: 7.5 percent lower productivity, 50 percent higher turnover, twice the hiring costs, and 800 percent higher direct training costs than in nonghetto plants.[30] Private corporations with involvements in the ghetto (including the companies participating in the Job Opportunities in the Business Sector Program to train the hard-core unemployed) report generally favorable labor performance. Most find their ghetto and nonghetto employees to be indistinguishable in terms of productivity, absenteeism, turnover, and learning rates.[31] Moreover, there is evidence that any correla-

---

26. Levitan, et al., *Economic Opportunity*, p. 64.
27. William K. Tabb, *The Political Economy of the Black Ghetto* (New York: Norton, 1970), p. 77.
28. William K. Tabb, "A Cost-Benefit Analysis of Location Subsidies for Ghetto Neighborhoods," *Land Economics*, February 1972, p. 51.
29. John T. Garrity, "Red Ink for Ghetto Industries?" *Harvard Business Review*, May-June 1968.
30. Ibid., p. 12.
31. For details, see The Conference Board, *Business and the Development of Ghetto Enterprise*, vol. 1., chap. 5; and The Conference Board, *Education, Training, and Employment of the Disadvantaged*, New York, 1969. For a summary, see Bennett Harrison, *Education, Training, and the Urban Ghetto* (Baltimore: Johns Hopkins Press, 1972), pp. 30–38.

tion between tenure and race[32] or quit-rates and race[33] disappears when the positive relationship between tenure/quits and wages is taken into account. Even so, Garrity's gloomy forecast indicates the difficulty of finding ventures inside the ghetto which are capable of generating sizable private profits. Moreover, a much more elaborate (and methodologically defensible) cost-benefit analysis of the Kennedy Plan was conducted by William Tabb;[34] even under the assumption that the average wage in a Kennedy plant would be only $3,000 (so that, while the plan might reduce ghetto unemployment, it would not by assumption reduce "working poverty"), Tabb concluded that "program costs would be two and one half times the net returns."

Thus, there seems to be considerable evidence that corporate branch-planting would be unprofitable. Assuming that it could be made profitable (perhaps through even larger subsidies than those envisioned by Kennedy), would ghetto residents benefit? What can be said about the external and dynamic effects of such a strategy?

These are questions which have been examined by Barry Bluestone.[35] The branch-planting strategy precludes ghetto organizations from influencing—let alone controlling—what the development economics literature refers to as "project selection." Different production processes—and indeed different products—generate different streams of external economies and diseconomies. Moreover, citizens have different feelings about the things which their neighborhoods produce, and (if they had the power to do so) might well establish those attitudes (however "irrational") as project selection criteria. Whether these externalities are technological (as, say, in the case of polluting industries) or attitudinal (perhaps the people of Watts didn't *want* to produce tents for use in the Vietnam War), branch-planting makes such issues moot from the point of view of the community. Westinghouse criticized the Special Impact Program on just these grounds:

> An important problem in East Los Angeles lies in the nature of the community's relationship to business, to unions, to governmental institutions which are supposed to serve it; the community has no control over these institutions. It doesn't even have the position of an equal partner. *Any special program*—be it job-oriented, educational or meant to stimulate housing—*will be of little consequence to the community if it does not take this state of affairs into account.*[36]

32. Peter B. Doeringer, "Ghetto Labor Markets," Program on Regional and Urban Economics, Harvard University, Discussion Paper No. 35, May 1968.
33. V. Stoikov and R. L. Raimon, "Differences in Quit Rates Among Industries," *American Economic Review*, December 1968.
34. Tabb, "A Cost-Benefit Analysis of Location Subsidies."
35. Barry Bluestone, "The Political Economy of Black Capitalism," in *Problems in Political Economy*, ed. David M. Gordon.
36. Westinghouse Learning Corporation, quoted in Faux, *CDCs: New Hope*, p. 41. Emphasis in the original.

Second, ghetto branch plants are able to get away with paying wages far below those which the company normally pays for equivalent work in its nonghetto facilities. Indeed, the Kennedy Plan explicitly reinforces such behavior by requiring only that firms pay the legal minimum wage or "the prevailing wage for the area," whichever is higher. For a variety of reasons (which are the subject of "dual labor market" theory—see above chap. 7, n. 1), and given the almost complete absence of unions in ghetto plants, the prevailing wage for the area is seldom above the poverty line. Even the unions have acquiesced thus far. "This [branch-plant] approach has enabled companies to set lower wage scales for the disadvantaged without meeting objections from union negotiators who—at least to date—have been willing to exempt *separated* operations from union scales."[37] The whole process, Bluestone argues, weakens the strength of union-negotiated nonpoverty wage floors in large corporations.

Finally, the participation of private corporations may be actually reducing public investment in the development of independent political and economic power in the ghetto, by redirecting that investment to the subsidization of private corporate profit. The private enterprise ethic, widespread faith in the ability of corporations to solve social problems, and the real power of these private interests, all conjoin to assure that if corporate groups want to direct the "war on poverty" they will be invited with open arms to do so. Bluestone also fears that, as the success of urban (especially ghetto) redevelopment programs becomes increasingly contingent upon the efforts of private corporations, the government will lose what little leverage it now has for enforcing antidiscrimination policies in the corporate sector.

The thrust of these critiques of the Kennedy Plan, together with the review of actual corporate experience in this area, can be easily summarized. Private nonghetto business has to play a role—probably several roles—in the redevelopment of the inner city. To let it dominate the redevelopment process, however, entails many risks. In any case, physically locating corporate branch plants in the black community appears for the most part to be an inefficient business decision. So long as modes of industrial organization emphasizing private profits form the basis of an urban redevelopment strategy, location in the inner city probably will mean "red ink for ghetto industries" and poverty-level wages for ghetto workers.

The Model Cities Program

TITLE I OF THE DEMONSTRATION CITIES and Metropolitan Development Act of 1966 (Public Law 89–754) authorized the U.S. Department of

---

37. Jules Cohn, p. 135.

Housing and Urban Development to undertake a "Model Cities Program" which would "concentrate public and private resources in a comprehensive five-year attack on the social, economic, and physical problems of slum and blighted neighborhoods," in order to "upgrade the total environment of such neighborhoods and significantly improve the lives of residents." The 150 cities participating in the program receive one-year planning grants to cover 80 percent of the cost of "planning comprehensive programs to raise substantially the levels of housing, education, health and medical treatment, employment and job training, income, and social services in the 'model neighborhood.'" This is a specific geographic target area defined by each city making application to HUD, according to the general criteria that it be largely residential and that "a substantial portion must be hard-core slums with a high concentration of low-income families." When plans are completed and approved, cities become eligible for a panoply of federal grants-in-aid and HUD "supplemental grants" to carry out their programs.

Of the $640 million invested by the public sector in Model Cities as of December 31, 1970,[38] only a fraction has been allocated to activities that could be classified as "economic development," e.g., the operation and support of new private and public enterprises or reconstruction of the housing stock. Indeed, the inability to generate much construction or rehabilitation business for minority building contractors has been one of Model Cities' most notable failures.

Model Cities is primarily concerned with the delivery of services and with combining direct public service employment with manpower training. Even with respect to the latter, while 83 percent of the approximately 25,000 regular salaried Model-Cities-funded workers in the Spring of 1971 were placed in jobs in various agencies of their local city and county governments, only about one quarter of the 83 percent worked in development-related agencies.[39]

Community Development Corporations (CDCs) are locally based, owned, and controlled organizations—some operated for profit, most not—which are directly involved in initiating and managing ghetto economic development programs. In their central concern for creating jobs, income, and economic and political power, they contrast sharply with the private profit and human capital orientations of the other approaches to urban poverty. We will study the CDC movement in detail later in this chapter.

CDCs have been woefully underfunded, especially as compared with City

38.   U.S. Department of Housing and Urban Development, *1970 HUD Yearbook* (Washington, D.C.: Government Printing Office, 1971), p. 19.
39.   National Civil Service League, unpublished survey data.

Demonstration Agencies (CDAs), the new local organizations (branches of the city or county governments) which operate Model Cities programs. The Bedford-Stuyvesant Restoration Corporation, the country's largest and *best*-funded CDC, received (by 1970) only about $20.4 million from the federal government and $6.2 million from private sources since 1967. By contrast, the Bedford-Stuyvesant Model Cities project has a cumulative budget of $65 million.[40]

It has been suggested that CDAs should use their own financial resources and strategic positions as regular agencies in local governments, with a special relation to Washington, to sponsor their own CDCs. In principle, this would appear to be a most promising approach.

The community, through the Model Cities process, can exert extensive control over the existence and actions of the development corporations [and over] criteria for their spending (job/capital/wage relationships), earmarking funds for specific projects (industrial parks, shopping centers, land acquisition), regulating staffing patterns and salaries (business packaging specialists, industrial recruitment specialists), and [determining] the . . . focus of the program (small business/medium and large enterprise, service/manufacturing/retail, neighborhood emphasis/larger economy).[41]

Several Model Cities projects have followed just such a course. The CDA in Winston-Salem, North Carolina, has created the Forsyth County Economic Development Corporation. Other programs have been launched in Butte, Montana; Atlanta, Georgia; and Fresno, California.[42] In 1971, the Boston CDA created a development corporation which, within a five month period, acquired five companies in the Roxbury ghetto (engaged in curtain and cosmetics manufacturing, wholesale grocering, taxi service, and retail men's wear) and loaned $69,000 to several smaller businesses owned by black residents of the area.[43]

Still, these efforts amount to precious little real economic development in the inner city. So far, the Model Cities Program has been a major disappointment to those who had looked to it as the instrument by which "our cities will be dealing simultaneously with the totality of problems of the slum areas and concentrating their resources on solving the problem."[44]

Nevertheless, the Model Cities Program still has great potential. It has succeeded in establishing one of the few new political institutions in American cities devoted to the interests of the poor. Through Model Cities

---

40.   Faux, *CDCs: New Hope*, p. 73.
41.   Charles E. Olken, "Economic Development in the Model Cities Program," *Law and Contemporary Problems*, Spring 1971, p. 211.
42.   Faux, *CDCs: New Hope*, p. 86.
43.   *Boston Globe*, Sun., December 19, 1971, p. 1.
44.   Henderson and Ledebur, *Economic Disparity*, p. 198.

(even more than was the case in the Community Action Program of OEO), a cadre of extremely capable, dedicated, articulate, and "savvy" professionals from the streets of the ghetto has been created. This is perhaps the most strategically valuable "human capital" the black community possesses.

But the realization of this potential will require major changes, including a real commitment from the White House. Even the administratively easier employment objectives of Model Cities have been seriously subverted by many local mayors and city counselors (see pp. 117–18).

Moreover, the program is currently out of favor with most local officials, who—after a number of "cool" summers—would like to unite the resources now earmarked for Model Cities and use them in meeting the general financial needs of their jurisdictions. And in early 1973, the President announced his intention to terminate the program altogether.

This is unfortunate. An economic development program sponsored by Model Cities could neatly complement the kind of community-based development strategy to be discussed below. It might include public improvement, housing construction and rehabilitation, and enterprise development projects, all with strong affirmative (antidiscriminatory) action and on-the-job training provisions. Especially promising would be the formation of modular housing corporations, to design, build, and operate low-income housing in the ghetto.[45]

Model Cities' special relationship with HUD might have made it possible to bring pressure to bear on city halls with respect to "the early provision of such public services [in the ghetto] as roads, lighting, water, sewers, and trees in an industrial setting. [This] can be the key factor in making a community's development effort successful."[46] HUD nominally has the authority to threaten uncooperative local jurisdictions with reduced support for general services.

In fact, some individuals in the agency have been trying for several years to mobilize this leverage to overcome employment and wage discrimination against ghetto residents in the Model Cities employment programs. In November 1970, Floyd Hyde, then the Assistant HUD Secretary for Community Development, issued "CDA Letter Eleven," requiring participating cities to give preferential hiring treatment in Model Cities-funded jobs to target area residents as a necessary condition for retaining HUD Model Cities funds. Except for an ineffectual threat to the city of Chicago, HUD has made no attempt to enforce this administrative order.

Thus, we conclude that the potential of Model Cities for promoting inner city economic development cannot be realized without significant changes

---

45.   Olken, pp. 216–18.
46.   Ibid., p. 220.

in public priorities, policies, and administrative practices. No responsible forecast on this score could possibly give an optimistic outlook.

The Case of Black Capitalism

THE TERM "BLACK CAPITALISM" first appeared in public discussion during the 1968 Presidential campaign, when Richard Nixon adopted it as a slogan to represent his interest in the development of minority entrepreneurship. A serious case for such an approach to the rebuilding of the ghetto was first—or, at any rate, most forcefully—made by a prominent business consultant, Theodore Cross,[47] who has since become an advisor to the Office of Economic Opportunity. Cross and most of those who follow him in advocating (or, for that matter, criticizing) black capitalism, use this term to mean the mobilization of both private and public resources to expand the scope of individual black (and other minority) ownership of ghetto businesses.

At least three reasons are given for advocating such a strategy. First, there is the matter of simple equity. Blacks and other minority groups have been disproportionately excluded from ownership of businesses, even within their own neighborhoods.[48] A national survey conducted in 1969 by the Small Business Administration (SBA) found that blacks owned only 2.25 percent of the more than 5 million private businesses in America. Sixty percent of these were in personal services and retail trade—the sectors least profitable and employing the fewest number of workers per establishment—compared with only 42 percent of white businesses.[49] Minority-owned activities were also both smaller and far less profitable than white businesses, as is shown by the results of two different surveys conducted by SBA and the National Business League (Tables 34 and 35).

These are national samples. In the urban ghettos, the relative disadvantage of minority businessmen is even worse. A 1964 study of North Philadelphia found over a third of the black businessmen engaged in hair-dressing and barbering, and many of the businesses would probably not survive if free family labor were not available. Four-fifths of the black-owned establishments in Harlem in the winter of 1967–68 had fewer than four employees, compared with only a little over 50 percent of the white businesses.[50] White businesses in the Harlem ghetto are also sig-

47.   See Theodore Cross, *Black Capitalism* (New York: Atheneum, 1969).
48.   For an historical analysis of this exclusion, emphasizing the uniqueness of slavery as an institution inhibiting the development of entrepreneurship, see Tabb, *The Political Economy of the Black Ghetto*, pp. 40–46.
49.   Ronald E. Bailey, "Introduction," in *Black Business Enterprise*, ed. R. E. Bailey (New York: Basic Books, 1971), pp. 8–9.
50.   Thomas Vietorisz and Bennett Harrison, *The Economic Development of Harlem* (New York: Praeger, 1970), p. 39.

TABLE 34
ENTERPRISE SIZE DISTRIBUTIONS, BY EMPLOYMENT AND SALES: 1969

Item	Minority-Owned	Other
Number of paid employees:	(Percent)	(Percent)
0	31	26
1- 9	64	55
10–49	4	13
50–99	1	3
100+	(a)	3
Gross receipts ($000):		
0- 9.9	33	19
10- 19.9	15	12
20- 49.9	19	19
50- 99.9	14	15
100- 999.9	17	26
1000–4999.9	2	9
5000+	(a)	(a)

(a) Less than 0.1 percent.
Source: Ronald W. Bailey, ed., *Black Business Enterprise*, (New York: Basic Books, 1971), p. 10.

TABLE 35
SELECTED CHARACTERISTICS OF BLACK-OWNED BUSINESSES: 1968

Type of Business	Number of Establishments	Employees Per Establishment	Receipts Per Establishment	Receipts Per Employee
Laundries, cleaning, and other garment services	38	4.8	$14,655	$3,053
Beauty and barber shops	102	2.5	6,678	2,671
Gasoline service stations	40	2.3	18,065	7,854
Food stores	82	3.1	28,258	9,115
Eating places	67	1.8	7,346	4,081
All services and retail trade	564	3.3	19,147	5,802

Source: Andrew F. Brimmer and Henry S. Terrell, "The Economic Potential of Black Capitalism," *Public Policy*, Spring 1971, p. 298. Data came from a 1968 National Business League survey.

nificantly more profitable than black businesses, as revealed by a study of tax records in 1968 (Table 36). A comparison of the gross sales receipts of black-owned businesses in the Buffalo ghetto in 1968 (Table 37) with the national minority distribution in Table 34 (blacks constitute almost 92 percent of all Census-designated "minorities") shows clearly that black ghetto merchants are even smaller and poorer than their national counterparts. A program of black capitalism would give minority entrepreneurs (to quote a 1968 Nixon brochure) "a bigger piece of the action."

Improvement of consumer welfare in the ghetto is another objective of the advocates of black capitalism. Larger, more efficiently managed businesses—even in the retail and service sectors—would (it is hoped) result

TABLE 36
BUSINESS RATE OF RETURN, BY RACE: HARLEM, 1965

	Number of Observations	Mean Return ($)	Mean Gross Sales ($)	Rate of Return on Sales (%)
Black-owned firms				
Total	41	8,690	83,319	10.4
—corporations	11	6,967	102,168	6.8
—small business corps.	7	26,305	177,363	14.8
—partnerships	6	6,963	91,829	7.6
—sole proprietorships	17	3,162	29,394	10.8
White-owned firms				
Total	55	18,610	149,089	12.5
—corporations	25	24,281	149,326	16.3
—small business corps.	7	19,068	303,444	6.3
—partnerships	13	15,382	132,948	11.6
—sole proprietorships	10	8,310	61,427	13.5
Spanish-owned firms				
Total	4	4,563	85,528	5.3
Other ownerships				
Total	5	4,527	21,825	20.7
Nonwhite ownership[a]				
Total	50	7,694	78,925	9.7

[a] Weighted average of black, Spanish, and other.
Source: James Heilbrun and Roger R. Conant, "Profitability and Size of Firm as Evidence of Dualism in the Black Ghetto," *Urban Affairs Quarterly*, March 1972, p. 264.

TABLE 37
GROSS SALES AND ORGANIZATIONAL FORM, BY RACE: INNER BUFFALO: 1968

Item	White-Owned	Black-Owned
Gross Sales	%	%
$0- 2,499	4.8	21.4
2,500- 4,999	4.5	14.0
5,000- 7,499	4.8	12.4
7,500- 9,999	4.5	7.6
10,000- 19,999	8.0	14.6
20,000- 49,999	20.9	16.1
50,000- 99,999	21.7	8.5
100,000-199,999	13.5	3.9
200,000+	17.3	1.5
	100.0	100.0
Form of Ownership		
Corporation	33.0	5.4
Partnership	13.0	10.8
Sole Proprietorship	54.0	83.0
Other		0.2
Do Not Know		0.6
	100.0	100.0

Source: Frank G. Davis, *The Economics of Black Community Development* (Chicago: Markham, 1972), pp. 43 and 61.

in relatively lower prices and higher quality of merchandise.[51] Lower
consumer prices are not possible in a private enterprise system without
economies of scale. One study produced evidence that "economies of scale
were important, as profits per worker rose an estimated $10 with a sales
increase of $1,000."[52] Thus the concern for increasing the size of individual
ghetto businesses.

Finally, it is hoped that expanded minority entrepreneurship would
contribute to the political stability of the ghetto. Absentee and white
ownership of the great majority of businesses in the black ghetto (over 80
percent, according to one national survey)[53] is a major source of political

---

51. Cf. Frederick D. Sturdivant, ed., *The Ghetto Marketplace* (New York: The Free Press,
1969).
52. Brimmer and Terrell, "The Economic Potential of Black Capitalism," p. 296.
53. Albert Reiss, Jr., "Minority Entrepreneurship," unpublished report, Office of Planning,
Research, and Analysis, Small Business Administration, June 30, 1969, p. 9.

disquiet in these areas. Anti-Semitic protests against Jewish merchants have been especially prominent; however,

a study of New Orleans, where the black ghetto businesses are heavily owned by Italians, showed the presence of strong anti-Italian feeling. In all cases hatred is aimed at the group which economically dominates the ghetto.[54]

The report of the Kerner Commission confirms that absentee ownership was a "major grievance" among ghetto dwellers prior to the 1967 urban riots. There is no question that the degree of absentee ownership in the black community is higher than in other ethnic enclaves. Glazer and Moynihan, for example, report that "the income of Chinese from Chinese-owned business is, in proportion to their numbers, *forty-five* times as great as the income of Negroes from Negro-owned businesses."[55]

To meet these objectives of equity in ownership, improved consumer welfare, and increased political stability, proponents advocate

good, old-fashioned, no-nonsense capitalism. It is up to those of us who have learned it and prospered from it to pass it on to those who would use it if they could but learn how. . . . Successful capitalists must go one at a time into the ghetto, find entrepreneurs, and work with them one at a time in the small businesses they seek to build.[56]

That outside private financial interests had little concern for ghetto merchants prior to the riots is understandable. The high risks associated with doing business in the inner city imposed disadvantages on individual entrepreneurs quite independent of their business competence. High risk means high interest rates, high collateral requirements, and difficulty in obtaining insurance. These diseconomies imposed by the ghetto environment on individual businesses (regardless of race or entrepreneurial capability) are by no means the only causes of high rates of business failure, but they make an important contribution.

However, prior to the riots, little help was forthcoming from the federal government, either. "A study of the ten and a half years of operation of the Philadelphia office of the SBA showed that out of 432 loans made through the fall of 1964, only seven had been to black businessmen."[57] Some additional effort was made after 1964, as part of the new antipoverty thrust of the Johnson Administration. SBA launched its "6x6" Program, to

54.   Tabb, *The Political Economy of the Black Ghetto*, pp. 41–42.
55.   Nathan Glazer and Daniel P. Moynihan, *Beyond the Melting Pot* (Cambridge: Harvard University Press, 1963), p. 34.
56.   Louis L. Allen, "Making Capitalism Work in the Ghettos," *Harvard Business Review*, May–June 1969; reprinted in Bailey, *Black Business Enterprise*. The quotation is from pp. 148 and 149 in Bailey.
57.   Tabb, *The Political Economy of the Black Ghetto*, p. 46.

provide $6,000 loans for six years to disadvantaged businessmen. Title IV of the new Economic Opportunity Act authorized SBA to make "Economic Opportunity Loans" to minority and low-income entrepreneurs using OEO funds, and to establish Business Development Centers to provide the recipients with technical assistance and managerial training. Nevertheless, the total effort was still quite small; in 1965, only $1.7 million was loaned to only 159 businesses.[58]

According to one former OEO official, the entrepreneurial assistance and human capital development programs of the "war on poverty" had a common theoretical basis:

Paralleling the manpower strategy applied to hardcore unemployment, the minority entrepreneurship strategy links individual minority businessmen with financial and business services provided by white institutions. Underlying both strategies is the assumption that the major problem is one of direct access by minorities to economic opportunities; once access is established, it is held that the economy at large will absorb the previously unemployed worker or businessman. Access to opportunities, of course, means access to white institutions.[59]

Public activity increased substantially after the riots. The Kerner Commission had called for "special encouragement [of] Negro ownership of business in ghetto areas." The federal government responded by expanding its existing programs—$30.4 million in Economic Opportunity Loans were provided to 2,897 businesses in 1968—and introducing a panoply of new ones. New SBA Administrator Howard Samuels gave high priority to what he termed "compensatory capitalism" through Project OWN, an approach administratively similar to Model Cities in its pooling of the resources of many existing federal programs—without, it must be said, any substantial *net* increment—and focusing them on ghetto businessmen. Under Samuels' aggressive leadership,

SBA accelerated its search for qualified black borrowers, instituting special outreach programs, lowering equity requirements (which in 1968 could be less than 15 percent), guaranteeing up to 90 percent of bank loans, and developing counseling programs in cooperation with volunteer groups such as the Service Corps of Retired Executives.[60]

President Nixon had campaigned in 1968 on a platform of expanded support for black capitalism. Immediately after his election, the President established an Office of Minority Business Enterprise (OMBE) in the De-

---

58. Faux, *CDCs: New Hope*, pp. 41–42.
59. Ibid., p. 41.
60. Tabb, *The Political Economy of the Black Ghetto*, p. 47.

partment of Commerce. A "national plan for minority enterprise" was announced, not much different from its predecessor, Project OWN. However, the "OMBE's performance during its first eighteen months was a disappointment if not a total failure," partly because the White House chose to separate it administratively from its major source of funding, the SBA. Thus, the two agencies became competitors for a relatively fixed overall small business development budget. Not only were lending and technical assistance targets not met, but losses and default rates among ghetto recipients rose rapidly. "In fiscal 1966 the loss rate was 3.6 percent. The next year it was 8.9 percent, and in fiscal 1968 the loss rate was nearly 12 percent of loan disbursement."[61]

OMBE's highest priority has been given to the establishment of Minority Enterprise Small Business Investment Companies (MESBICs). These are organizations generally operated by "large, established white firms, which could put up the initial capital contribution and provide the administrative support." Like the Small Business Investment Companies (SBICs) which preceded them (without any emphasis on *minority* entrepreneurship per se), the function of MESBICs is to supply venture capital and long term financing to small businessmen, through purchase of stock or securities issued by the latter. SBA will then "leverage" (supplement) this initial capital. "Since MESBICs are treated as separate entities for SBA loans and for income tax purposes, they are an attractive investment for large corporations."[62] However,

The game is "rigged". . . . Any firm the MESBIC invests in must make a 100 percent to 500 percent profit increase before the MESBIC benefits. [Moreover], SBICs which are capitalized for less than $1 million have rarely been successful. . . . It is very difficult for a minority group to find financial backing for $1 million. . . . This is too much to expect from the overwhelming number of businesses which ask MESBICs for investment capital.[63]

There are many other administrative requirements which make MESBICs something less than the ideal vehicle for black economic development. No SBIC of *any* kind can invest more than a fifth of its capital in any single venture; this "eliminates ventures of significant scale and encourages only 'Ma and Pa' tokenism." Moreover, MESBICs may not invest in cooperatives, a particularly promising organizational form in many areas of business

---

61. Ibid., p. 47.
62. Otto J. Hetzel, "Games the Government Plays: Federal Funding of Minority Economic Development," *Law and Contemporary Problems,* Winter 1971, p. 76.
63. Ibid.

operation.[64] These and many other limitations have motivated two Harvard Business School professors to suggest: "Let's write off MESBICs."[65]

Despite the criticism and the limitations of the program, President Nixon continued to give it top priority. On March 14, 1972, he sent a five-page message to Congress, recommending legislation to expand OMBE, to permit MESBICs to organize as nonprofit corporations "in order to attract foundation investments and tax-deductible gifts," and to give these nonprofit MESBICs tax-exempt status.[66]

The Brimmer Critique

ONE OF THE MOST VOCAL AND INFLUENTIAL CRITICS of the strategy of black capitalism—and, indeed, of any program of investment in the urban ghetto—has been Andrew Brimmer, a member of the Board of Governors of the Federal Reserve System.[67]

According to Brimmer, investment in the ghetto is inefficient, and therefore socially wasteful, given the "unfavorable economic climate." Yet this "climate" is largely a result of the underinvestment in the economic base of the ghetto. Improvements in the local economy will improve the "climate." To be sure, unsubsidized *private* investment is unlikely (at least in the beginning) because of the present state of underdevelopment. But that is not a valid argument against *public* investment.

Similar reasoning applies to Brimmer's contention that, since "the high incidence of crime in ghetto areas is certainly a factor retarding the growth of minority businesses,"[68] investments in minority enterprise should be

---

64. Ibid., p. 77.
65. Richard S. Rosenbloom and John D. Shank, "Let's Write Off MESBICs," *Harvard Business Review*, September-October 1970. MESBICs are not the only federal programs that have come in for criticism. Otto Hetzel, Professor of Law at Wayne State University and Associate Director of its Center for Urban Studies, believes that "the government's administration of these programs often constitutes a series of 'games' imposed on those minority group members who attempt to utilize the financial resources offered." The game includes "Come Play with Me," "See if You Qualify," "Gotta Play with Those Guys," "Gotta Bring Your Own Ball," "Only One Game at a Time," "Change the Rules," "No Mistakes Allowed," and "Rig the Game." See Hetzel's article for an amusing and informative survey of the administrative machinery in the programs of SBA, OEO, HUD, and the Economic Development Administration (EDA).
66. "Nixon Urges Business Aid to Minorities," *The Washington Post*, March 20, 1972, p. A-1.
67. Cf. Andrew F. Brimmer and Henry S. Terrell, "The Economic Potential of Black Capitalism," a paper delivered to the 82nd Annual Meeting of the American Economic Association in 1969, reprinted in *Public Policy*, Spring 1971. The rebuttal in the text is based largely on Charles Tate, "Brimmer and Black Capitalism: An Analysis," *The Review of Black Political Economy*, Spring-Summer 1970; reprinted in Bailey, *Black Business Enterprise*.
68. Brimmer and Terrell, p. 297.

avoided. To the extent that "economic crime" is at all related to poverty and social disorganization, investments which increase ghetto economic welfare will reduce the necessity and motivation for at least part of the crime which—Brimmer quite accurately observes—makes it so difficult for ghetto businessmen to survive economically.

This "chicken and egg" problem appears still a third time in Brimmer's analysis of capital shortage in the ghetto:

> It is axiomatic in economics that the real wages of labor increase directly with the amount of complementary capital. The self-employed Negro manager . . . by being limited mainly to the small amount of complementary capital available from the low level of ghetto savings, will have a substantially lower expected income.[69]

One answer to this problem would seem to be the subsidized provision of greater quantities of capital to ghetto-based entrepreneurs.[70]

Brimmer is, as we saw in Chapter 7, certainly incorrect when he asserts that ghetto development is infeasible due to "the high cost and unavailability of adequate land area."[71] The central cities have substantial under-utilized and vacant land per se, and have hardly begun to tap that additional resource: three-dimensional space.

As an alternative to public or private assistance to minority entrepreneurs, Brimmer advocates expanded human capital development programs. Well educated and trained black workers "will be attracted to the higher expected returns and the greater job security in firms operating in the national economy."[72] While it is desirable to be attracted, the central question is whether these upgraded workers would be hired. All of the evidence presented in previous chapters is most uncongenial to Brimmer's forecast.

A Radical Evaluation of the Atomistic Enterprise Development Strategy

A DEVELOPMENT STRATEGY IN WHICH "the estimated eventual loss rate [on government loans to ghetto businesses] is [now] 38 percent on

---

69. Ibid., p. 304.
70. For a more sophisticated critique of capital subsidies for ghetto businesses, see Robert Crandall and C. Duncan MacRae, "Economic Subsidies in the Urban Ghetto," *Social Science Quarterly*, December 1971. Their analysis, it seems to me, can be criticized for the naivete of their assumptions about technology, their use of a "revealed preference" approach which ignores the existence of capital market failure, and their unwillingness to consider the prisoner's dilemma in which large-scale capital investments which no individual firm would risk could, if taken together, create a more profitable economic climate for everyone.
71. Brimmer and Terrell, p. 306.
72. Ibid., p. 293.

direct loans and 20 percent on loans with bank participation and SBA guarantees"[73] can hardly be called successful.

Some critics believe that atomistic enterprise development is hopeless on technical and political grounds—that some other approach is needed:

> The odds facing the minority entrepreneur in the ghetto constrain his ability to act as a developer of the ghetto economy. . . . The ghetto businessman has all he can do to keep his own business afloat. He has neither the time nor the resources to plan for anyone but [himself]; he does not have the ability to design "linkages" between businesses and housing, training, consumer and other programs.
>
> Individual entrepreneurs are not equipped to cope with the political nature of ghetto programs. For example, securing land in the inner city for commercial development is essentially a political process. Developers have to deal with a multitude of city government agencies and officials as well as with neighborhood planning and advisory boards, which, if they cannot exercise veto power, can cause intolerable delays.
>
> Small business entrepreneurship programs are also weak as builders of institutions. . . . [Their] impact on minority employment and, perhaps more important, [their] influence as an example for the ghetto population as a whole, is [also minimal].[74]

The critical importance of mutual support—one of the many forms of "linkage"—is illustrated by the case of the Big V supermarket chain operating in the Washington Metropolitan Area.[75] Big V takes over stores in black neighborhoods which have been vacated by the big chains and operates them as "affiliated independents." While each supermarket is individually and privately owned, they share common costs such as advertising and merchandising, and often obtain these and other services from a single source (such as the National Council for Equal Business Opportunity) and at quantity discounts. Recently, one owner broke away from the coalition, which did not force him to honor the one-year contract he had signed with them. Shortly thereafter his business failed, and a consultant to Big V commented: "The independent in today's market has an impossible row to hoe. [Bob X] just tended to be a loner, and the game's not for loners." Four of the remaining five stores in the Big V coalition are making a profit.

Militant black intellectuals and community leaders have been alternately suspicious and critical of black capitalism. They clearly want something more likely to have an impact on the entire community, not merely on

---

73. Faux, *CDCs: New Hope*, p. 45. More recent data on the programs of OMBE indicate somewhat greater success. A growing number of individual (but not community-owned) black businesses are receiving assistance from the program. Cf. U.S. Department of Commerce, *Progress of the Minority Business Enterprise Program* (Washington, D.C.: GPO, January 1972).
74. Faux, *CDCs: New Hope*, pp. 45–47.
75. "Black Capitalism Venture is Failure," *The Washington Post*, February 24, 1972, p. E-1.

the small segment consisting of owners of private businesses. As radicals such as Robert E. Wright put it, "If 'Black capitalism' is the kind of capitalism that Richard Nixon is talking about, where Blacks merely exploit other Blacks or where Blacks merely become cogs in the traditional Western monopoly capitalist system, then we must oppose it without a doubt."[76] Julian Bond, the prominent young black legislator from Georgia, argues,

What we need is not Black capitalism but something more properly called "community socialism," that we may have profit for the many instead of the few; so that neighborhoods and communities shall have the major say in who gets what from whom.[77]

Earl Ofari fears that labor-intensive black capitalists will be exploitative of necessity, if not by choice; they will be "in a position to pay, at best, a few black workers at $1.25 an hour or maybe with a little luck the minimum wage." The "piece of the action" demanded by black capitalists, Ofari believes, is merely a chance to share in the exploitation.[78] And Barry Bluestone is convinced that black capitalism is supported by powerful public and private interests explicitly in order to create a counterrevolutionary middle class in the ghetto whose newly-created and insecurely-held vested interest in political stability can and will be manipulated by those outside interests to deter the formation and growth of a movement for political and economic "liberation" or "community control."

Thus far, black capitalism appears to have been as unsuccessful in catalyzing ghetto economic development as have the other orthodox strategies reviewed in this chapter. Radicals are neither surprised nor dismayed. To quote Charles Tate once more,

The real potential of Black economic development must be measured in terms of its capability to produce the leadership in the Black ghettos for organizing the human and capital resources to take control of local institutions. Neither mom-and-pop style Black capitalism nor token employment of Blacks in salaried positions in the white corporate economy constitute viable alternatives.[79]

Community Economic Development

THE STRATEGIES FOR GHETTO DEVELOPMENT that we have just studied effectively place decision-making power in the hands of established interests. Even such ostensibly "new" institutions as the Model Cities agencies

---

76. Robert E. Wright, "Toward Controlled Development of Black America," Negro Digest, December 1969; reprinted in Bailey, Black Business Enterprise. Quotation is from Bailey, p. 159.
77. Julian Bond, "Foreword," in Bailey, Black Business Enterprise, p. x.
78. Earl Ofari, The Myth of Black Capitalism (New York: Monthly Review Press, 1970). p. 85.
79. Tate, "Brimmer and Black Capitalism," in Bailey, Black Business Enterprise, p. 179.

are revealed to be substantially controlled from outside the ghetto. Major decisions with respect to what, where, and how to develop the local economy are made by outsiders.

While it had its origins in the federal War on Poverty, the demand for local control of ghetto economic institutions was not an intended part of that effort. When it became clear that the poverty program itself would not provide a vehicle for self-determination, many organizers who had worked in that effort began to search for a new institutional mechanism.

The vehicle which emerged from this experience is the Community Development Corporation (CDC).[80] While its specific functions vary from one area to another, reinvestment of at least part of the surplus in other community-based ventures constitutes perhaps the major distinction between the CDC and the typical profit-oriented white corporation.[81]

The emergence of the CDC is consistent with an analysis of the prospects for inner city economic development by Harvard University's Program on Technology and Society. A team of social scientists and management experts concluded that, given their existing fragmentation, local governments are unlikely to organize development efforts.[82] Moreover, existing corporate structures and goals will not allow the private sector to invest to any significant extent in community development.[83] Thus, some kind of wholly new institution is needed; the CDC is such an institution.[84]

Community development corporations engage in a wide variety of projects:

a shopping plaza, an electronics plant, a sewing plant, a chain of small supermarkets and a housing project in Philadelphia; a rubber plant, two restaurant

---

80. In December 1966, Senator Robert F. Kennedy said of the new Title I-D ("Special Impact Program") amendment to the Economic Opportunity Act which he and Senator Jacob Javits were cosponsoring: "The measure of the success of this or any other program will be the extent to which it helps the ghetto to become a community—a functioning unit, its people acting together on matters of mutual concern, with the power and the resources to affect the conditions of their own lives. Therefore, the heart of the program, I believe, should be the creation of CDCs. . . . A critical element in the structure, financial and otherwise, of these corporations should be the full and dominant participation by the residents of the community concerned." Quoted in Arthur I. Blaustein and Geoffrey Faux, *The Star-Spangled Hustle*, p. 116.
81. For example, the policy of Operation Bootstrap, a CDC in the Watts ghetto of Los Angeles, is to allocate commercial profits as follows: "10 percent goes to Bootstrap, 40 percent is reinvested, and 50 percent is divided equally among the workers." Center for Community Economic Development, *Profiles in Community-Based Economic Development* (Cambridge, Mass.: 1969), p. 33.
82. Ivergen Schmandt, "The Urban Crisis: Its Technological and Political Context," in *Social Innovation in the City*, eds. Richard S. Rosenbloom and Robin Marris (Cambridge, Mass.: Harvard University Press, 1969).
83. Robin Marris, "Businesses, Economics, and Society," in *Social Innovation in the City*.
84. Richard S. Rosenbloom, "Business, Technology, and the Urban Crisis," in *Social Innovation in the City*.

franchises, a housing project and development of a combination shopping plaza and public housing project—the first of its kind in the country—in Cleveland; a housing project and an electronics plant that cleared a sizable profit in its second year of operation in Rochester; investments of over $4 million in forty-three separate businesses, several housing programs, and commitments from the New York banking community for a $100 million mortgage pool for ghetto home buyers in Bedford-Stuyvesant in Brooklyn.[85]

The Bedford-Stuyvesant Restoration Corporation has also brought into the ghetto an IBM plant which, in 1970, employed "some 400 individuals, over ninety-five percent of whom live within a mile of the plant," renovated nearly 1,500 private homes through the employment of 900 unskilled youths, and constructed a series of "superblocks" in the middle of the ghetto: blocks whose housing has been rehabilitated, and which have been closed to auto traffic and provided with trees, new lighting, and playgrounds.[86] Restoration recently purchased the air rights above a Brooklyn day care center, and is constructing new apartments in this location.

The Harlem Commonwealth Council, a CDC located in the Harlem ghetto,[87] has assets of more than $15 million, including an office building; a factory manufacturing wood, metal, and plastic interiors for supermarkets; an office equipment and furniture company; a data processing facility; a foundry; a contract construction company; a pharmacy; and a sewing/hi-fidelity store.[88]

Not all of the CDCs are black. The East Boston CDC (EBCDC) was organized in 1971 in a predominantly Italian, white working-class community, around the continuing struggle against the expansion of a nearby airport. EBCDC is currently engaged in housing rehabilitation and the planned redevelopment of part of the Boston waterfront for commercial and industrial use.[89] The Denver CDC operates in four largely Mexican–American neighborhoods of that city, where it is engaged in the manufacture of upholstered furniture, toys, and the operation of supermarkets and restaurant franchises.[90]

CDCs vary in the size of their constituencies (or target areas) and in

---

85. Geoffrey Faux, *CDCs: New Hope*, p. 6.
86. Kilvert Don Gifford, "Neighborhood Development Corporations: The Bedford-Stuyvesant Experiment," in *Agenda for a City*, eds. Lyle C. Fitch and Annmarie Hauck Walsh (Beverly Hills, Calif.: Sage Publications, 1970), pp. 433–37.
87. Cf. Bennett Harrison, "A Pilot Project in Economic Development Planning for American Urban Slums," *International Development Review*, March, 1968; reprinted in *Black Business Enterprise*.
88. C. Gerald Fraser, "Antipoverty Unit Adds to Holdings," *New York Times*, August 5, 1972, p. 1.
89. Center for Community Economic Development, *Newsletter*, March 15, 1972, pp. 19–22.
90. Center for Community Economic Development, *Profiles in Community-Based Economic Development*, pp. 65–66.

their legal organizational structure. The East Central Citizens' Organization of Columbus, Ohio—one of the very earliest CDCs—has a target area of only 7,000 people. The Bedford-Stuyvesant Restoration Corporation covers an area of Brooklyn containing well over 400,000 residents. Restoration and the Inner City Business Improvement Forum in Detroit are examples of CDCs which concentrate on the development of independent, privately owned businesses. The Hough Area Development Corporation in Cleveland, and FIGHT in Rochester, have stressed community ownership. The Harlem Commonwealth Council (HCC) is a nonprofit "planning" agency with a for-profit affiliate, the Commonwealth Holding Company, which wholly owns the enterprises invested in by the Council.

In many (perhaps most) cases, the investment program of these organizations has developed without a systematic plan (or has moved in directions other than those indicated in the plan), in response to the sudden opening of specific opportunities, such as the offer of a subcontract from a large white corporation, or a government offer to turn over a local piece of property to the community as a gesture of political good will. Nevertheless, a surprising amount of theoretical planning has taken place, and many CDC directors indicate a preference for turning increasingly to planned (i.e., time-phased and functionally articulated) investment strategies once their survival is assured.

Economic planning theory suggests that we distinguish between the reorganization of existing activity and the creation of new investments, folding both programs into a systematic development strategy which emphasizes the technical and behavioral linkages between activities.[91]

CDCs have provided a variety of aids to existing ghetto businesses. HCC provides loans to local pharmacies whose owners are penalized by delays in state processing of the Medicaid forms which customers trade in lieu of cash. The Bedford-Stuyvesant Restoration Corporation assists local contractors to obtain bonding, so that they may compete for those larger contracts which require such a guarantee. In Detroit, the Inner-City Business Improvement Forum provides technical assistance (especially managerial training) to private entrepreneurs, and operates an emergency revolving fund for small loans.

Consultants to HCC attempted to measure the extent of institutional consumption that characterizes large cities like New York.[92] Schools, hospitals, churches, and office buildings all consume large quantities of paper and metal products, photographic and repair services, etc. Another project was undertaken to acquaint HCC with federal government pur-

---

91.   Vietorisz and Harrison, *The Economic Development of Harlem*, chap 3.
92.   Ibid., chap. 4.

chasing procedures, and with the Commerce Department's "set-aside" program which reserves a share of procurement contracts for small businesses.

In either case, existing ghetto enterprises are generally too small and inefficient to fill such contracts punctually and at reasonably competitive cost. One proposed solution is the reorganization of existing businesses into networks of "affiliated independents." These are a form of limited producers' cooperatives, in which independently owned and operated business engage in joint purchasing of merchandise, joint advertising, and the pooling of other overhead costs. Between 1946 and 1972, the white affiliated independents in the retail grocery industry increased their share of all retail stores from 23 to 33 percent. Their share of total retail grocery sales rose during the same period from 29 to 44 percent.[93] This success appears to have been built on a combination of the economies of large-scale purchases characteristic of the chain stores, and the high motivation and flexible adaptation to local conditions characteristic of independent entrepreneurs.

The new commercial investments produced by CDCs fall into three general categories: incorporated businesses (owned either by individuals or by CDC affiliates); producers' and consumers' cooperatives; and "turn-key" plants, initially built by outside white corporations to be turned over later to the CDC.

The variety of new incorporated CDC activities is enormous. The Bedford-Stuyvesant Restoration Corporation is developing a series of large manufacturing facilities, which it will sell to the employees or local investors once they become profitable; the first of these ventures is a modular housing factory. The East Los Angeles Community Union, a Chicano CDC, hired a former mattress industry production worker to manage a new CDC mattress factory; "mattresses were chosen because of complaints from welfare mothers that the Welfare Department made them purchase from large downtown stores cheap mattresses that did not last more than a few months."[94] The Black People's Unity Movement in Camden, New Jersey, developed a garment factory with its own retail outlet. In Hough, the CDC has constructed a mixed-zoning project, the Martin Luther King, Jr. Plaza, consisting of low-income elevated town houses built over a shopping mall. Another shopping center project—Progress Plaza—is part of the complex of programs in North Philadelphia created under the leadership of Reverend Leon Sullivan. The complex includes Progress Aerospace Enterprises, Inc., which manufactures high-technology components. In Seattle, the United

93. *Progressive Grocer*, April 1973, p. 100.
94. Faux, *CDCs: New Hope*, p. 81.

Inner City Development Foundation is building an industrial park for large service enterprises and light industrial facilities, including a community-owned construction company. FIGHT, the Rochester CDC, has developed a profit-making, wholly owned manufacturing facility which produces electrical transformers, metal stampings, and power supplies, and does welding and light assembly work. Many of these new activities are linked through contracting arrangements with large private corporations or the federal government; in many cases (such as the "sheltered market" provided for FIGHT by the Xerox Corporation), these contracts were won by overt political struggle.

Cooperatives are still reserved largely for rural agricultural development; many well-known products (including Sunkist and Ocean Spray) are produced by farmer-owned cooperatives. The Southwest Alabama Farmers' Cooperative Association is one of the few rural CDCs in the country. New industrial cooperatives are beginning to appear, some of them under CDC auspices, in such areas as pharmaceuticals and furniture production and sales. Cooperative grocery and supermarket outlets are expanding in large cities, due in part to the growing power of wholesale co-ops large enough to finance the retail expansion. The newest experiment in manufacturing is Crawford Enterprises, a community-owned, cooperatively operated factory in Crawfordville, Georgia, which produces modular housing and is now integrating forward into the acquisition of real estate.[95] Cooperative housing is another growing industry, and one in which CDCs are increasingly engaged. The Mutual Ownership Development Foundation of San Francisco has sponsored sixty-three co-op communities on the West Coast. The newest, Co-op Village in Pasadena, California, includes a mutually-owned five-acre shopping center, with a supermarket, shops, a bank, and a medical group.[96]

The first and most famous of the ghetto turnkey operations was Operation Bootstrap's Shindana doll factory (Shindana is Swahili for "competitor"). The Mattel Toy Company built the factory, trained local managers, and then turned the entire project over to the community. Other "parent" corporations seem to have held onto their facilities for a longer period, before divesting themselves of control. Examples include the Watts Manufacturing Company (Aerojet-General Corporation), the Hough Manufacturing Company (Warner and Swasey), and Progress Laboratories, Inc., in Los Angeles (International Rectifier Corporation). IBM does not at the

---

95. James M. Phemister and James L. Hildebrand, "The Use of Non-Profit Corporations and Cooperatives for Ghetto Economic Development," *Journal of Urban Law*, Issue 1, 1970-71, pp. 200-202.
96. Dorothea M. Brooks, "Cooperation Seen Key to Cooperative," *The Washington Post*, April 15, 1972, p. D-17.

present time plan to turn over its computer cable facility in Bedford-Stuyvesant to the community.[97]

The initial Harlem development "plan" proposed an enterprise development strategy based upon maximizing linkage effects. Many economists have observed that economies of scale in production no longer constitute the main barrier to free entry, having been replaced in relative importance by scale economies in advertising and dealerships. Therefore, the planners recommended a strategy of beginning with the control of the local distribution system (especially retail stores), gradually integrating backward into wholesaling and manufacture of at least some of the items sold in those stores. This strategy motivated the following time-phased development sequences: cooperative supermarkets and affiliation of existing grocers, extended back into food canning and even further back to contracts with farm co-ops in other regions; and stationery and office equipment supplies ("sheltered" by state and city government procurement contracts), integrated back into printing and metalworking operations.[98]

Such an articulated strategy has in fact been implemented (although not in Harlem). The Watts Labor Community Action Committee has established a

produce farm where vegetables, fruits and flowers are grown by Watts youth on previously vacant land beneath the city's high tension power lines . . . a poultry ranch . . . two auto service stations . . . an auto repair center with training facilities for mechanics [and] a chain of . . . supermarkets. . . .

A highly significant feature of these enterprises is the extent to which their operations have been integrated. For example, the poultry ranch supplies the produce farm with fertilizer; the products of both entities are transported on trucks fueled and serviced by the WLCAC gas stations and repair center; the . . . supermarkets and the new general hospital serve as outlets for the products of both the ranch and farm.[99]

The strategy of backward integration from distribution to manufacturing is also advocated by a prominent black organizer from Detroit, the Reverend Albert Cleague, Jr. Cleague has called for the development of black cooperatives on the Swedish model, to take the place of the existing retail and service opportunities open to Detroit black consumers. This would be followed by backward integration into the production of durable goods and agricultural produce to be sold in the stores.[100] Other ghetto leaders speak of controlling local housing and then integrating backward into the

---

97.   The Conference Board, *Business and the Development of Ghetto Enterprise* (New York: The Conference Board, 1971), vol. 2.

98.   Victorisz and Harrison, *The Economic Development of Harlem*, chaps. 4 and 5.

99.   Center for Community Economic Development, *Profiles in Community-Based Economic Development*, pp. 51–52.

100.   Henderson and Ledebur, *Economic Disparity*, p. 98.

development of construction and rehabilitation companies.[101] According to an economic analysis of the potential for such a development strategy, the commodities which ghetto consumers purchase in large enough quantities to make large-scale production for local distribution feasible include (in order of relative expenditures) food, clothing and accessories, and furniture.[102]

Among the most attractive new investments being considered by a number of CDCs are those involving the processing and communication of information. The original Harlem Development Project investigated at least two possible areas for community investment: (1) an electronic data-processing bed monitoring service for local hospitals, and (2) the operation of one or more local cable television franchises.[103] The latter has become the object of increased attention in the United States. In 1970, a Presidential Commission headed by Professor Edward S. Mason of Harvard recommended that at least some of the cable franchises rapidly being created by municipal governments across the country be reserved for community groups. In 1972, The Urban Institute inaugurated a Cable Television Information Center to help local governments solve their franchising problems with respect to cable television. An earlier exploratory project (under the direction of Charles Tate) was concerned with the practical application of cable systems to community economic development.[104]

A fundamental issue in the community development movement—and in its technical literature—concerns the trade-off between commercial profits and community benefits. No single subject more clearly distinguishes this approach to inner city development from those discussed earlier than the avowed commitment of most CDC leaders to give high priority to such "external" outputs as manpower training, consumer education, improvement of the ghetto environment, reduction of anomie (especially among young black men), and consolidation of political "clout" in the community's relations with city hall, the state house, the federal bureaucracy, and the private sector.[105] CDCs speak of trading off profits for community welfare, so that profits become just one of the goals of development. Even those groups ostensibly committed to "hard-headed" profitability have indicated their intention to reinvest the surplus in nonprofit activities. Thus, for

---

101.   Faux, *CDCs: New Hope*, p. 49.
102.   Frank G. Davis, *The Economics of Black Community Development* (Chicago: Markham, 1972), p. 193.
103.   Vietorisz and Harrison, *The Economic Development of Harlem*, chap. 5.
104.   Charles Tate, ed., *Cable TV in the Cities: Community Control, Public Access, and Minority Ownership* (Washington, D.C.: The Urban Institute, 1971).
105.   Faux, *CDCs: New Hope*, pp. 48–55.

example, James Dowdy, President of the Harlem Commonwealth Council, argues that "the first responsibility of a local development group is to generate profits. . . . It's cold, up and down business." However, he says, "Profits generated by HCC's businesses will be used for social purposes."

One of the most consequential types of "market failure" arises from the "jointness" in the relationship between the production of output and the provision of on-the-job manpower training. Pigou first developed the theorem that competitive markets will invest suboptimally in activities which generate external economies. The implications of this particular externality—the indivisibility between production and training—have been virtually ignored by human capital theorists, who assume that decentralized markets are able to allocate training investments efficiently, e.g., by "optimally taxing" workers, through discounted wages, for the "specific training" they receive on the job. In fact, with "neoclassical" production functions this is not possible; the indivisibility makes it impossible to uniquely allocate costs between the joint products.[106]

In community development programs, political considerations often force attention to the training "product," and implicit values are assigned to the "production" of a trained ghetto labor force equipped to deal with modern technology. This demand by ghetto leaders has become more insistent as evaluations of conventional manpower training programs have shown that the jobs for which ghetto dwellers are normally trained very closely resemble the unskilled, low-wage jobs which the trainees or their peers held in the past.[107] The Harlem Development Project referred to "green-house industries": community-owned or sponsored manufacturing, commercial, and service enterprises selected as much for the nature and extent of the on-the-job training they are capable of providing as for the product and profits they would generate.[108]

To the extent that the production of external benefits of any kind costs foregone profits, subsidies are necessary.[109] This widely known proposition in welfare economics appears to be well understood by ghetto leaders.

---

106.   Richard Eckaus, "Investment in Human Capital: A Comment," *Journal of Political Economy*, October 1963; Marris, "Businesses, Economics, and Society," pp. 22–23.

107.   Harrison, *Education, Training, and the Urban Ghetto*, chap. 5 and pp. 171–75.

108.   This is, in fact, one of the strongest principal justifications for the "new institution," the CDC. In appending supporting bundles of consumer-oriented service activities to the core of an industrial project, for example, adding credit unions, "do-it-yourself" repair stalls, and insurance claim service "clusters" to a computerized automotive diagnostic center, the CDC will necessarily trade off profits for the sake of community service benefits. It is difficult to imagine how any institution other than the community development corporation would be willing and able to accept the curtailed profits and unorthodox operating procedures necessarily associated with such an experiment.

109.   Cambridge Institute, *Conference on Community-Based Economic Development*, Occasional Bulletin No. 2, June 1970, p. 10.

Consider, for example, the analysis of Bernard Gifford, former Director of FIGHT and currently President of the New York City RAND Institute:

In Rochester, we had to explain to both the black and the white communities what FIGHT meant by "profit". . . . If we take ten welfare mothers off the welfare rolls . . . we save the . . . Department of Social Services $50,000. . . . We have about eighteen brothers working with us who were ex-cons. If you go by the statistics, you'll find that about 75 percent of the brothers who leave the slam get remanded in less than nine months. We found out that nobody with us went back to the slam; those who left us went on to better jobs. So we put that in our [benefit-cost] statement. . . . We have these people off welfare and out of the slam getting training with us at FIGHT-ON and then going on to Kodak and Xerox. . . . So we go back to Kodak and Xerox and say, "Dig it, man. Here we are subsidizing you because we're training these people and sending them on to you, pushing them into the mainstream, and not getting any payback. So when we want to bid on some Kodak machinery at less than cost we trade off."[110]

Whether the subsidies are private (as Gifford says), public, or both (as would be appropriate in Gifford's example, since the public at large as well as the white corporations receive benefits from the activities of FIGHT), community development is impossible without them. Yet some critics of the CDC program (especially the government's more "business-minded" consultants) call for greater efficiency in project selection in order to phase out public subsidies as quickly as possible.

This debate over project selection criteria and subsidization goes to the heart of the economic development problem. The central issue is summarized by the former Director of Economic Development at OEO:

The notion that CDCs are meant to become financially self-sustaining in the near future is a common one. It is also an attractive one. . . . If self-sufficiency is the goal of a CDC, the enterprises in which it invests not only must make profits, they must return sufficient profits to the CDC to cover the latter's expenses. A recent Abt [Associates, Inc.] report evaluating the performance of 16 OEO-funded CDCs declared, quite logically, that if self-sufficiency is the goal, then CDCs should attempt to maximize the profitability of their investments even if they have to forego [impacting] the community. Thus, CDCs were advised not to hire local management or the hard-core unemployed if there were extra costs associated with doing so (which, of course, there are). Maximizing the return on investments means that CDCs have to forego social investments in training, or in establishing community facilities, in favor of those things that generate profits. It may also mean that values such as community participation and local control will have to be abandoned. . . . In sum, the goal of self-sufficiency requires that the CDC play the role of venture capitalist rather than that of community developer.[111]

Methodologically, the difficulty in selecting ghetto development projects lies in the combination of quantitative and qualitative objectives, and in

110. Ibid.
111. Center for Community Economic Development, *Newsletter*, May 15, 1972, pp. 2–3.

the externalities—e.g., production function interdependences, indivisibilities, and economies of scale—that link different projects together. An operational solution to the second problem has been employed by development planners for several years; it is the use of a complex of interrelated activities as the unit of project planning. This unit is variously referred to as an "industrial complex," an "activity complex," a "module," or simply a "project."[112] Work is presently underway to attack the first problem through the design of decision models involving man-machine interactions.[113]

Financing Ghetto Development

PRECISE ACCOUNTS OF THE TOTAL public and private resources invested in the CDC movement are simply not available, but scattered records imply that the total is still very modest.

In 1969–70, the average OEO Special Impact grant was $600,000 per CDC (not counting the Bedford-Stuyvesant Restoration Corporation, which has received about $5 million per year since 1967 from all sources).[114] Cumulative Special Impact investment in 23 urban CDCs through fiscal 1973 amounted to $89.8 million.[115]

As indicated earlier, some CDCs have developed contacts with outside white corporations, which provide a source of technical assistance, occasional loans, and, most importantly, procurement contracts. Foundations (notably Ford) have provided some support. Nevertheless, most CDCs continue to rely on assistance from the federal government. The Special Impact and Community Action programs of OEO, together with HUD's Model Cities Program, are nearly the ghetto's *only* sources of equity capital. The administrative staffs of the CDCs themselves are financed by OEO, Model Cities, and the Technical Assistance Program of the Commerce Department's Economic Development Administration (EDA). Debt-financing is provided by the Small Business Administration, by HUD (for housing loans), and by EDA's Business Loan Program. EDA and SBA provide technical assistance. SBA and the Labor Department finance

---

112.   Cf. Walter Isard, Eugene Schooler, and Thomas Vietorisz, *Industrial Complex Analysis and Regional Development* (New York: Wiley, 1959); Thomas Vietorisz, "Decentralization and Project Evaluation Under Economies of Scale and Indivisibilities," *Industrialization and Productivity* [Journal of the United Nations Industrial Development Organization], Bulletin 12, 1968; Joel Bergsman, Peter Greenston, and Robert Healy, "The Agglomeration Process in Urban Growth," *Urban Studies*, October 1972.
113.   An ingenious—if tentative—solution to the first problem has been suggested by Thomas Vietorisz, "Quantized Preferences and Planning by Priorities," *American Economic Review*, May 1970. The formal model is presented in an appendix to this chapter.
114.   Abt Associates, Inc., *An Evaluation of the Special Impact Program: Phase I Report* (Cambridge, Mass.: Abt Associates, 1972), vol. 1, p. 24.
115.   Center for Community Economic Development, *Newsletter*, Aug. 1973, p. 4.

manpower training within CDC projects. Federal (especially military) procurement contracts are channeled into the ghetto through SBA's Section 8-A "set aside" program.[116]

The bureaucratic procedures imposed upon minority entrepreneurs in general (see note 65) affect CDCs as well. Federal agencies are willing to provide administrative support, but they strongly prefer debt to equity financing. This has forced many CDCs to acquire seriously excessive debt-equity ratios, which hampers their ability to grow through reinvestment of profits. HUD seems especially reluctant to pay the "brick and mortar" costs of economic development.[117]

In June of 1970, a new quasi-public institution was created to help finance both independent black capitalists and organized CDCs: the Opportunity Funding Corporation (OFC).[118] OFC was developed by a New York attorney, Theodore Cross, under the auspices of OEO. In 1969, Cross had been invited to Washington by the new Administration to design an institution to implement the financial concepts set out in his influential book, *Black Capitalism*. Cross assumed that the government alone would never provide adequate capital to fund minority economic development programs, and that techniques would therefore have to be found for "leveraging" such resources from the conventional private capital markets. Government, in his scheme, would provide incentives, guarantees, equity insurance, rediscounting and subsidies to induce the private sector to invest in the ghetto.[119]

OFC is funded principally by OEO's Special Impact Program—at the expense, it must be noted, of additional direct capital flows to CDCs. As a concession to the latter, whose directors were not surprisingly distressed by OEO's decision to reallocate Special Impact funds to the new institution, Cross agreed to initially reserve OFC support for the OEO-funded ghetto development corporations. OFC is in the process of trying to raise additional funds through public offerings of its own securities. Cross now serves as a consultant to the organization he created; the current Chairman

---

116. Faux *CDCs: New Hope*, p. 113.
117. Ibid., p. 86.
118. This section is based on Samuel I. Doctors and Sharon Lockwood, "Opportunity Funding Corporation: An Analysis," *Law and Contemporary Problems*, Spring 1971.
119. "The solution lies in ignoring the propaganda of black militants and in doggedly pursuing the route of clear logic and justice: the forced injection of credit, risk capital, and entrepreneurial skills into the ghetto economy" (Theodore Cross, *Black Capitalism* [New York: Atheneum, 1969], p. 69). Geoffrey Faux's study of CDCs concludes with this rebuttal to Cross: "Few CDC leaders would agree with Mr. Cross. For years the residents of the nation's ghettos and barriers have been subject to the forced injection of urban renewal, minority capitalism, antipoverty programs, training projects, and subsidized housing, all of which have probably left things in worse shape than they were before. The hostility these experiences have generated makes it unlikely that anything is going to be successfully "forced" on the ghetto economy. If there was a time when that kind of tactic would have been effective, it is long past" (Faux, *CDCs: New Hope*, p. 117).

of its prestigious board of directors is David Hertz of McKinsey and Co., a prominent management consulting firm.

OFCs earliest activities included the provision of bonding to minority contractors in Los Angeles and the District of Columbia, consumer credit to low-income citizens in the Special Impact areas, and supplementary funding for target area minority banks and credit unions. Gradually, OFC will offer a variety of incentives to private investors to inject capital into ghetto activities, including the establishment of a secondary market for SBA- and EDA-backed obligations and other commercial paper. OFC will purchase these obligations, repackage them, and resell the new securities to pension funds, churches, and similar institutions, a function similar to that performed by the Federal National Mortgage Company in the mortgage market. For the time being, OFC proposes to limit its activities in any one ghetto area to no more than one or two ventures.

Several new approaches to funding community economic development have been recommended. There is, for example, the black demand for "reparations." The demand for large-scale income transfers from white to black Americans as repayment for the foregone earnings associated with slavery and, more recently, with racial discrimination was first made in 1969 at the National Black Economic Development Conference in Detroit.[120] Both political and economic arguments are made to support the claim; Robert Browne, for example, reports estimates of compounded foregone earnings of slaves ranging as high as $995 billion.[121] He would allocate part of the reparations payments directly to blacks, as transfer income, and use the rest to finance various economic development efforts (including CDCs).

Duran Bell is critical of this rationale for redistribution.[122] He argues that the main beneficiaries of slavery and post-slavery discrimination have been working-class whites. If we insist upon true reparations—redistribution of income from the beneficiaries to the victims—then logically we should tax the white working class most heavily of all whites. That, says Bell, is neither politically feasible nor, in his opinion, desirable. It would serve only to satisfy a sense of revenge. Redistribution to blacks can and should be defended on substantive grounds, such as their disproportionately high incidence of poverty.

A number of blacks, observing the magnitude of the income generated

---

120.   James Forman, "The Black Manifesto," in *Black Business Enterprise*, ed. Ronald W. Bailey.
121.   Robert S. Browne, "The Economic Case for Reparations to Black America," *American Economic Review*, May 1972. See also Richard America, "A New Rationale for Income Redistribution," *The Review of Black Political Economy*, Winter 1972.
122.   Duran Bell, "The Beneficiaries of Slavery and Discrimination," *The Review of Black Political Economy*, Spring 1972.

by "policy" or "the numbers" in low-income communities, have proposed that locally controlled CDCs "set up and operate legal numbers games for the purpose of financing their community welfare activities."[123] Ghetto operations would successfully compete with organized white crime, provided that law enforcement and other public agencies lent their support. The cost to individual players would be modest ("adult and late teen-aged ghetto residents in New York bet an average of $3 to $5 a week"),[124] and could be considered a community development tax.

An important potential source of nontransfer income for ghetto development projects is city hall itself. Local governments could allocate a share of their procurement contracts to ghetto enterprises (foregoing competitive bidding, if necessary), and could place at least some of their financial accounts in banks willing to invest in the ghetto economy. In New York City, for example, "with a half-billion dollar annual expenditure for purchases and small contracts, a set-aside of roughly 10 percent of this amount could provide . . . an estimated 50 million dollars" for ghetto businesses.[125] Similarly, even a small share of the city's "$20 million to $100 million day-to-day demand deposits" would significantly increase the lending capacity of local banks, who might then be induced to lend to ghetto businesses and development corporations. Indeed, city deposits might be linked to (i.e., made conditional upon) such investments.[126] This is, of course, fundamentally a redistribution device, since some of the existing recipients of government contracts and demand deposits would have to be cut off. The authors do not discuss this aspect of what they call the "Ghediplan," and the political feasibility of implementing it is surely sensitive to this redistributional aspect. Nevertheless, the concept certainly deserves further investigation and experimentation. The argument often employed by government agencies (and by liberal economists generally), that location-specific inducements represent unacceptable "beggar-thy-neighbor" policies, is irrelevant since the existing allocation of location-specific resources already has its own distributional impact. That the bulk of existing government contracts go to nonghetto producers beggars the ghetto. This inseparability of allocation and distribution is an important part of the emerging "radical critique" of economic theory.[127]

123. Daniel B. Mitchell, "Black Economic Development and Income Drain: The Case of the Numbers," *The Review of Black Political Economy*, Autumn 1970, p. 54.
124. Ibid., p. 50.
125. Dunbar S. McLaurin and Cyril D. Tyson, "The *Ghediplan* for Economic Development," in *Black Economic Development*, eds. William F. Haddad and G. Douglas Pugh (Englewood Cliffs, N.J.: Prentice-Hall, 1969), p. 133.
126. Ibid., p. 134.
127. Cf. Michael Zweig, "Bourgeois and Radical Paradigms in Economics," *The Review of Radical Political Economics*, Summer 1971.

Recognition of the limits of existing programs led a group of senators, congressmen, lawyers and black leaders (notably Roy Innis) to meet in the spring and summer of 1968 to draft a piece of legislation—The Community Self-Determination Act (S.33)—designed to create an entirely new structure to finance ghetto development.

The bill provided for federal chartering of CDCs and Community Development Banks; creation of a nationwide Community Development Bank as a secondary financing institution; authorization of favorable tax status for CDCs as well as "turnkey" tax incentives for cooperating outside businesses; and managerial and technical assistance money for CDCs through the SBA.[128]

Although the bill received support from politicians associated with an extraordinarily broad range of ideological views (including Richard Nixon, Senators Muskie, Humphrey, Tower and Goodell—the chief sponsor), it languished in committee for two years, never even coming up for a vote.

The original Act has been severely criticized, partly on the merits and partly by groups jealous of the central role of Innis' Congress of Racial Equality. Among the more serious substantive criticisms are the attack on the bill's insistence that subsidized investments be spatially confined to the ghetto, in order to minimize competition with established concerns.[129] If the Development Bank sells stock to private corporate investors, then—to the extent that the latter oppose the community control movement, e.g., out of fear that whites will emulate the black ghettos in this respect— individual ghetto projects may ultimately be subjected to outside interference.[130]

A substantially revised bill, the Community Corporation Act of 1970, was subsequently prepared by the staff of the Senate Subcommittee on Employment, Manpower, and Poverty. Many of the defects of the original bill (especially the spatial constraints on investment) were corrected. Nevertheless, the new legislation has not fared any better than the old. In spite of its self-characterization as an "avid supporter" of "minority economic development," the Nixon Administration has failed to support the creation of a permanent financial "delivery system" for a CDC-based development effort.

---

128. Faux, *CDCs: New Hope*, p. 114.
129. Phemister and Hildebrand, "The Use of Non-Profit Corporations," pp. 187–88. "This geographic restriction reduces the possibility of developing chain organizations capable of reaping the advantages of quantity purchasing, centralized warehousing, management specialization, multiple-unit advertising, and other efficiencies" (Frederick D. Sturdivant, "The Limits of Black Capitalism," *Harvard Business Review*, January–February, 1969, p. 124). In view of the Congress' motivation for prohibiting ghetto-based companies from investing in "outside" assets, Kain's argument that public investment in low-income neighborhoods constitutes inefficient and politically undesirable "ghetto-gilding" seems ludicrous.
130. Ofari, *The Myth of Black Capitalism*, p. 120.

Evaluation and Outlook

THE RELATIVE SPACE ALLOCATED in this monograph to the community economic development strategy reflects the variety and spontaneity of effort underway, not an implicit conclusion that the strategy has been successful. It is much too soon to be able to subject this approach to a definitive performance evaluation. The very diffuseness of its stated objectives makes evaluation difficult.

One preliminary study was recently completed by Abt Associates, Inc. The OEO Special Impact Program was evaluated in terms of three objectives: venture development, the ability to "leverage" private financial support through public funded CDCs, and the institutionalization of community control.

On the first objective, the evaluation is generally favorable; a great deal of new enterprise development has taken place. However, "less than 13 percent of the employees were previously dependent upon welfare and unemployment compensation,"[131] profits have been foregone due to the recruiting of inexperienced managers, and the "50 percent rate of failing to reach break-even in four years is too high, in the evaluators' opinion."[132]

CDCs have demonstrated a significant ability to obtain private funds to complement their federal grants: "CDCs have leveraged about fifty cents on each dollar of [the Special Impact Program] grant into CDC-sponsored ventures."[133] Real estate investments have been the most successful in this regard.

The CDCs have *not*, according to Abt, promoted community control, either in the development of new broad-based political institutions or in diffuse ownership or management of CDC-related enterprises. The leadership of CDCs and their ventures consists largely of the minority middle class. Nevertheless, concludes Abt, "all CDCs studied enjoy a high level of support by residents. . . . Over half of the [ghetto] residents interviewed recognized the CDCs and felt that they are engaging in activities that are beneficial to the community."[134]

---

131. Abt Associates, *An Evaluation of the Special Impact Program*, vol. 1, p. 7.
132. Ibid., p. 8.
133. Ibid., p. 10.
134. Ibid., p. 15. A committee of CDC representatives, invited to review the Abt evaluation, was most critical of Abt's selection of the objectives to be evaluated. In particular, the nonpecuniary aspects of community development (such as job—including managerial—training and political organizing) were not considered; "the evaluators have consistently confused the economic development process with the more narrow activities associated with short-term financing of business enterprise" (ibid., p. 29). (The CDC critique is published as an Appendix to the Abt report itself.) Had such targets been considered (argues the committee), Abt's finding that many ventures were not achieving short-term break-even status

The number of activities which CDCs could usefully pursue in order to promote local development is literally limitless. It has, for example, been suggested that they become subcontractors to public agencies, or direct recipients of federal public service employment grants, in order to produce and distribute public goods and services within the ghetto.[135] Apart from meeting environmental and other direct output goals, this would enable CDCs to provide larger numbers of jobs to their constituents, thereby increasing their political legitimacy within the black community.

A study of property taxation in Boston found that assessments of ghetto residential property in 1960 averaged more than 70 percent higher than assessments elsewhere in the city. Statistical analysis identified three explanatory factors: (1) systematically higher assessment of multifamily dwellings throughout the city, with the ghetto having a disproportionately high incidence of such dwellings; (2) failure of officials to adjust downward for reductions in value over time throughout the city, with the ghetto being penalized because it used to be a middle-income area; and (3) a residual (responsible for 40 percent of the variance) interpreted as reflecting racial discrimination.[136] A CDC might usefully acquire control of (or at least participate in) the local assessment process to assure that declining property values are accounted for. Also, it might lobby for changes in tax laws, so that land rather than improvements are taxed.

The diversity of inner city development programs and their vitality (although not necessarily their demonstrable successes) reinforces an earlier conclusion of this monograph, that the "either-or" perspective on development versus dispersal which is held by many liberal economists and elected officials is short-sighted. Thousands of individuals and many organizations across the country are committed to the creation of new institutional approaches to local development. However reluctantly, many members of the establishment are addressing the previously ignored issue of "investment

---

would not have been interpreted so negatively. Moreover, that CDCs have been able to mobilize the new black professional class should be considered a major achievement, rather than an implied failure to meet the objective of "community control." Without a professional class, they argue, ghetto institutions cannot possibly compete successfully with outsiders.

In a different approach, officials of the CDCs were invited to join with staff members of The Urban Institute to define the criteria by which the CDCs would ultimately be evaluated. In Congressional Hearings on the 1970 Community Corporation Act, the author and a colleague suggested that provision for such "self-defined success criteria" be institutionalized into the entire poverty program (Thomas Vietorisz and Bennett Harrison, "Ghetto Development, Community Corporations, and Public Policy," *The Review of Black Political Economy*, Autumn 1971, pp. 36–37).

135.   Geoffrey Faux, "Public Service Employment: Who Decides?" in *The Political Economy of Public Service Employment*, eds. Harold L. Sheppard, Bennett Harrison, and William Spring (Lexington, Mass.: Heath-Lexington Books, 1972).

136.   Alan A. Altshuler, *Community Control* (New York: Pegasus, 1970), pp. 150–51.

in place" as a complement to the strategy of "investment in people" which has dominated official antipoverty policy for over a decade.

The severity of the impact of job decentralization on urban minorities will depend to a considerable extent on the success of these new experiments in inner city economic development.

APPENDIX: QUANTIZING COMMUNITY PREFERENCES AND PLANNING PRIORITIES

THOMAS VIETORISZ HAS SUGGESTED a solution to the problem created by the qualitative nature of some of the goals of ghetto development.[137] A "project" is defined as a particular activity complex. Project variants are identified by engineering analysis according to their alternative process designs (which, in neoclassical fashion, may for expository purposes be summarized by their factor proportions). One variant of each project will be included in the development plan or it will not; no project can be operated at less than full scale. This is the sense in which the decision-making process is said to be "quantized."

Each project is assigned a numerical priority ranking by the political decision-makers, reflecting their subjective valuation of the expected community benefits (including profitability) associated with each. All of a project's technical variants share a common priority ranking. The unidimensionality and ordinal scaling of this kind of "planners' preference function" make it relatively easy to estimate; indeed, such a system of priority orderings has been a prominent feature of both regular Soviet and wartime U.S. planning.

Construction of the model is illustrated in Figures 16 and 17, the coordinates of which refer to generalized inputs f_1 and f_2. It is necessary to consider only the most f_1-intensive and f_2-intensive ("extreme") variants of each project, although all linear combinations of the "full-scale" activity levels are in fact feasible. The two extreme variants of the highest-ranked project are represented in Fig. 16 as vectors 1A and 1B. Thus, the resource costs associated with implementation of project 1 are given by the convex hull of these vectors.

Since the second project can not (by assumption) be undertaken until the first is completed, the extreme variants for project 2 are represented

---

137.   Thomas Vietorisz, "Quantized Preferences and Planning by Priorities," *American Economic Review,* May 1970.

FIGURE 16

QUANTIZED PRIORITY PLANNING MODEL

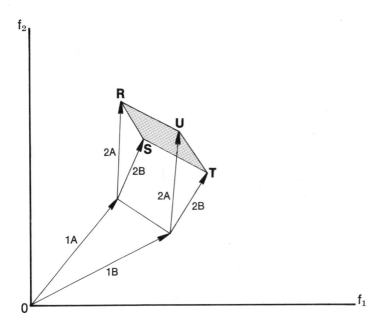

Source: Thomas Vietorisz, "Quantized Preferences and Planning by Priorities," *American Economic Review,* May 1970, pp. 67-68.

FIGURE 17

QUANTIZED PRIORITY PLANNING MODEL

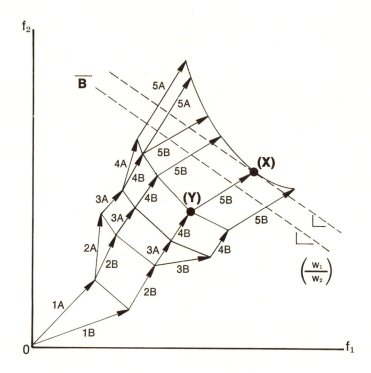

Source: Thomas Vietorisz, "Quantized Preferences and Planning by Priorities," *American Economic Review*, May 1970, pp. 67-68.

as vectors originating at the two previous possible resource allocation points. The convex hull of project 2 is given by RSTU. Only linear combinations along RST are efficient, however; variants represented by RUT are unnecessarily expensive. The extreme variants for project 3 are therefore "built" upon R, S, and T, and so on for the n projects in the plan.

Now define a simple budget constraint with slope $-(w_1/w_2)$, representative of a set of financial, technical, and even behavioral constraints expressed in terms of resource prices w_1 and w_2. Then static optimization over the entire plan may be approached either as the development of the entire set of n projects at minimum cost (which, with $n = 5$ as in Fig. 17, leads to the full plan resource utilization indicated by point X), or the development of the maximum number of projects subject to a given budget. In the latter case, because of the 0-1 nature of the project designs, affordable resources may remain slack. With a budget of $\bar{B}$, for example, only the first four projects can be built. Given that constraint, engineers will select the variant of project 4 consistent with the lowest cost, indicated by the corner tangency between a line with slope $-(w_1/w_2)$ and the efficient portion of the convex hull of project 4—point Y in Fig. 17.[138]

Suppose the process is to be implemented formally as a mathematical programming model in which the number of priority-ordered projects is maximized subject to resource constraints. The sequencing constraints involve integer variables, but the problem can be reformulated as a chain of linear programs in which the scale of the first m projects is set to unity $(1 \leq m \leq n)$. The scale of the $(m + 1)$th project is treated continuously and maximized; the scales of all lower-priority projects are set to zero. By trial and error with m, the maximum number of feasible projects m° can be identified. For any $m > m^\circ$ no feasible solution will exist. For $m < m,^\circ$ the scale of the $(m + 1)$th project will exceed unity.

Vietorisz proposes the introduction of a feedback mechanism (or man-machine interaction), whereby those who originally set the priorities would be confronted with the implications of their preferences, and invited to revise them, after which the program would be rerun. This process would continue iteratively (parametric conditions for convergence have not yet been studied). The mechanism makes use of the shadow prices in the model, which "can be interpreted as a subsidy to the lowest-ranked feasible

---

138. Vietorisz treats these loci of efficient portions of convex hulls as "indifference curves," à la Kelvin Lancaster, since the planners are assumed to be indifferent between alternative variants of a project with a given priority ranking. The "indifference map," or set of such loci, is therefore unique up to a specified priority ordering, scale (i.e., the size of n), and the structure of the indivisibilities for each project (i.e., the length of each project's vectors). This is not a high order of uniqueness, but it is computable.

project, enabling it to break even at the resource prices of the optimal solution."[139] By parametrically varying the budget constraint, so that $m°$ takes on successive values of $1, 2, \ldots, n$, the opportunity costs of any given priority ordering (already measured qualitatively by the number of infeasible projects) can be given a quantitative dimension in terms of the relative subsidies of the included and excluded projects associated with each budget.

---

139. Vietorisz, "Quantized Preferences and Planning by Priorities," p. 69.

PART IV

CONCLUSIONS

Chapter 9

THE URBAN CRISIS AS A FAILURE OF POLICY

MOST POLITICAL SCIENTISTS AGREE THAT URBAN AREAS in the United States, and, indeed, in many foreign countries, continue to operate under institutional rules which are manifestly antiquated. This is especially true of the set of arrangements by which the production and distribution of public goods and services in cities are financed.

It is this institutional inflexibility which is ultimately responsible for the increasing fiscal difficulties of central cities. The fundamental problem is neither one of incremental resource misallocation nor of race. What we face is the inability or unwillingness of constituted governments to design new political institutions and fiscal instruments to meet new conditions created at least in part by actions of those very governments. I call this a "failure of policy."[1]

The outward expansion of most of our older cities is certainly at an end, and even the younger cities are likely to find it politically more difficult to annex peripheral territory in the future. Development by a widening of the economic base—by simply doing "more of the same" over a larger area—has therefore become impractical. City development will have to occur increasingly as a *deepening* of activity, involving higher densities, new technologies and new administrative forms (such as multilevel govern-

---

1. This interpretation is clearly at variance with that of Edward Banfield. That "government cannot solve the problems of the cities and is likely to make them worse by trying" is his central thesis. From this point of view, future urban problems are more likely to be attributable to an excess than to a failure of policy. Edward C. Banfield, *The Unheavenly City* (Boston: Little, Brown and Co., 1970).

ment). New political mechanisms will be needed to finance this new form of urban development.

If I am correct in interpreting these phenomena as portents of an era in which urban development will proceed in a qualitatively different fashion than it has historically, then the role of social science will involve more than simply describing the transition. We can—and should—actively promote what Adolph Lowe and Robert Heilbroner call "instrumental economics." We must help governments to design, implement, and evaluate planned experiments in the management and financing of this new form of urban development. As with the income maintenance, education voucher, public service employment, and housing allowance experiments conducted by the Office of Economic Opportunity, the Department of Labor, and by HUD, new experiments are needed with respect to multilevel urban government, revenue-sharing, user charges on some central city public services, and public ownership and allocation of urban land. We must also be more vocal in our advocacy of expansionary fiscal and monetary policies, given what we have learned about the relationship between urban growth and national aggregate demand.

There is also a very important role for academic research. Perhaps the first among the issues to be investigated should be the updating of the statistical series analyzed in Part I, to reflect the 1970–71 recession. The updated series would provide another turning point in our attempts to refine the important cycle hypothesis. Moving in this direction, researchers at the University of Pennsylvania are currently simulating the effect of national business cycles on the rate and composition of employment decentralization in Philadelphia.[2] A study of plant location in the New York SMSA, focusing on the 1970 turning point, is contained in a recent Yale doctoral dissertation.[3]

At The Urban Institute, a research team directed by Joel Bergsman has identified a large number of "industrial clusters" which seem to locate in groups. Where one member of a group is found, the others will also tend to appear. Conversely, SMSAs in which the number of jobs in certain industries is low tend systematically to have little employment in certain other linked industries.[4] This is an area where much more research is needed. So far, the phenomenon has been measured only for intermetro-

---

2.   An early version of the model is presented in Norman J. Glickman, "An Area-Stratified Regional Econometric Model," Regional Science Research Institute Discussion Paper No. 58, October 1972.
3.   Robert A. Leone, Location of Manufacturing Activity in the New York Metropolitan Area (New York: National Bureau of Economic Research, forthcoming).
4.   Joel Bergsman, Peter Greenston, and Robert Healy, "The Agglomeration Process in Urban Growth," Urban Studies, August 1972.

politan data, but it seems likely that there are similar indivisibilities in intraurban industrial location. Identification of the intraurban clusters would greatly facilitate both the forecasting of job decentralization and its control. If certain activities are known to be decentralizing, then there is a high probability that other activities linked to the first group will also decentralize. Thus, strategic locational control of a set of activities might be achieved by directing public policy towards "key" members of the group.

In Chapter 2, we stratified John Kain's original data by age, size, and rate of growth of city. An additional dimension along which urban areas may well stratify in their decentralization patterns is industrial structure, by mix and by industrial organization (e.g., do the headquarters cities of multinational corporate headquarters display greater or lesser decentralization of jobs in industries which are in competition with the "multinationals" for urban space?).[5]

Data sources now exist with which to study the process rather than simply the results of nonwhite suburbanization. With such longitudinal studies as the Parnes (Ohio State) and Survey Research Center (University of Michigan) files, it is now possible to "track" a small number of persons who resided in central city poverty areas in one year and then moved to the suburbs the next. From the 1970 Census, researchers can identify suburban residents who lived in the central city (although not necessarily in poverty areas) five years earlier, together with their former occupations and industries (but not earnings). How is the employment status of these new suburbanites affected? It should also be possible with 1970 Census data to calculate for various locations throughout an SMSA the number of jobs within a given commuting range. One thing which the latter exercise may well show is the relative superiority of central city residential locations in providing access to the greatest number of job sites. Moreover, even though some industries may be growing more rapidly in the suburbs than in the core, it is quite possible that the average length (in time or distance) of the intrasuburban journey to work exceeds the length of the intracore journey. Most suburban areas are not known for outstanding public transit.

Public expenditures create employment in two distinct ways: through direct production of goods and services, and through procurement of such goods and services from the private sector. Some of the differences between central city and suburban job growth might be explained by the location patterns of firms doing business with the government. These procurement networks need to be studied in detail—so far as I can tell, they have never

---

5.   The impact of multinational headquarters on central city economies is currently under study by a research team at The New School for Social Research in New York.

been studied at all. At the same time we need to extend the work already begun on the growth and location of the public sector jobs themselves.[6]

Conclusion

THERE IS NO QUESTION that much of the new "action" is in the suburbs. Yet before we allow ourselves to be swept up in the romanticism of this newest American "frontier movement," let us look again at the continuing role of the central cities in the American economy. It can be argued that central cities have been, and will continue to be, the birthplace of much new social, economic, and technological innovation.[7] The cities have been and may after all still be playing the role of staging areas for the rural population—social instruments for upgrading the skills, aspirations, and political prowess of the underclass.[8] The central cities still account for a major share of national production and wealth. As of 1968, for example,

29 large cities whose population makes up half that of their metropolitan areas and one-fourth of that of the Nation as a whole, account for two-thirds of the production of goods and services in their metropolitan areas, and more than one-third of that for the nation as a whole. With anticipated growth in productivity, but little growth in jobs, they may still be expected to account for one-fourth of future national growth in output in the decade of the 1970's.[9]

In 1970, 30 percent of the American people (a quarter of the whites and over half of the blacks) still lived inside the central cities of our 212 metropolitan areas.[10] Virtually all of the political institutions which minority groups (especially blacks) have so laboriously fought to create are located in central cities.[11] Finally a great deal of research on whether or not our major cities have grown too large and have exceeded some optimum city size seems to have led scholars to the conclusion that no such optimum has yet been reached—if indeed one exists at all. Brian Berry summarized the situation in testimony delivered to the Ad Hoc Subcommittee on Urban Growth of the U.S. House of Representatives in December 1970:

6.   Cf. Bennett Harrison and Paul Osterman, "Public Employment and Urban Poverty: Some New Data and a Policy Analysis," *Urban Affairs Quarterly*, March 1974.
7.   Jane Jacobs, *The Economy of Cities* (New York: Random House, 1969).
8.   For a discussion of this point and a call for further historical research on the question, see Charles Tilly, "Race and the Migration to the American City," in *The Metropolitan Enigma*, ed. James Q. Wilson (Cambridge: Harvard University Press, 1968).
9.   Alexander Ganz, "Our Large Cities: New Directions and New Approaches," reprinted by the Ad Hoc Subcommittee on Urban Growth, House Committee of Banking and Currency, *Hearings*, 91st Congress, second session, 23 September 1970, p. 122.
10.   U.S. Bureau of the Census, *Current Population Reports*, Series P-23, No. 37, "Social and Economic Characteristics of the Population in Metropolitan and Non-metropolitan Areas: 1970 and 1960," U.S. Government Printing Office, Washington, D.C., 1971, Table A.
11.   Frances Fox Piven and Richard A. Cloward, "Black Control of Cities," *The New Republic*, September 30, 1967 and October 7, 1967.

There is no evidence that very large cities encounter significant diseconomies of scale, or that there is any particular optimal city size. On the contrary, the evidence indicates that the larger the city, the greater the returns to innovative enterprise, the more compelling the growth impulses it diffuses downward to successively smaller centers in the urban hierarchy and the higher the incomes and the greater the range of economic, social, and cultural opportunities provided.

This suggests that policies to combat the growth of the largest cities may be counter-productive in the long run.[12]

For all of these reasons, I conclude that caution should be exercised in confronting the policy prescriptions of those who see in the suburbanization phenomenon "a massive, nationwide social and economic movement" which it would be expensive and irrational to attempt to reverse. This perception of reality has led many to advocate the freezing of all inner city redevelopment efforts and the large-scale relocation of ghetto dwellers to new homes in the suburbs. The caution I advocate is bolstered by the finding, reported above, that minorities already residing in the suburbs of our largest metropolitan areas near the height of the Kennedy-Johnson "boom" in the mid-1960s enjoyed levels of economic welfare which were not significantly greater than those of their brothers and sisters in the core city ghettos.

For many Americans, particularly those who are black, there is a strong presumption that the future lies in the cities, after all. After what I hope has been a careful and reasonably thorough analysis of the record, I must conclude that the suburbanization phenomenon in itself need not be inconsistent with, let alone vitiate, this vision. What *will* prove fatal to the aspirations of city dwellers is a continuation of the failure of policy which is responsible for the dire straits in which the cities now find themselves.

---

12. Brian J. L. Berry, Testimony before the Ad Hoc Subcommittee on Urban Growth, *Hearings*, pp. 330–31.

SELECTED BIBLIOGRAPHY

Articles

Bergsman, Joel. "Alternatives to the Non-Gilded Ghetto." *Public Policy*, Spring 1971.

Bergsman, Joel; Greenston, Peter; and Healy, Robert. "The Agglomeration Process in Urban Growth." *Urban Studies*, August 1972.

Canty, Donald. "Metropolity." *City*, March–April 1972.

Cohen, Benjamin I. "Trends in Negro Employment within Large Metropolitan Areas." *Public Policy*, Winter 1972.

Downs, Anthony. "Alternative Futures for the American Ghetto." *Daedalus*, Fall 1968.

Droettboom, Theodore, Jr., et al. "Urban Violence and Residential Mobility." *Journal of the American Institute of Planners*, September 1971.

Edel, Matthew B. "Development or Dispersal? Approaches to Ghetto Poverty." In *Readings in Urban Economics*, edited by Matthew B. Edel and Jerome Rothenberg. New York: Macmillan, 1972.

———. "Planning, Market, or Welfare? Recent Land Use Conflict in American Cities." In *Readings in Urban Economics*, edited by Matthew B. Edel and Jerome Rothenberg. New York: Macmillan, 1972.

Frieden, Bernard J. "Blacks in Suburbia: The Myth of Better Opportunities." In *Minority Perspectives*, edited by Lowdon Wingo. Baltimore: Johns Hopkins University Press, 1972.

Furstenberg, George M. von. "Place of Residence and Employment Opportunities within a Metropolitan Area." *Journal of Economic Issues*, June 1971.

Ganz, Alexander. "Our Large Cities: New Directions and New Approaches." Reprinted in *Hearings* of the Ad Hoc Subcommittee on Urban Growth, Committee of Banking and Currency, U.S. House of Representatives, Ninety-First Congress, second session, 23 September 1970.

Glickman, Norman J. "An Econometric Forecasting Model for the Philadelphia Region." *Journal of Regional Science*, April 1971.

Harrison, Bennett. "Education and Underemployment in the Urban Ghetto." *American Economic Review*, December 1972.

———. "Ghetto Economic Development." *Journal of Economic Literature*, March 1974.

———. "Ghetto Employment and the Model Cities Program." *Journal of Political Economy*, March–April 1974.

———. "The Participation of Ghetto Residents in the Model Cities Program." *Journal of the American Institute of Planners*, January 1973.

———. "A Pilot Project in Economic Development Planning for American Urban Slums." *International Development Review*, March 1968. Reprinted in *Black Business Enterprise*, edited by Ronald E. Bailey. New York: Basic Books, 1971.

Harvey, David. "Revolutionary and Counter-Revolutionary Theory in Geography, and the Problem of Ghetto Formation." In *Perspectives in Geography*, vol. 1, edited by Harold McConnell and David W. Yaseen. DeKalb, Ill.: Northern Illinois University Press, 1972.

Hetzel, Otto J. "Games the Government Plays: Federal Funding of Minority Economic Development." *Law and Contemporary Problems*, Winter 1971.

Hoch, Irving. "The Three-Dimensional City." In *The Quality of the Urban Environment*, edited by Harvey S. Perloff. Baltimore: Johns Hopkins University Press, 1969.

Innis, Roy. "Separatist Economics: A New Social Contract." In *Black Economic Development*, edited by William F. Haddad and C. Douglas Pugh. Englewood Cliffs, N.J.: Prentice Hall, 1969.

Kain, John F. "The Big Cities' Big Problem." *Challenge*, September–October 1966. Reprinted in *Negroes and Jobs*, edited by Louis A. Ferman et al. Ann Arbor, Mich.: University of Michigan Press, 1968.

———. "The Distribution and Movement of Jobs and Industry." In *The Metropolitan Enigma*, edited by James Q. Wilson. Cambridge, Mass.: Harvard University Press, 1968.

———. "Housing Segregation, Negro Employment, and Metropolitan Decentralization." *Quarterly Journal of Economics*, May 1968.

Kain, John F., and Persky, Joseph J. "Alternatives to the Gilded Ghetto." *The Public Interest*, Winter 1969.

Kasarda, John D. "The Impact of Suburban Population Growth on Central City Service Functions." *American Journal of Sociology*, May 1972.

Lewis, Wilfred, Jr. "Urban Growth and Suburbanization of Employment: Some New Data." Washington, D.C.: The Brookings Institution, 1969. Unpublished manuscript.

Mills, Edwin S. "Urban Density Functions." *Urban Studies*, February 1970.

Mooney, Joseph D. "Housing Segregation, Negro Employment and Metropolitan Decentralization: An Alternative Perspective." *Quarterly Journal of Economics*, May 1969.

Newman, Dorothy K. "The Decentralization of Jobs." *Monthly Labor Review*, May 1967.

Noll, Roger. "Metropolitan Employment and Population Distributions and the Conditions of the Urban Poor." In *Financing the Metropolis*, edited by John P. Crecine. Beverly Hills, Calif.: Sage, 1970.

Northam, Ray M. "Vacant Urban Land in the American City." *Land Economics*, November 1971.

Offner, Paul, and Saks, Daniel H. "A Note on John Kain's 'Housing Segregation, Negro Employment, and Metropolitan Decentralization.'" *Quarterly Journal of Economics*, February 1971.

Olken, Charles E. "Economic Development in the Model Cities Program." *Law and Contemporary Problems*, Spring 1971.

Piven, Francis Fox, and Cloward, Richard A. "Black Control of Cities." *The New Republic*, 30 September 1967 and 7 October 1967.

Tabb, William. "A Cost-Benefit Analysis of Location Subsidies for Ghetto Neighborhoods." *Land Economics*, February 1972.

Tate, Charles. "Brimmer and Black Capitalism: An Analysis." *The Review of Black Political Economy*, Spring-Summer 1970. Reprinted in *Black Business Enterprise*, edited by Ronald E. Bailey. New York: Basic Books, 1971.

Tilly, Charles. "Race and Migration to the American City." In *The Metropolitan Enigma*, edited by James Q. Wilson. Cambridge, Mass.: Harvard University Press, 1968.

Ulmer, Melville J. "The Limitations of Revenue-Sharing." *The Annals of the American Academy of Political and Social Science*, September 1971.

Vernon, Raymond. *The Changing Economic Function of the Central City*. New York: Committee for Economic Development, Supplementary Paper No. 6, January 1959. Reprinted in *Urban Renewal: The Record and the Controversy*, edited by James Q. Wilson. Cambridge, Mass.: Harvard University Press, 1966.

Vietorisz, Thomas. "Quantized Preferences and Planning by Priorities." *American Economic Review*, May 1970.

Vietorisz, Thomas, and Harrison, Bennett. "Ghetto Development, Community Corporations, and Public Policy." *The Review of Black Political Economy*, Autumn 1971.

Books and Monographs

Advisory Commission on Intergovernmental Relations. *Urban and Rural America: Policies for Future Growth*. Washington, D.C.: U.S. Government Printing Office, 1968.

Alloway, David N., and Cordasco, Francesco. *Minorities and the American City*. New York: David McKay, 1970.

Bailey, Ronald E., ed. *Black Business Enterprise.* New York: Basic Books, 1971.

Birch, David L. *The Economic Future of City and Suburb.* New York: Committee for Economic Development, Supplementary Paper No. 30, 1970.

Blaustein, Arthur I., and Faux, Geoffrey. *The Star-Spangled Hustle: White Power and Black Capitalism.* New York: Doubleday, 1972.

Bosselman, Fred, and Callies, David. *The Quiet Revolution in Land Use Control.* Washington, D.C.: Council on Environmental Quality, 1971.

Burton, Richard P. *The Metropolitan State.* Washington, D.C.: The Urban Institute, 1970.

Committee for Economic Development. *Reshaping Government in Metropolitan Areas.* New York, 1970.

Doeringer, Peter B., and Piore, Michael J. *Internal Labor Markets and Manpower Analysis.* Lexington, Mass.: Heath-Lexington Books, 1971.

Faux, Geoffrey. *CDCs: New Hope for the Inner City.* New York: The Twentieth Century Fund, 1971.

Fremon, Charlotte. *Central City and Suburban Employment Growth, 1965–1967.* Washington, D.C.: The Urban Institute, 1970.

———. *The Occupational Patterns in Urban Employment Change, 1965–1967.* Washington, D.C.: The Urban Institute, 1970.

Furstenberg, George M. von; Horowitz, A.; and Harrison, B.; eds. *Patterns of Racial Discrimination* (Lexington, Mass.: Heath–Lexington Books, 1974).

Gordon, David M., ed. *Problems in Political Economy: An Urban Perspective.* Lexington, Mass.: D.C. Heath, 1971.

Harrison, Bennett. *Education, Training, and the Urban Ghetto.* Baltimore: Johns Hopkins University Press, 1972.

———. *Public Employment and Urban Poverty.* Washington, D.C.: The Urban Institute, 1971.

Kalachek, Edward D., and Goering, John M., eds. *Transportation and Central City Unemployment.* St. Louis: Washington University, Institute for Urban and Regional Studies, 1970.

Mayor's Committee on Economic and Cultural Development. *Mid-Chicago Economic Development Project.* Washington, D.C.: U.S. Economic Development Administration, 1970.

Neenan, William B. *The Political Economy of Urban Areas.* Chicago: Markham, 1972.

Owen, Wilfred. *The Accessible City.* Washington, D.C.: The Brookings Institution, 1972.

Rosenbloom, Richard S., and Marris, Robin, eds. *Social Innovation in the City.* Cambridge, Mass.: Harvard University Press, 1969.

Sheppard, Harold L.; Harrison, Bennett; and Spring, William; eds. *The Political Economy of Public Service Employment.* Lexington, Mass.: Heath-Lexington Books, 1972.

Tabb, William K. *The Political Economy of the Black Ghetto.* New York: Norton, 1970.

Tate, Charles, ed. *Cable TV in the Cities: Community Control, Public Access, and Minority Ownership.* Washington, D.C.: The Urban Institute, 1971.

Vietorisz, Thomas, and Harrison, Bennett. *The Economic Development of Harlem.* New York: Praeger, 1970.

Wertheimer, Richard F., II. *The Monetary Rewards of Migration within the United States.* Washington, D.C.: The Urban Institute, 1970.

SUBJECT INDEX

AUTHOR INDEX